DUDLEY PUBLIC LIBRARIES

The loan of this book may be renewed if not required by other readers, by contacting the library from which it was borrowed.

CP/494

ALSO BY HOWARD MARKS

Mr Nice
The Howard Marks Book of Dope Stories

HOWARD MARKS

Señor Nice

Straight Life from Wales to South America

VINTAGE BOOKS
London

Published by Vintage 2007

4 6 8 10 9 7 5

First published in Great Britain in 2006 by Harvill Secker

Vintage
Random House, 20 Vauxhall Bridge Road,
London SW1V 2SA

www.vintage-books.co.uk

Addresses for companies within The Random House Group Limited
can be found at: www.randomhouse.co.uk/offices.htm

The Random House Group Limited Reg. No. 954009

A CIP catalogue record for this book
is available from the British Library

ISBN 9780099453932

Penguin Random House is committed to a sustainable future for
our business, our readers and our planet. This book is made from
Forest Stewardship Council® certified paper.

MIX
Paper from
responsible sources
FSC® C018179

Printed and bound in Great Britain by Clays Ltd, St Ives plc

Dedicated to the memory of my mother, Edna Rhyfelgar Marks

Acknowledgements

I would like to thank Giles Cooper, who has been my close friend and a perfect manager of my live shows for the last eight years. Without his tenacity, kindness, and understanding, this book would never have been started.

The following family members, friends, and associates deserve far more than mere acknowledgements. You know what you did. Thank you so much.

Jamie Acott; Richard Allen-Turner; Martyn Baker; Angelina Basco; Dave Beer; Dafydd Bell; Crofton Black; Martin Blackhall; Scott Blakey; Ernesto Blume; Leroy Bowen; Charlie Breaker; Mike Broderick; Arthur Brown; Alun Buffry; Tina Butler; Mary Carson; Anna Collings; Tim Corrigan; Dave Courtney; Tel Currie; Bernie Davies; Suzanne Dean; Dirty Sanchez; George Duffin; Briony Everroad; Emily Faccini; Claudette Finnegan; Mark Gehring; John Goad; David Godwin; Goldie Lookin Chain; Maria Golia; Adenor Gondim; Simon Greenberg; Lee Harris; Lisa Harvey; Rhys Ifans; JC001; Les Johnson; Ian Johnstone; Justin Kerrigan; Jimmy Knight; Marty Langford; Christian Lewis; Nick Linford; Kelly Major; Patrick Marks; Amber Marks; Francesca Marks; Myfanwy Marks; Polly Marshall; Mike and Claire McCay; Biff Mitchell; Amanda Monroe; Les Morrison; Claire Nicolson; *Observer* Travel Section; John Oliver; Jimmy Page; Jason Parkinson; James Perkins; Johnny Pickston; Werner Pieper; Joey Pyle; Justin Rees; Mark Reeve; Bruce Reynolds; Charlie Richardson; Sharon Robbins; Susan Sandon; Jim Shreim; Phil Sparrowhawk; Frank Steffan; Stereophonics; Super Furry Animals; Pauline Townsend; Marcus van der Kolk; Hywel Williams; Stuart Williams; Clare Wilshaw.

A very special thank you to Caroline Brown and to my editor Geoff Mulligan.

Contents

When a person endeavours to recall his early life in its entirety, he finds it is not possible: he is like one who ascends a hill to survey the prospect before him on a day of heavy cloud and shadow, who sees at a distance some feature in the landscape while all else remains in obscurity. The scenes people events we are able by an effort to call up do not present themselves in order but in isolated spots or patches, vividly seen in the midst of a wide shrouded landscape. It is easy to fall into the delusion that the few things thus distinctly remembered and visualised are precisely those which were most important in our life and on that account were saved by memory. Unconscious artistry sneaks in to erase unseemly lines and blots, to retouch, colour, shade, and falsify the picture.

Far Away and Long Ago, W. H. Hudson

One

THE SHOW

Wherever I travelled, whatever scam or profession I was engaged in, I always returned to my birthplace Kenfig Hill: as an Oxford student on vacation, a source of pride to my parents and no doubt mystery and resentment to my friends; in the 1970s before skipping bail while awaiting an Old Bailey trial for smuggling tons of hashish in the equipment of rock bands such as Pink Floyd; in the 80s celebrating my acquittal, having been charged with importing fifteen tons of Colombian marijuana into the UK (I persuaded the court I was working for the Mexican secret service); in the 90s, having served a lengthy sentence at the maximum-security US Federal Penitentiary, Terre Haute, Indiana, to spend time with my parents, who had hung on to life just long enough to share my experience of freedom.

Winter 2001. Paddington, looking like an airport with its check-in facilities, escalators and shopping malls, was wet and windy – a foretaste of South Wales, to where its trains, on the hour every hour, were constantly bound. I bought a ticket to Bridgend, 200 miles away, gateway to the coal mining valleys and the nearest railway station to Kenfig Hill. Notices depressingly announced that all Great Western services were now strictly non-smoking. Outside the ticket office a conveyor belt of sushi and sashimi plates trundled around in front of delayed passengers. I sat down, took half a spliff out of my top pocket, lit it, and stared at the raw fish and rice whizzing around.

'Sorry, sir. No smoking,' the sushi chef commanded abruptly.

How could anyone purporting to be Japanese disallow smoking? Japan has always had the highest cigarette consumption in the world and the lowest rate of lung cancer, a fact I found most comforting.

'Are you Japanese?' I asked the menacing, knife-wielding chef.

'Korean.'

'Maybe that explains it.'

Irritated, even slightly enraged, I ambled off to the platform, got on the waiting train, and sat down at an empty table as the train began to fill with people off to see Wales play England at rugby at Cardiff's Millennium Stadium.

'*Swt Mai*, Howard?' It was Gruff Rhys, lead singer and guitarist of the Super Furry Animals, on his way to Cardiff to record his next album. 'Going to see the folks or down for the match?'

'No. Dad's dead, and Mam is very ill. She's living in Yorkshire now with my sister. And these days I've completely lost faith in the Welsh rugby team. In the 1970s no one could beat us; now, we can't win a match.'

'It must have been great back then. Did you play when you were at school?'

'I was never any good, Gruff, but yes, I did.'

'What position?'

'Second row forward. In fact, two of the school's front row, John Lloyd and Geoff Young, went on to play for Wales and the British Lions when they beat the All Blacks.'

'So you've had your head stuck between a couple of very famous arses.'

'That's one way of putting it, Gruff, but I'm not here for sport; I'm doing a show tonight at the Pavilion, Porthcawl.'

'Yeah? Great! Can me and a couple of the boys come?'

'Of course, I'll put you all down on the list.'

'*Diolch*, Howard. I'll get us a couple of beers now.'

My rehabilitation has taken a curious path which never ceases to branch out in unexpected directions, of which one is a career as a stand-up comic. This evolved from fulfilling vaguely contractual commitments to promote and publicise my autobiography, *Mr Nice*, by appearing on TV and radio shows, being interviewed by book reviewers and other journalists, and reading passages from the book in bookshops. Many authors arrogantly take the view that their creative output speaks for itself and excuse themselves from such duties. I couldn't begin to take that risk and am a firm believer in blatant self-promotion, but I found it difficult to come to terms with bookshops as suitable venues for any event. First, the reading has to take place during normal working hours, when most of the staff want to get home and most of the potential punters can't attend. Second, the booze is in short supply and of poor quality. Third, the reading takes place against a background of all the competition, which seems to me an absurd marketing strategy. Admittedly, some book-shops go out of their way to create a sensible ambience at an appropriate hour, but generally book readings are sterile, boring affairs. Getting a laugh from the audience always helps, so I included as many funny passages as I could find. The reading would be followed by a question-and-answer session, which was invariably more stimulating than the reading itself.

This was during the mid-1990s, when other writers such as Irvine Welsh, Nik Cohn, Roddy Doyle and Nick Cave were beginning to do readings in pubs and clubs. I attended a few and was encouraged to do the same, but I felt the authors invariably made two important errors: they would insist the bar till stayed inactive when reading so no booze could be purchased, and they would read passages precisely as they were written. Very few if any authors write prose with the thought that one day they might have to read it standing on a stage in front of an audience hell bent on having a good time. I modified my extracts severely, bearing the listeners in mind, and let the cash tills ring and the booze flow all night. It worked.

Mr Nice did not draw a veil over my consumption of drugs and my desire to see them legalised, so much of each question-and-answer session was devoted to that topic. This suited me perfectly as probably for the first time in my life, I had a sincere social agenda. Organisations devoted to drug legalisation invited me to speak. Universities asked me to debate. At the end of each debate or talk I would be asked to sign copies of *Mr Nice*. It couldn't have turned out better if it had been planned: I could use the book readings to advance my social agenda and use my agenda to sell books.

I did both talks and readings without charging – it never occurred to me to even ask for a fee – but in August 1997 I read at the Edinburgh International Book Festival and was approached afterwards by comedy promoters Avalon, who offered to finance a series of one-man shows and pay me £500 a gig. I agreed. Within a few months I had sold out at Shepherd's Bush Empire more times than anyone except Abba. A year later, I did twenty-three consecutive shows at the Edinburgh International Festival. I enjoyed learning how to banter with audiences, battle with hecklers, cope with cock-ups and experiment with multimedia.

But tonight would be the real test. I had to perform in front of a home crowd at the Royal Pavilion, Porthcawl, four miles from Kenfig Hill, where I was born. I was last there thirty-five years ago as one of a number of drunken yobs participating in an Elvis impersonators' contest. I came close to last. Would they remember? I was now playing the part of a prison-hardened gangster in front of people who terrified me as a schoolboy. How could they possibly take me seriously? Worse still, the whole performance was going to be filmed for a *Mr Nice* DVD.

Gruff stepped down from the train at Cardiff, lighting a cigarette as soon as his foot touched the platform. Twenty minutes later, I did the same at Bridgend and took a taxi to Kenfig Hill. The semi-detached house in Waunbant Road had been empty for just a few months, but already the home-made weathercock was dangling from the rotten chimney, and the front gate had almost come off its hinges. A carpet of decaying litter covered what used to be the front lawn. I knew there was a garage behind the brambles and ivy; I just couldn't see it. My key still turned the lock, but the damp door didn't want to open. I forced it and stumbled through a pile of mail to switch on the light then walked up the stairs and into the infinite familiarity of my parents' bedroom, where fifty-five years previously I had first breathed in harmony with the universe. Now both my parents had gone. Just the house lived on. It couldn't stay empty forever; it would have to be sold or rented. No rush. First, it would need to be emptied of boxes and several generations of memorabilia – but some other time. It was mid-afternoon, and cameraman Martin Baker, son of Welsh actor and director Stanley Baker of *Zulu* fame, was due any moment.

The doorbell rang.

'Who is it?'

'Martin.'

It wasn't Martin Baker but my oldest friend and first dope-smuggling employee, Marty Langford. I had been home for twenty minutes. Word gets around.

'Julie from the shop just told me you were home. Why didn't

you call me? All this author and performer stuff has gone to your head, hasn't it? Put the kettle on, then. I'm dying for a brew and a blast. Got anything decent?'

'I've got some excellent hash for a smoke, Marty, but there's no milk in the house for tea.'

'I knew I should have bought some milk at Julie's. And hash is no good for me, Howard. I don't smoke tobacco, and I can't be messing with pipes and buckets and things at my age. Haven't you got any skunk?'

'A bit, just a third of a spliff, actually. We could smoke it and go down the pub.'

'What! For a cup of tea?'

'I thought they sold everything in pubs now from Thai food to cappuccino.'

'Not round here, Howard; it's still just beer and crisps. But we might as well go down. I fancy a walk. Haven't been for months and months. I usually stay in these days – on the computer.'

The pub was a good twenty-minute walk. On our left we passed the furniture shop, once Kenfig Hill's only cinema, and then the Institute, where we had been taught snooker by miners working nights and where I had first dared imitate Elvis in public. The skunk hit hard. Marty and I looked at each other and started giggling like the children we still were. On our right we could see the Prince of Wales and the old Victoria Inn, both smothered in scaffolding on account of their being converted into flats.

When I was in my mid-teens Kenfig Hill had a population of just over 5,000, one church of Wales, one Roman Catholic church, four Welsh Nonconformist chapels – Baptist, Presbyterian, Methodist and Welsh Congregationalist – and nine pubs. Since then, housing estates and new streets have sprung up but the population is approximately the same; the accommodation is just less crowded. Television keeps the elderly at home while cars and motorbikes have enabled the

young to get away from the prying eyes of family and
neighbours. Accordingly, there are now two fewer pubs and
one less place of worship. The chapel that bit the dust was the
Welsh Congregationalist one, named Elim, the first chapel in
Kenfig Hill. Members of my family attended Elim for several
generations, preaching, deaconing, singing hymns and playing
in the tiny orchestra, but lack of interest closed its doors a few
years ago. At the tender age of ten, I was taken to Elim and
introduced to the serious side of God. Until then he had been
little more than a powerful Father Christmas figure from
whom one occasionally asked for serendipitous gifts and
various forms of assistance. Learning that God is everywhere
at once and saw everything had conjured up the idea of a
wonderfully active and clear-sighted person.

Unlike my father, my mother was deeply religious, and she
insisted I went to Sunday school in the afternoon and to either
the morning or evening service. My mother also insisted my
father went with her to the evening service. I hated both
Sunday school and services. I opted to attend in the morning
alone rather than go in the evening under the watchful eyes of
my parents, partly to get the chore behind me, but mainly
because I could get away with not going at all. I would leave
the house at 10 a.m. and go to Marty's place for an hour to
chain-smoke cigarettes and listen to 78s on his impressive
radiogram. Eventually I was grassed up by one of Marty's
neighbours and forced to attend the evening service.

Thousands of unhappy Sunday walks flooded through my
memory as Marty and I turned the corner at the Victoria Inn.
This used to afford the first sight of Elim, a dull grey roof
pointing hopelessly at heaven.

'See what's happened to Elim, Howard?'

'Jesus!'

Elim Welsh Congregationalist Chapel had been replaced by
red-brick houses surrounded by manicured gardens and little
fences.

'That must mess with your memory circuits, Howard.'

'I used to hate the place. I feel worse about the Vic being turned into a house.'

'C'mon, there must be some good memories. That's where you first got married, right, in 1967? On a Thursday, wasn't it?'

That was, indeed, a good memory. Loads of people turned up to witness my marriage to Latvian beauty Ilze Kadegis. It was followed by a hard-core drinking competition in Kenfig Hill's pubs between the Welsh and visiting Latvians. Both sides definitely lost.

Not only was Elim Chapel where I had lost my bachelorhood, it was also where I had lost my virginity some years earlier. This had happened on a Saturday.

On Friday evenings during the early 1960, the vestry of Elim Welsh Congregationalist Chapel served as the only youth club in the community. This weekly transformation was achieved by pushing the pews and chairs to the side, placing a Dansette record player on a bench, and setting it to continuous full volume. I and other village teenagers brought our 78s, and taught each other to jive before snogging and smoking in the dark rooms and cellars adjoining the vestry. As I was one of the very few kids who was both a member of the youth club and the chapel, I was entrusted with the keys, and it was my duty to go there every Saturday morning to tidy up.

On one particular Friday, a new girl, Susan Malone, whom I had asked for a date a few days before, came to the club. I went up to her and asked her to dance just as the Shirelles were singing those very same words. We jived furiously to Danny and the Juniors' 'At the Hop', then moved into one of the unlit rooms for a frantic snogging session that left us breathless but wanting more, lots more. I asked if I could walk her home, and she agreed with far more enthusiasm than I had expected. Susan lived in a caravan and was the daughter of an Irish construction engineer who had just started a three-month contract at Port Talbot. I secured another date for the next afternoon, but I had no idea where to take her. It was bound to be raining, and we were too young for the pubs. Overnight I had a brainwave. I would leave the club-tidying chore until the afternoon and take Susan with me.

We sneaked into the damp vestry. Cigarette butts and sweet wrappings littered the wet floor, but the chapel was much warmer, ready for Sunday's services. I switched on the organ and, out of respect, played some classical chords. Then I played 'The Twist'. We lay down on the front pew. And then I shagged her. We had a few more dates over the next month, after which she left the locality as suddenly as she had arrived.

'Shall we go to the Oak, Howard? The Masons has just been pulled down.'

Marty and I walked into the public bar of the Royal Oak. We were completely ignored; everyone was transfixed by the rugby match on television. Wales lost; nevertheless, the pub would still stay open continuously for two days and play host to hundreds of tales of successful and heroic Welshmen, past and present. As the drink flowed, the tales got taller.

'Well, now they finally have the proof,' said Eddie Evans, the village sage. 'Elvis was Welsh.'

'You mean Tom Jones, don't you, Eddie,' said Ivor Prior, who loved to catch Eddie out. 'And you are right, Eddie. Tom was born in Treforest. His real name is Tommy Woodward.'

'I'm not talking about him. I'm talking about the real original Elvis, Elvis Presley.'

'How do you mean, Eddie?' I asked.

'Well, it's obvious, isn't it? His mother's name was Gladys, and they've now found out that his surname a few generations back was Preseli, same as the mountains in Pembroke where the stones in Stonehenge come from.'

'But Elvis is hardly a Welsh name, Eddie,' I protested, a

little discomfited to hear that my god's grandfather might have
been a neighbour of my grandfather.

'Of course it is, Howard. I thought you would have known
that, having been to Oxford. Elvis was the name of the bishop
who baptised our patron saint, St David. The parish of Elvis
still exists. It's very small, but it's definitely there. No doubt at
all. It's not far from St David's itself, which, as you should
know, is the smallest city in the world.'

'How did they move those bloody huge stones from
Pembroke to Salisbury then, Eddie? There's a question for
you,' said Ivor Prior.

'There's two theories. One is they were taken by boat; the
other is that the great wizard Merlin moved them. Take your
choice, Ivor.'

'How the hell can a boat get to Salisbury? It's not even on
the coast.'

'Ever heard of rivers, Ivor?'

'There's no river from Pembroke to Salisbury, Eddie,' said
Ivor a little uncertainly.

'Obviously not, but there is a river from Pembroke to the
bloody sea, and there is another river from the bloody sea to
Salisbury.'

The pub liked this explanation.

'Merlin was Welsh,' added Eddie.

'Doesn't sound like much of a Welsh name,' teased Ivor.
'You're not getting mixed up with Mervyn, are you?

'Merlin is what the bloody French call him,' explained
Eddie. 'His real name was Myrddin, and he was born in
Carmarthen, which is shortened from Caer Myrddin. He died
near there as well, after ruling the roost for a bit at Stonehenge.
Awful boy he was too.'

'In what way, Eddie?' I asked.

'Well, just think a bit about it. Merlin's father was the Devil.
His mother was a virgin. And he ends up telling Arthur, the
ruler of the first Christian kingdom, how to run the country.

Don't forget Camelot was very close to here – in Caerleon, just by Newport, in fact.'

'That's really interesting, Eddie. I wish I could stay and listen to more, but I'd better go now. I'm doing a show tonight at Porthcawl.'

'As if we didn't bloody know that already,' said Eddie. 'The whole village has been talking about bugger-all else. Why anyone should pay good money to listen to you chopsing on a stage about smoking weeds is beyond me. What a waste of an Oxford science education. What a bloody waste!'

'Would you prefer I was a nuclear physicist, Eddie?' I said walking to the door.

'You've got a point. No, I'm only joking. Good luck tonight, boy *bach*. Break a leg, as your understudy might say. That's where the saying came from you know: a Welsh actor was once performing . . .'

Marty and I left. Eddie's voice receded as my mobile picked up several voice messages: Martin Baker was waiting in his car in Waunbant Road; Christine from Lloyds asked if she could have twelve tickets to give the bank staff; Polly, the area's best skunk grower for the last ten years, wondered if she should bring some buds along tonight; Leroy, my Jamaican friend from Terre Haute prison and current security man, had called from Birmingham to say he had got lost driving from London but knew the way now; and Kelly Jones of the Stereophonics asked if I could ring him back.

'Hi, Kelly. Howard here.'

'All right, butt? Tell you why I called: I heard you were doing a show tonight.'

'That's right. You want to come along?'

'Aye, but any chance of another ticket as well, like? I can have a lift down then.'

Kelly is one of the country's highest-paid rock stars and could probably have a fleet of limousines on twenty-four-hour call without noticing the cost, but you can't take the valleys out of that boy. It was hard enough getting him out of the valleys.'

'No worries, Kelly. You can have more if you want.'

'No, two is fine, butt. Thanks, How. Good luck for the show.'

'Hello, Polly. Just got your message. Everything all right?'

'Oh hello, Howard. Yes, everything is fine, thanks. Do you want me to bring something along tonight?'

'Of course.'

'Right, I will. You'll never ever guess what it is: it's my first crop of your Mr Nice Seedbank's Super Silver Haze. I haven't tried it myself yet, but it looks as if it's going to be the best I've ever grown or known.'

Back outside the house, I introduced Marty to Martin.

'Hello, Marty. I've heard a lot about you. Any chance of filming an interview with you later?'

'Oh, I don't know about that,' answered Marty. 'Last time I answered any questions about his nibs here, I was put in jail for a few years. Sorry. No offence, but I'd better say no right away and be on the safe side. Well, I'll be off now to pick up my mother from bingo. See you later, How. Best of luck and all that.'

I led Martin Baker into the house.

'I find that a lot of people I was hoping to interview take the same attitude, Howard. I hope Leroy won't be the same. Do you think he'll agree to be interviewed?'

'If he ever gets here, yes. Just keep off his past.'

'Shit! There's nothing else I want to know about him other than his past. I'd better get to the venue; it's five o'clock. I'm late as it is. Ian's there already, I suppose?'

'Yes, of course. He's been there since two.'

'I should have guessed. See you later. Good luck.'

Ian Johnstone was my tour manager. His duties, invariably executed with complete professionalism, included setting up the lighting, sound equipment and props, ensuring the dressing room had ample booze, fags and cigarette papers, determining from the venue's management their attitude to tobacco and dope being smoked on stage, in the dressing room and in the auditorium, and lastly every tour manager's nightmare – managing the guest list and any after-show activities. The show had been hosted by venues ranging from subterranean ecstasy clubs to pristine theatres staffed by old aged pensioners wearing evening dress. Rules varied. The Royal Pavilion, Porthcawl was a council-subsidised music and pantomime venue. The management might be difficult. It was time I called Ian.

'They don't seem too bad here, Howard. All the props are on stage, the dressing room is equipped as usual; smoking is allowed in the auditorium; but they want you to sign a declaration that you won't use any illegal substances. Apparently, there's going to be a demonstration against your appearing here. The management want to cover their backsides.'

This was nothing new. I had done well over 200 shows. At each of them I had smoked either a bong of marijuana or a joint of hashish on stage. Although venue personnel and the odd season ticket holder must have called the authorities dozens of times, local police had not once done anything about it. But it was always possible they might. Accordingly, licence holders and the like often wanted to ensure they weren't compromised. This was easily achieved by my signing a piece of paper stating that I would behave myself. It never stopped me lighting up, obviously, but it made matters easier for them. And we actively encouraged demonstrations by out-of-touch parents; it was great publicity.

'No worries, Ian. I'll sign the paper as usual. There probably won't be more than a handful of demonstrators. Just give them free tickets; it'll liven up the show a bit.'

'Well, I think we are more than sold out, Howard. I trust you don't have too much of a guest list.'

'I'll bring it down with me. There might be a few, I'm afraid.'

'Fuck! They might have to stand at the back. I'll send a cab to pick you up?'

Outside the venue, the long queue waiting for the doors to open jeered at the small group of protesters carrying placards decrying the dangers and evils of drugs. A smaller line clutching copies of *Mr Nice* was outside the stage door. Ian was by an unmarked door, flashing his torch at the cab. He had done his research, as always. The door opened. Then an almost invisible figure jumped out of the shadows.

'Hello, Taff. How are you? I didn't expect to see you here.'

Taff was rarely seen working anywhere outside a festival or holidaying anywhere outside a tepee village.

'Not so bad, How. Remember last Glastonbury you said I could come to one of your shows?'

'Yes, of course I do.'

'Well is it all right if me and six of my friends come to the show tonight?'

'Sure, Taff. Just give the names to Ian here.'

'But he's the cunt who just told me to fuck off.'

'OK, give them to me then. Ian probably didn't realise you were a friend of mine.'

'No, I suppose not. But I did tell him, like. Anyway, thanks a lot, How. Good luck for the show.'

I had a look at the stage. Cameras, lights and props were all in place. The microphone worked and was at the right height. The way to and from the dressing room was clearly marked by strips of shiny white tape stuck to the stage floor. I gave the OK for the venue doors to open, put my guest list into Ian's hands, and walked off the stage as Ian began playing the first track from the walk-in CD, 'I Just Want to Smoke It' by the Super Furry Animals.

Leroy greeted me in the dressing room.

'Hey, mon, di road signs a bullshit. Mi tek more dan six hours fi gu.'

Leroy Bowen is a mustee, fifteen sixteenths black and one
sixteenth white. I first met him while serving my prison
sentence at the United States Federal Penitentiary, Terre
Haute, Indiana. Born in Jamaica, he survived a cut-throat
childhood in Kingston's Spanish Town and rose to become a
sergeant major in the army, a special security policeman and
finally the governor of Jamaica's personal bodyguard. While
holidaying in the United States Leroy inadvertently overstayed
his visa and was sent to Oakdale Aliens' Detention Center for
deportation. He witnessed several incidents of physical and
mental abuse of his countrymen by the institution's staff and
began to complain. The complaints turned into an organised
prisoners' protest; the protest turned into a riot. The prison
was burned down, and Leroy sentenced to several years'
imprisonment at Terre Haute. We spent most of those years
together and were deported the same day from Oakdale in
Louisiana, where his problems had begun. It was the most
important day in both our lives. I remember so well how we
looked at each other and at the prison space we were leaving
behind. Then we looked again at each other.

These were no mere glances; they were attempts to understand the intense emotions suddenly swamping our minds, the
confusing but comforting knowledge of a common destiny, a
shared future. Had I known Leroy in every previous lifetime
but only, at that moment of intense farewell, just started
looking through his eyes rather than at them? Would we one
day work or scam together? We had both been shafted enough
by those we had trusted in our respective lives, those for whom
we would have gladly risked our lives, done our time inside,
not grassed and never cheated. Could we ever trust anyone
again, ever correctly predict anyone's actions or ever even give
a fuck? Leroy and I hadn't dared talk about scamming – too
many hacks, too many grasses, too many listening walls and
far too many nosy troublemakers. But through those 10,001
games of Scrabble, chess and backgammon, we had learnt

each other's deviousness, ruthlessness and courage. We had
always respectfully looked away when the other had tears to be
stifled; we had never dared share a bad mood and had always
tried to find somewhere else to shit. 'Su dis a Wales. Yeah,
mon. At las. Mi finally dyah.'

Several decades ago Leroy's family had set out from Jamaica
for Britain, and had come to Tiger Bay, Cardiff for fortune
and fun. That was the last Leroy had heard of them. Until we
became friends Leroy had not even realised his last name was
Welsh – Bowen is an abbreviation of ap Owen – or that Tiger
Bay, the first-ever British Jamaican community, was in the
heart of Wales's capital city.

'So dis a yo home town, mon. Yo mus feel irie.'

'I feel more nervous performing here than anywhere else in
the world, Leroy.'

Ian barged in looking hassled. 'Howard, they're saying
sixty-five is far too big a guest list. There just isn't room, even
if they all stand. And they are absolutely adamant about no
more than twelve in the dressing room at any one time.'

'Don't worry, Ian. Lots of them won't turn up. You know
what it's like. And Leroy can control the numbers in and out
of the dressing room. But can you ask them if they can put
aside a special room for an after-show party? That will take the
heat off a bit.'

'Not off me it won't. But I'll do what I can. Some local
papers want to interview you. I told them to wait until after
the show and that I couldn't promise anything. By the way,
there's someone called Polly outside. She says you know
her.'

'Oh yes. Get her in as soon as possible. She has something I
need. Take Leroy with you.'

Soon afterwards, Polly walked in with a few of her friends,
closely followed by Taff and his motley gang. Polly handed me
a packet of skunk. I asked Taff to skin up while I got my scripts
together. Leroy came in with some letters left for me at the

stage door. Most were invitations from people to go to their houses after the show for a smoke and a chat; some were requests for autographs and signed photographs; all wished me good luck for the show. But there was one long letter from an ex-workmate of my father's about how Dad would turn in his grave if he knew the extent of my depravity in encouraging drug use among the youth of today. The twat obviously didn't know my father very well; nevertheless, the letter made me even more nervous.

'Twenty minutes before show,' yelled Ian from the other side of the dressing-room door.

I offered drinks all round and downed a pint of bitter.

'Here you are, How. You have this one, and I'll roll one for us lot. It looks excellent stuff, by the way,' said Taff, handing me an unlit spliff.

Ian yelled again as I sparked it up: 'Ten minutes. Who the fuck is Psychic Dave?'

'He's one of my oldest friends, Ian; you have to let him in. Leroy's on his way to get him.'

Psychic Dave was Dave Leatham. Back in the late 1960s he and Marty Langford were my first dope-smuggling employees. Unlike Marty, Dave escaped imprisonment and he became a fortune-telling fugitive on the streets of New Orleans. Now he was trying out his mystic skills in Tenerife in the winter and Cardiff in the summer. He had asked if he could come to my dressing room with his tarot cards and tell people's fortunes and I had agreed.

Psychic Dave came in, accompanied by Leroy and Martin Baker. 'Well at least Psychic Dave has agreed to do an interview, as long as I let him read my palms,' said Martin, looking at my smoking spliff. 'That smells fantastic. Can I have some?'

'Sure. Be careful, though, it's really strong.'

'Five minutes,' shouted Ian. 'Everyone out of the dressing room, please.'

I always needed five minutes of peace before the show to collect my thoughts and calm the butterflies in my stomach. I achieved this in various ways: shouting at myself in the mirror, snorting a line of cocaine or briefly meditating.

My guests left, each wishing me good luck. I sat down and smoked the rest of Polly's Super Silver Haze spliff. Christ, it was strong. I started giggling. I thought of my dead father and dying mother and cried a bit. I paced up and down and gulped some whisky.

'Okay, mon. Dem a wait pon yo.'

I followed Leroy to the side of the stage.

'Ladies and gentlemen, please welcome on stage Mr Howard Marks.'

Adrenalin pumped through my brain and body. Shouts, hoots and catcalls greeted me as I took my place behind the microphone. The noise subsided.

'Are there any plain-clothes cops here?' I asked the audience. 'Because if so, now's your fucking chance. Just fucking try it, motherfuckers.'

Loud cackles of laughter cut through clouds of marijuana smoke. I picked up my script and began reading 'The Dope Dealer and the Terrorist', my stage version of the passages in *Mr Nice* about my dope importing activities into Ireland with self-professed IRA gunrunner Jim McCann. September 11, 2001 had just happened, so the piece was appropriately topical and outrageous. My Belfast accent left a lot to be desired, but the show was working.

'I've cracked it, H'ard. Send me all the fucking dope you want. I got the man I needed. He fucking examines everything coming into Shannon Airport and, if he values his fucking Guinness, he'll let through what I tell him to. His name's Eamonn. He's a true Republican.'

'Does he know we're going to bring in dope?'

'Of course he fucking doesn't, you Welsh arsehole. He

thinks he's bringing in guns for the IRA cause. He's dead against dope.'

Relieved to be speaking to a responsive audience, I relaxed and looked around the stage. Behind his camera, which was pointing at the ceiling, Martin Baker had gone white. Leroy was at the side of the stage looking at him with concern and worry wrinkling his magnificent face. Suddenly, Martin lost his legs and began falling into a giant spaghetti of electrical cables. Leroy dived, caught him, saved his life, and carried him off. Martin had done a whitey on Polly's skunk. Fuck! I hoped no one else had. It would be bad publicity. And what would happen to the DVD? Never mind, the show had to go on.

'Jim, the consignment's left and it's addressed to Juma Khan, Shannon, Ireland.'

'You stupid Welsh cunt, what did you put my fucking name on it for?'

I suddenly realised the similarity in pronunciation between the names Jim McCann and Juma Khan.

'Jim, Khan is like Mister in the Middle East. And it's Juma, not Jim. Juma means something like Friday in their language.'

'Jim McCann might fucking mean Man Friday in Kabul, but in Ireland Jim McCann means it's fucking me, for fuck's sake.'

I announced the end of the first half and went back to the dressing room. The sight that greeted me was appalling.

Martin Baker was trying to convince two St John's Ambulance men that he had suffered a migraine attack while Leroy kept repeating, 'Im woulda dead, mon. Im woulda dead, mon.' Polly was lying semi-conscious on a sofa and whispering over and over again, 'Never happened to me before, and I've been smoking dope for over forty years, and I grew this myself.' Psychic Dave was reassuring three other comatose bodies with carefully worded predictions of their imminent recovery based on the tarot cards, while Marty and Taff at his side were crying with laughter.

'Ten minutes to show time,' cried Ian.

The ambulance men shuffled out scratching their heads.

'Taff, can you skin up another joint?' I asked. 'Better use the hash this time. It's for me to smoke on the stage during the second half.'

Ian popped his head around the door.

'Five minutes. Clear the dressing room.'

This time I just snorted a huge line of cocaine.

Leroy came to get me, still repeating, 'Im woulda dead, mon.'

'Ladies and Gentlemen, please welcome back on stage, Mr Howard Marks.'

I decided not to read an extract about life in a United States penitentiary as originally planned. I would read the Egyptian delegate's speech to the League Of Nations Second Opium Conference (1926) on the need to make hashish illegal. That always went down well and would be more in line with my legalisation agenda, which judging by the dressing room needed some support.

'Hashish is a deadly poison against which no effective antidote has ever been discovered. Users suffer from two serious medical conditions: one, acute hashishism and two, chronic hashishism . . .'

I pulled out the spliff from my top pocket, lit it and smoked it until nothing but ash remained. The crowd went wild. Leroy and the Pavilion's own security looked around anxiously. I put a red fez on my head.

'The chronic hashish user eventually becomes hysterical, neurasthenic and completely insane. Hashish is beyond any doubt the principal cause of insanity occurring in Egypt.'

To rapturous applause, I sat down for the question-and-answer session, which always started with the same questions:

'*What's the strongest dope you have ever smoked?*'

'Nepalese hash from a place called Mustang.'

'*Do you have any regrets?*'

'No.'

'*Who was your best shag?*'

'Your mother.'

'*What is your favourite method of hiding cannabis?*'

'In a container.'

'*What are your favourite munchies?*'

'Sugar Puffs.'

'*Which is the easiest skunk to grow: White Widow, Purple Haze or Jack Herrer?*'

'I don't know; I'm not a gardener. I just deal with the finished product.'

Then some peculiarly local questions:

'*What do you think of today's performance by the Welsh rugby team?*'

'Complete shite. If they wanted to score, they should have given me a call.'

'*If Wales was independent, would there be a better chance for us to legalise marijuana?*'

'Absolutely. Tom Jones has already sung our new anthem, "Green, Green Grass of Home".'

Ian's voice boomed from the side of the stage: 'One more question.'

'*Howard, how can we beat the piss test?*'

I was hoping this would be asked. Now American-style piss tests were becoming the bane of every pot smoker's lifestyle. Convicts on parole, kids on probation, members of the armed forces and even ordinary employees of certain corporations were being asked with increasing regularity to demonstrate that their urine contained no traces of drugs. The British government had considered plans for police to be given the power to randomly stop any car and insist the driver step outside and piss into a bottle. Pot heads throughout the world had been experimenting with all sorts of foodstuffs, chemicals and minerals in the hope of neutralising evidence of dope in their urine. None seemed to work but recently, while on parole, Gerry Wills, my former Californian marijuana smuggling partner, had successfully invented a contraption to beat the test. Gerry called it the Whizzinator and sold them for $500 each. For old times' sake he had given me one for nothing. The Whizzinator is an extremely lifelike false rubber penis (in a range of colours and sizes) which contains a small plastic bag of drug-free urine. Straps hold it in position. The instructions suggest you find some people who don't take drugs, and take the piss out of them. When asked to do a piss test, all the smoker has to do to produce a stream of clean urine is to pull it out and squeeze it.

I took out the Whizzinator and explained the principles to the guffawing audience.

'Show us how. Demonstrate it,' someone yelled.

Clumsily, I stuck the Whizzinator down my trousers, pulled it out through my fly, stuck it in an empty pint glass and squeezed. It worked perfectly, but I couldn't stop the flow. Nor could I pull the fucking Whizzinator out of my trousers without taking my clothes off. There was no chance of my doing that in front of the home crowd, who were now roaring with uncontrollable laughter. Ian switched off the stage lighting and put on the walk-out CD, and Leroy took me back to the dressing room, my trousers drenched with pristine piss.

The dressing room had recovered but, as a result of my enormous guest list, was quickly filling up and well on the way back to its former emergency-ward status. Everyone except

Leroy ('Mi neva touch di shit, mon') and Martin Baker was smoking a joint. Polly had fully recovered from her whitey but not from the embarrassment.

'According to the tarot cards, you are both going to make it really big time in show business,' said Psychic Dave to the bemused Kelly Jones and Gruff Rhys.

'That Whizzinator stunt is pathetically sexist,' a female reporter from *Wales on Sunday* complained to Taff. 'How on earth could that rubber cock possibly help women beat the piss test?'

'Look, love,' said Taff, a master of lateral thinking, 'if your car was stopped by the Old Bill, you were asked to do a piss test and you pulled the Whizzinator out of your knickers, the cops would soon be on their bloody way. They'd fuck off, I can promise you that.'

Letters, cards and little presents were thrust into my hand. They included lighters, home-made Welsh cakes laced with hashish, home-brewed booze, several expertly crafted spliffs, a box of Sugar Puffs (the donor had seen the show in Liverpool the week before), a Welsh lady's traditional top hat to be worn at future Welsh gigs instead of the fez, jars of honey and a bag labelled *Goddess Juice Grail Drop Mushrooms*. I quickly tore it open. Inside were about a hundred tiny Welsh psilocybin mushrooms – about two full doses. These would definitely come in handy. Governed by the operating hours of local public transport, many people began to leave, much to Ian's relief, and soon there was just the hard core that had been there from the beginning.

'I'm knackered, Ian. I think I'll stay in the same hotel as you rather than go back to Kenfig Hill. Which one is it?'

'The Seabank. It's just up the road.'

'Mi wi tan de, too, mon. Maybe mi wi fin mi family ya. Ow far Cardiff de?' asked Leroy.

'Only about twenty-five miles. I might go there myself; I don't have a show for a few days.'

'I'll see you tomorrow afternoon, Howard,' said Marty. 'I'm busy in the morning.'

One by one they disappeared into the blustery night air. I took my bag of goodies to the Seabank and fell asleep listening to the crashing of the waves.

After a sleep full of dreams of ships and Welsh fezzes, I got up, had a full Welsh breakfast and took a cab back to Kenfig Hill. In the attic I rummaged through the bookshelves and cabin trunks and sifted through mounds of school exercise books, cuttings from magazines and yellowing documents that had once held some significance for a now-forgotten ancestor. I knew little about my family history and for the first time in my life wanted to learn more. I had better start soon before all my aunts and uncles passed away.

The oldest surviving member of my maternal family was my Grandpa Ben's sister, Afon Wen, as precious as the roughest of diamonds. Much to her dismay, she now lived in an old people's home set between Kenfig and Kenfig Hill, close to the M4 and adjacent to a sewage farm which she referred to as the perfume factory. By the strangest of coincidences, *Afon Wen* was also the name of the deep-sea salvage tug that during December 1979 landed fifteen tons of the finest Colombian marijuana on the western Scottish island of Kerrera. I was accused of masterminding the operation but after a nine-week trial was cleared of the charge by an Old Bailey jury, having persuaded them I was a spy. Although it was just a bizarre coincidence, I feel convinced that if Her Majesty's Customs & Excise had been aware that the offending boat had the same, very unusual, name as my great-aunt, my acquittal would never have happened.

I walked into the home and found Aunt Afon Wen's room.

'Good God all bloody mighty! Howard *bach*! What the hell are you doing down here?'

'Hello, Auntie 'Fon. I did a show last night at the Royal Pavilion in Porthcawl.'

'Never! Well, I don't know. No one lets me know bugger all these days now I'm stuck here with all these half-dead moaners and groaners. I'd have come along. Our Glyn would have given me a lift, I'm sure. Although I don't know; I haven't seen that bugger either for months. Come to think of it, why the hell didn't you let me know yourself? I sent you a bloody Christmas card every year when you were in jail.'

'I know. And yours was always the first I received. I'm sorry.'

'Never mind. You're here now. And looking all right too, except for that bloody hair of yours. I always used to tell your mam she should cut it in the middle of the night when you were sleeping. I'll just make us a cup of tea. Help yourself to a fag. I think I'm going to have to give those up soon too. I'm coughing like a bloody hyena. But it's hard to break an old habit, isn't it? I've been smoking for over seventy years now.'

'Well, I'm not the one you should ask for help. You know that.' It was time to ask the question. 'Auntie 'Fon, is there anyone famous in our family on Mam's side?'

'I don't think so at all, unless we count you, of course. If they weren't down the pits digging coal for the bloody English, they were writing poetry – a load of tommyrot most of it was, too.'

'So none of them actually became famous?'

'None except Dyfnallt Owen, who was a great-uncle of Nanna Jones, your mother's mother. He became the bloody archdruid of Wales. A bit of a wizard, too, according to Nanna Jones.'

'A wizard?'

'Well, you know how people talk, Howard *bach*. How much to believe is another thing. But there were no end of stories from Nanna Jones about him boiling up magical potions and doing all sorts of tricks with them, tricks he had learnt from his mother's father, Dafydd Rhys Williams, a brother or first cousin of none other than Edward Williams, better known as Iolo Morgannwg.'

'Well, he's definitely famous, Auntie 'Fon. I've heard of him.'

'I'm sure, but it's pushing it a bit to say he's part of the family, he's a very distant relation if any at all. Mind, I'm not surprised you have heard of him. He was a bloody opium addict. Clever though, by all accounts. They say Iolo invented the eisteddfod. That's how Dyfnallt Owen became its archdruid. It's always been the same, hasn't it, Howard *bach*? It's who you know not what you know. There's a book about Iolo on the shelves somewhere. Have a look when I get some milk for the tea.'

Iolo Morgannwg (Ned of Glamorgan), born 1747, was and is a glorious pain in the arse. Dead for nearly 200 years, this bard, visionary, genius, literary forger, field archaeologist, opium head and jailbird is still the cause of passionate debate in Wales and elsewhere. The arguments usually revolve around perceptions of Iolo's establishment of the Gorsedd of the Bards in 1792 at Primrose Hill, north London, where he and a few of his mates stood within a circle of pebbles brought from Wales and mirrored Druidic rites that Iolo claimed to have uncovered in ancient manuscripts. They spoke prayers, sang hymns and founded the still-existing Gorsedd to promote Welsh language, folk culture, literature and the arts. Some historians now think that he wrote the rites while serving a prison sentence for debt and that the material derived from his opium-crazed imagination. Nevertheless Iolo's rituals are still performed every August as part of the Welsh National Eisteddfod and his Gorsedd prayer is still used by Druids. Recent initiates to the Gorsedd include Dr Rowan Williams, archbishop of Canterbury, while the Queen is an ovate, and actor Richard Burton and prime minster David Lloyd George were past members.

To many, Iolo is the victim of an English revisionist attempt to oppress Welsh culture and tarnish the image of what was once a great civilisation. To others, he lived in times so dangerous for an outspoken republican anti-slavery campaigner, pacifist and hater of English tyranny, he had to hide behind the names of dead poets and writers to mask the subversive nature of his literature. He was followed by spies, arrested for sedition and widely viewed as a heretic. Ensuring he offended the tastes of everyone in power during his lifetime, he was also an opium eater, a vociferous religious dissenter, a political liberal and a supporter of the American rebels and the French Revolution. Iolo was also a witty guest and a brilliant storyteller, who wrote anti-war poems and drinking songs. He was a vegetarian, herbalist and tea addict, and walked the length and breadth of Wales accompanied by his horse, which he rode just once in his life. Although he received money from wealthy patrons in London and Wales, every now and then Iolo had to work for a living. During his life he was a stone mason, a farmer, a bookshop owner, and a grocer selling 'East Indian Sweets: Uncontaminated by Human Gore'. Iolo's main ambition was to cross the Atlantic in search of the Welsh Red Indians referred to in various manuscripts by Sir Walter Raleigh and other European explorers. By way of preparation he slept rough in the fields near his home but became ill, never recovering enough to make the trip. During his last days Iolo begged the surviving members of his family to fulfil his unfinished ambition.

'So, Auntie 'Fon, is there no one else interesting in our family on Mam's side?'

'Come to think of it, Dyfnallt's ancestor William Owen was quite famous in his time. Well, infamous would be a better way of describing him, as it would with you. They say he was the greatest-ever Welsh smuggler, not drugs mind. He was executed in Carmarthen. I think he wrote an autobiography, too. They discovered it quite recently. Now that's a coincidence, isn't it?'

I later found out the previously unknown autobiography of William Owen had turned up in 1982. After a few successful smuggling runs between Wales and the Isle of Man, Owen worked in South America for a well-armed worldwide smuggler known as The Terrible. My own smuggling activities had centred largely on Europe and Asia. Though I didn't know it, I'd soon be heading for his old stamping ground. Owen's sexual liaisons resulted in illegitimate children of all colours, and his chronicle of scams, acquittals and debauchery would put any modern-day smuggler or playboy to shame.

'This gets better and better, Auntie 'Fon. Any others?'

'Well there's my mother's half-brother Madoc. I can't go into it too much. I think there was a bit of incest going on. There was more of that in those days. But he's the bugger who gave me my name, Afon Wen, which I've never been bloody keen on. You know what it means, don't you?'

'Of course. It's Welsh for White River.'

'That's right. A bloody good name for a squaw, don't you think? Madoc always claimed he was a Red Indian brought up in a wigwam with totem poles outside it.'

'Perhaps he was an opium addict too?'

'Maybe. He did have some crackpot ideas. Thought he was a direct descendant of a Welsh prince who was also the first of the Incas. He used to say the Incas were his bloody cousins. I ask you! Mind, Madoc was all bloody there all right, and he certainly had Red Indian blood in him from somewhere.'

'Do you know which tribe?

'No idea. They spoke Welsh, according to Madoc. God knows how.'

'What happened to Madoc in the end?'

'He wanted to go to Patagonia and join the Welsh colony there. A lot of people from the valleys round here had gone to Patagonia for a new life, and they got on very well with the Indians, by all accounts. Madoc got jealous because he had always felt he belonged on the other side of the Atlantic with the Red Indians and their wigwams. He never made it though, poor bugger. He got killed by lightning.'

I drank my tea, smoked a couple of fags and bid Auntie 'Fon goodbye.

'Don't leave it so bloody long next time.'

I never saw her again.

The oldest surviving member of my paternal family was my grandfather's eldest sister, Katie Marks. She was ninety and lived in her own flat in Kenfig Hill. I had never known her very well and hadn't seen her for about fifteen years. Maybe she would have some stories to tell.

'Auntie Katie.'

'Hello, Howard *bach*. Lovely to see you after all these years. You must be glad to be back from America. What are you doing with yourself these days?

'Writing and doing shows. I've turned over a new leaf.'

'That's right, Howard *bach*, put the past behind you.'

'Well, actually, Auntie Katie, it's the past I wanted to talk to you about.'

'Oh dear! How can I help?'

'Who was my Grandfather Tudor's father?'

'Dafydd Marks. He owned half of Kenfig Hill.'

'And who was his father? Was that Patrick Marks?'

'That's right. Patrick Marks, a very religious man in the end. He is buried up the road in Siloam chapel, Cefn Cribbwr.'

'And his father? Who was that?'

'Well, that's where it does get a bit confusing. It seems that Patrick changed his name from McCarty to Marks.'

'Why?'

'There are three theories. One was to inherit a lot of money from a German Jewish family called Marks who worked the coal mines round by here. Another was to hide himself because he had made a lot of money abroad in a way he shouldn't have, and the foreign police were after him.'

'How did he make his money?

'Now that I don't know. He made it somewhere in America.'

'North or South America?'

'I don't even know that. But the third theory, and this is the one I think is true, was to get rid of the bad name and reputation of his relative, who was Billy the Kid, of course.'

'What! How closely related were they?'

'Patrick's father, who was also called Patrick, was Billy the Kid's father as well, but with another woman.'

'This is incredible. My great-great grandfather was Billy the Kid's brother.'

'Half-brother, I think, isn't it? But there's more, Howard *bach*, lots more. The McCartys were also in Jesse James's gang and got together with Butch Cassidy and the Sundance Kid in Patagonia, a Welsh colony and the headquarters of all the Irish and Welsh cowboys in those days. It was there that Patrick learned Welsh. Anyway, after years out in South America, he decided to come and live here in South Wales under another name. I'm sure Denny, your dad, was given everything that Patrick wrote. Probably in a box somewhere in your house. Not that changing his name did Patrick much good, mind. His son, your great-grandfather Dafydd's brother, Willie Bevan Marks, became a notorious Chicago gangster. He was Bugs Moran's first lieutenant. I wasn't a bit surprised you became a famous smuggler, not a bit.'

'Is this true, Auntie Katie?'

'Every word. Why do you think your Grandfather Tudor's brother Tommy called all his children something Bevan Marks, including the girls? He was hoping Willie would leave them his money.'

'Did he?'

'Not a penny.'

I decided to check the veracity of this avalanche of information

about my ancestry and called into Kenfig Hill library to surf
the Net.

Billy the Kid was born in 1861 in New York to Patrick and
Catherine McCarty and named William Henry McCarty. A
few years later Patrick left Catherine, who married William
Antrim and died when young Billy was thirteen. Billy became
an outlaw, teaming up with Welshman Jesse Evans, the leader
of a gang of rustlers called The Boys. To avoid capture, Billy
changed his name to William H. Bonney.

At the beginning of Prohibition, Willie Marks joined Dean
O'Bannion's North Side Gang of Chicago and was best
friends with fellow member George 'Bugs' Moran, who later
became leader of the gang and made Willie Marks his second
in command. His duties included the management of the
gang's South American interests. Willie Marks narrowly
missed being murdered in the St Valentine's Day massacre but
was later fatally machine-gunned by Al Capone's James 'Fur'
Sammons, a well-known psychotic who was convicted of the
rape, mutilation and murder of an eleven-year-old schoolgirl.
Willie Marks is buried in Woodlawn Cemetery in Forest Park,
Illinois.

I was about to research Prince Madoc, the Mandans, the
Welsh Incas and the ever-increasing connections with
Patagonia when the familiar figure of Marty Langford ambled
into the library.

'I heard you were here. You know the council has
withdrawn funding for the Royal Pavilion since last night's
shenanigans, don't you? You've stirred the place up again.
There'll be no more of your shows round here.'

'Oh no! Never mind. Fancy a pint?'

Two

WELSHMEN

The scene which greeted us back at the Royal Oak bore a marked likeness to that of the day before. The television was showing precisely the same rugby match, although a highlighted version. Ivor Prior and Eddie Evans were sitting in the same seats waiting for the match to end so they could get on with the regular Sunday afternoon quiz. The rest of the pub's customers were watching the match as intently as they had been twenty-four hours earlier, displaying no sign they already knew the result.

'Well, what an achievement!' said Eddie. 'Getting the local council to withdraw financial support for the Royal Pavilion. The end of an era, that's what it is. I've spent all my bloody life trying to bring culture to the masses down by here, and you ruin it in one night. Now there isn't anywhere in the area where we can put on plays, operas and concerts. I hope you're pleased with yourself.'

'You're being too harsh on him, Eddie,' said Ivor, springing to my defence. 'If the council wanted to put on your daft bloody plays, they wouldn't let something like Howard puffing on a stage get in the way.'

'You're probably right, Ivor,' conceded Eddie unexpectedly.

'They were just looking for an excuse. I was only joking, Howard. The Porthcawl councillors are nothing but a load of tossers. Anyway, it's quiz time in a few minutes. Get your brains working.'

The match finished, and the viewers, every bit as disappointed with Wales's dismal performance as before, took their seats for the quiz. Eddie perched on a high stool at the bar to preside over proceedings.

'We'll start with one for you sports fans. Where and when did the first ever sports event under floodlights take place?'

The question met with silence. I could see from Marty's facial expression he knew the answer but was too shy to shout it out. There was little about Wales and matters Welsh Marty didn't know, but he had taught himself and had little experience of vocalising his wealth of knowledge.

'Well, I thought you lot would know that, at least. I deliberately started with an easy one. The first ever sports event under floodlights took place in Cardiff in 1877 at a Cardiff-versus-Newport rugby match.'

Marty nodded and smiled.

'Next question. You all eat cornflakes, I'm sure. What's the origin of the name Kellog's, the cereal company?'

Another silence.

'Come on. You probably had some this morning. All of you. Think of the packaging.'

Again, it was obvious that Marty knew the answer, but he still kept his peace.

Eddie carried on: 'Kellog comes from the Welsh for chicken, *ceiliog*. There's a picture on every packet.'

And so it continued, every question asked and answered by Eddie, every one another Welsh fact.

The final question: 'Who won the first ever recorded libel case? I'm not even going to bother to ask if anyone knows the answer. I know no one does. It was—'

'I know,' interjected Marty, finally plucking up the courage to speak. 'The first ever recorded libel case was won by Henry Morgan.'

'You are right, boy *bach*. Well done! Henry Morgan the buccaneer, probably the greatest Welshman ever, much more impressive than Alexander the Great in my opinion, sued the Dutchman Esquemeling for writing that he was sent overseas because of his criminal behaviour. The Dutchman was right, mind, but that's another tale. You should write Henry Morgan's life story, Howard; it's a lot more impressive than yours.'

'Where was he born, Eddie?' I asked out of genuine interest.

'Somewhere on the border between Glamorgan and Monmouth, I think. His family lived in a big mansion near where the M4 is now. It's still there.'

'There was something else I wanted to ask you, Eddie.'

'Go ahead. I'm always happy to quench an Oxford graduate's thirst for knowledge.'

'Yesterday afternoon you were talking about Merlin advising King Arthur.'

'That's right, I was. I'm pleased you remember. I thought you would have forgotten everything other than the fact that Elvis was of Welsh descent. I know you are a big fan. Not that he could sing all that well. His version of "O Sole Mio" is diabolical, absolutely diabolical.'

'I preferred the old Elvis,' Ivor put in, 'when he was younger.'

'That doesn't make too much sense, Ivor. Think about what you are saying for once,' said Eddie.

'I'm saying I liked Elvis's early songs, before he joined the army. Mind, we've all passed a lot of water under the bridge since then. And one man's meat isn't everyone's cup of tea, of course. I accept that.'

'You are mixing your metaphors a bit too much there, Ivor. But let's get back to the point. Yes, Howard, the first ever Christian kingdom's throne was Camelot, which was at

Caerleon, a city the Romans built on an old Druidic site just outside Newport. Caerleon had a huge amphitheatre, much of which is still visible today. Arthur had twelve knights doing his bidding in the same way the twelve disciples served Jesus Christ.'

'But Eddie,' I asked, 'why did Christianity take off here, if it did, rather than anywhere else in the world?'

'Well, it took off, as you put it, in all sorts of places, but here was the first country that had a Christian king – Arthur.'

'So why was that?'

'It's something I've done no end of research into. I have my own theories, of course, all backed by historical fact, but every time I mention them, I'm called a blasphemer.'

'I promise not to.'

'I couldn't give a bugger if you did. I've been called worse by better. I'll explain. What's the name of the Catholic church here in Pisgah Street?'

'St Joseph of Arimathea,' I answered.

'Correct. And who was Joseph of Arimathea?'

'The guy who paid for Jesus' tomb in Jersualem.'

'Yes, everyone knows that, but who was he? Where did he come from?'

'Arimathea?' Ivor conjectured.

'I mean what family, Ivor, as you well know.'

'No idea, Eddie. Unless Arimathea is the old name for Kenfig Hill.'

'No need for sarcasm, Ivor. What I'm going to say is funda-mental, absolutely fundamental. Joseph of Arimathea was the same person as Joseph, husband of Mary, mother of Jesus.'

'Why doesn't the Bible say that, then?' asked Ivor. 'I just can't believe the lies you are coming out with lately.'

'Ivor, the Bible doesn't say that wasn't the case, and it doesn't say that Joseph, husband of Mary, came from anywhere else, does it?'

'Maybe not; I don't know. But what's a carpenter from

Arimathea, what ever that is, doing buying and selling tombs in Jersualem? The Bible said Joseph was a carpenter. I know that much, Eddie.'

'Simple, Ivor. It's a mistranslation: it shouldn't be carpenter; it should be mason. That's where a lot of this freemasonry rubbish comes from. I'll continue. Howard and Marty here are genuinely interested. In AD 33 Joseph brought the body of his son Jesus, as well as the Holy Grail, to Glastonbury, where he planted his staff, which grew into the famous thorn tree there. Glastonbury was an important place in ancient Britain.'

'Glastonbury is in England, not Wales.' Ivor looked pleased with his point.

'Ivor, as I have pointed out on more than one occasion in this very room, the ancient Britons were the Welsh. Ancient Britain, the first country in the world to move into the Iron Age in about 1000 BC, was a cultured country whose language, Welsh, was spoken throughout what is today the United Kingdom and was understood in most of Europe.'

'I bet they didn't speak it in Scotland.'

'Of course they did, Ivor. Don't show your ignorance. Taliesin, the greatest ever Welsh poet, spent all his life near Glasgow, which itself is a Welsh word meaning blue meadow. What I've said so far most people know and accept as fact; what a lot of people don't know, however, is that Joseph and Jesus had visited ancient Britain years before. The family owned extensive tin mines in Cornwall and often came to oversee matters.'

'You're opening a real tandoori box now, Eddie. I doubt if many people will believe that,' said Ivor.

'Well, the brilliant William Blake did, Ivor.' Eddie then suddenly burst into song:

> 'And did those feet in ancient time
>   Walk upon England's mountains green?

And was the holy Lamb of God
    On England's pleasant pastures seen?

And did the Countenance Divine
    Shine forth upon our clouded hills?
And was Jerusalem builded here
    Among these dark Satanic mills?'

The rest of the pub looked puzzled – just ten minutes ago they had been singing 'Sospan Fach' to the accompaniment of the rugby highlights – but at the beginning of the next verse they joined in with full power.

'Bring me my bow of burning gold:
    Bring me my arrows of desire:
Bring me my spear: O clouds, unfold!
    Bring me my chariot of fire

I will not cease from mental fight
    Nor shall my sword sleep in my hand,
Till we have built Jerusalem,
    In England's green and pleasant land.'

Shelves of bottles and hanging lampshades resonated furiously with the strong harmonies that only a Welsh male voice choir can provide. Then came an impromptu 'Bread of Heaven', followed by another final rendition of 'Sospan Fach'. Silence eventually fell but it was broken after less than a minute by Ivor: 'Anyway, I don't believe Jesus came back from the dead.'

'That's entirely another matter, Ivor,' said Eddie. 'Some people do; they believe Jesus suffered on the cross for our sins.'

'Suffered on the cross!' protested Ivor. 'Jesus' sufferings were nothing like as bad as the pain millions of people have had to put up with. If I was as sure of living for ever as Jesus was, I wouldn't mind being nailed to a bloody cross for a few nights.'

'Now show some respect, Ivor, please. It is a Sunday, after all.'

But Ivor was in top gear. 'There isn't another world. We haven't got any bloody souls. You see all this stuff in front of you with your eyes, and when you shut them or go blind, you don't see any of it anymore. It's exactly the same with our brains. When our brains decay, we forget everything. When we die, everything dies with us. It's the same for us as for all other animals. You all know this. You're just kidding yourselves.'

No one took any notice. They had heard it all before.

'What was in that Holy Grail, Eddie?' I asked, thinking of the mushrooms I had been given the previous night.

'I can't pretend to know the exact ingredients, but whoever drank a single drop would either die like a demon, live for ever, or pass on a bit of divinity or a kingdom to his son or grandson, depending on who the mother was. Joseph's grandson, the Welsh hero Caradoc, was born very near here and became king of ancient Britain. Caradoc refused to bow his head to the Romans and was taken to Rome as a prisoner. The Romans respected him, cut him loose and gave him a taste of the high life. After a while Caradoc came back to Wales and brought with him none other than St Paul, who set up his church in Caradoc's parish, Llanilid, just outside Bridgend.

'Caradoc is a direct ancestor of King Arthur and of Hywel Dda, who, despite being a nasty bit of work, first gave a system of law to Wales. Obviously, Joseph gave Caradoc a sip from the Holy Grail. Caradoc gave the same to his son, and so on until Hywel Dda. The Holy Grail is the same as the divine right of kings. That's why Henry VII – Henry Tudor – bent over backwards to show he was descended from King Arthur, fulfilling Merlin's prophecy that a Welsh king with the essence of Arthur would once again rule Britain.'

'That can't be right,' I said. 'If King Arthur had drunk from the Holy Grail, why did he send his knights out to find it? Did someone steal it?'

'Actually, yes; Merlin did. Not only did he steal it, he also drank more than his fair share from it.'

'Ah! I see.'

Something among all the madness made sense to me, but I didn't know what it was. None of it made sense to Ivor.

'Eddie, shut up for Christ's sake. Even if anyone could understand you, they wouldn't know what the hell you are on about.'

Four pints later, Marty and I left the pub to roll a skunk spliff in the shelter by the old railway line.

'Marty, I want to take a strong dose of these mushrooms called Goddess Juice Grail Drops someone gave me last night. Can you be with me in case I go weird?'

'Of course. An honour and a privilege.'

'Unless you want to take some, too?'

'No, thanks; I still haven't recovered from that acid you gave me nearly forty years ago.'

We walked to the 'ton', the hill that distinguishes Kenfig Hill from nearby Kenfig. I ate the mushrooms and after about twenty minutes a stream of unconsciousness drowned me with profundity and madness. I started thinking of females and God and Merlin, Eddie Evans and Elvis, and the setting sun.

'What the hell are you thinking about, Howard.'

'Christianity, I suppose. And all that stuff Eddie Evans was talking about. Mad, isn't he?'

'Well much of what he says is true. The first Christian kingdom did happen around here, as did the Druid religion thousands of years earlier.'

'I don't know anything about the Druids, to be honest.'

'Well, it was the first worldwide religion. Pythagoras, for example, was a Druid.'

'Marty, are you saying the first religious person ever was Welsh?'

'No, I'm not saying that. Seth, the third son of Adam after Cain and Abel, founded Druidism somewhere in Iraq. He used the name Gwyddon Ganhebon. Seth's devotee, Hu Gadarn the Mighty, a contemporary of Abraham, brought Druidism to ancient Britain. There are loads of similarities between Druidism and Christianity.'

'I thought Druids sacrificed virgins. Doesn't sound too Christian to me.'

'There's plenty of sacrificing going on in the Bible, Howard. And don't forget the Holy Trinity – the Druids had that idea, but to them it was simply the past, present and future. No Holy Ghost stuff. Druidism had its headquarters here for two thousand years. Going from Druidism to Christianity is not as traumatic as some people try to make out.'

'But I read that the first Christian kingdom was Georgia, where red wine, Jesus' favourite drink, was first produced. The Georgian alphabet is based on the stages of growth of the vine.'

'Is Georgia anything to do with Saint George?'

'Yes, he's their patron saint as well.'

'Well, there you go, Howard. Don't forget the red dragon is the same as red wine from the true vine. St George killed the red dragon, a triumph of evil over good, of the English over the Welsh, and Merlin did say the Welsh would have their day. They probably just read books about it in Georgia when they got pissed; we Welsh experienced it.'

'OK, Marty, thanks. Can we go back to the pub? I'm dehydrating and sweating.'

Again, not much had changed at the pub, although Eddie Evans was on the point of leaving.

'It's Howard and Marty back. You've been a while; I won't ask what you've been up to. But here's something interesting

which I only found out today and forgot to tell you earlier:
America was named after a Welshman.'

I felt confident enough to contradict: 'You're wrong there,
Eddie. America was named after Amerigo Vespucci.'

'Oh really! Have you heard of Richard Americ?'

'No, I can't say I have, Eddie.'

'I'll leave you to research that one, Oxford boy.'

The mushrooms, the beer, the skunk, last night's cocaine
hangover and today's overdose of information had left me
exhausted. Marty and I went to our separate Kenfig Hill
homes. Sleeping was difficult – too many images of pirates,
kings, rock singers, angels, mistletoe and wizards. I gave up,
switched on my laptop, went online, and searched for websites
referring to Richard Americ.

I discovered that Italian mariner Giovanni Caboto (John
Cabot) had visited Bristol to meet wealthy merchants willing
to fund a voyage of discovery to the west. Henry VII had given
Caboto authority to claim lands on his behalf. Richard
Americ, King's Customs Officer and Sheriff of Bristol, provided most of the finance on condition that any land claimed
would carry his name. Americ was born in Wales, and his
name is derived from the Welsh ap Meuric (son of Maurice).
Caboto set out and made landfall five weeks after leaving
England. On his return with proof of a new world, America,
Henry VII gave Caboto a bigger fleet of ships to exploit his
discovery. As a result of the meanderings of their own Italian
mariner Christopher Colombus, the Spanish had other ideas
about who discovered America. On hearing of Caboto's
voyage and the naming of America, the Spanish sent the
notorious pirate Hojeda to sink Caboto's fleet. One of
Hojedas's crew was another Italian, Amerigo Vespucci.
Caboto's fleet never returned.

Still surfing, I found the Americ family coat of arms: it was
the stars and stripes. I needed no further proof. America was
named after a Welshman, and the United States flag was

derived from his coat of arms. Why was this not commonly known? Was this further evidence in support of Marty's favourite hobby horse – the suppression of all things Welsh by the English?

I rummaged around the attic again. Dozens of boxes contained belongings of mine from days gone by – old school textbooks, chemistry and Meccano sets, unopened wedding presents from my 1967 marriage to Ilze, psychedelic rock posters, hundreds of letters and reams of pretentious philosophical ramblings from the days when I thought my only possible career was as an academic. One box was from Terre Haute Penitentiary. It had lain unopened since 1995 and contained all the photographs, books and letters sent to me during my years as a prisoner and which the authorities had judged detrimental to maintaining good order in the prison. One was a photograph of my son Patrick aged two taking his first swim. It hadn't been allowed to get through because he wasn't wearing a swimming costume. There were several inoffensive books on drugs, crime, sex and politics, computer magazines and various articles on subjects ranging from racism in America to the Super Furry Animals. American prisons take no chances. Some books contained dedications to me handwritten by the authors. These were automatically banned; books had to be sent to the prison in virgin condition direct from the publishers. My attention was drawn to a book entitled *Madoc – The Legend of the Welsh Discovery of America*. The author, Gwyn A. Williams, had signed a copy for me. An envelope of articles and pamphlets on the same subject peeped out from inside the book. I settled down to read, highlighting and scribbling frantically.

Prince Madoc, the illegitimate son of Welsh king Owain the Great, had become disillusioned with royal life. In 1170 he and some of his friends set sail from Abergele, currently a small village and large caravan park near Colwyn Bay, and landed in Alabama. Both Abergele and Mobile, Alabama have plaques to Madoc's memory. Leaving behind a small group, Madoc returned to Wales with tales of the warm, luscious land he had found. He picked up supplies and more ships full of like-minded fellow countrymen and was never seen again.

Advisers to Henry Tudor's granddaughter, Elizabeth I, used the tale of Madoc to assert British sovereignty over American territory already claimed by Spain. The house of Tudor was proud of its Welsh roots and had ample evidence to argue its case. Explorers, including Sir Walter Raleigh, had written about a tribe of Native Americans who spoke Welsh. In 1669 the Reverend Morgan Jones of Jesus College, Oxford and a party of five were taken prisoner by Native Americans. One of the tribe heard Reverend Jones praying in Welsh, whereupon the men were released unharmed by the braves, who claimed descent from Madoc. Around a hundred years later French fur trader Jacques d'Eglise found a tribe of Native Americans who lived in beehive-shaped lodges similar to those found in Wales and fished in round skin and wickerwork boats exactly like Welsh coracles. Clerics, traders, missionaries and anthropologists such as George Catlin all came into contact with the tribe, who referred to themselves as the Madogwys – men of Madoc. In 1782 Oconosto, chief of the Cherokee nation, stated that a series of pre-Columbian forts on the shores of the Alabama River were built by 'a people called Welsh and they had crossed the Great Water'. Chief Oconosto called their leader Madoc. Archaeological research has shown that one of the forts was identical in setting, layout and method of construction to Dolwyddelan Castle in Gwynedd, the still-standing birthplace of Prince Madoc.

One pamphlet claimed that Madoc, on his second visit, landed and settled in Mexico; there were several Welsh words in the Aztec language. One of these was the name of a strange new bird, the *penguin*, Welsh for 'white head' (*pen gwyn*). At this point I took a break from my research to smoke a spliff. I thought of penguins and realised they had black heads. My heart fell. I had been reading a complete load of bollocks. I drifted asleep, weary and depressed.

I woke up with a crystal-clear mind. The penguin problem had provoked doubts about the existence of Welsh Native Americans but the rest made perfect sense. Back online, I searched for 'white-headed penguins' and came across the great auk (*Pinguinus impennis*), a big, northern hemisphere penguin with a white patch on its head. Great auks, extinct for over 150 years, had lived in great numbers on islands off Britain, Iceland and Greenland and were sources of food and down, especially for mariners crossing the Atlantic. Almost all seabirds had black heads, so the great auk could be distinguished by its white patch. When Welsh settlers came across southern hemisphere penguins, the striking similarity in shape between these and great auks resulted in the name penguin being used for both. I felt relieved. Until this moment I had been inclined to dismiss Great-Aunt Afon Wen's story of Welsh Red Indians as a flight of fancy, possibly her own, but here it was confirmed in works of scholarship. Could she also have been right about the Incas? That would just be too much to take. Within minutes, I was back in the attic.

In 1908 the Reverend John H. Parry of the University of Durham published *Manco Capac the First Inca of Peru, Being a Critical Inquiry into the Pretensions concerning the Discovery of America by Prince Madawg Ap Owen Gwynedd with Reflections upon the Final Discovery of that Continent by Christopher Columbus; and upon some of the Historical Antiquities of America*, which argued that Madoc became known as Manco Capac. Accompanied by Mama Ocello (a corruption of *Mama Uchel* – 'High Mother'), Manco Capac had arrived on the shores of Peru a few weeks after Madoc's disappearance from Wales. The couple are the progenitors of the Incas. The

natives saw them as children of the sun because they had
come from the east. Manco Capac became a leader, set up a
dynasty and taught the natives to live in houses, cultivate
trees and plants, and rear flocks of animals. He made Cuzco
the capital of Peru and reigned there for forty years before
heading south down the Andes and disappearing. He
brought a lot with him: he developed structures of authority
and justice remarkably similar to those of Hywel Dda in
Wales. Elements of Christianity were present in the Incas'
worship of the sun. Words and place names were similar to
those used by Welsh Druids.

There was a knock on the door. It was Marty. 'I've got the car
for a couple of days if you fancy a bit of an excursion.'

Three

THE CARIBBEAN

'Please come this way, ladies and gentlemen. On the walls of this magnificent dining room are portraits of Morgan family members. As you can see, scattered around the room are various bits of china and silver, some of which are extremely valuable. That Elizabethan salt cellar, for example, is worth almost twenty thousand pounds. These chairs are worth—'

'Who is that in the picture by the door?' interrupted Marty.

'Ah! That's the black sheep of the family, Henry Morgan the pirate. We try not to mention him. He did disgrace the family quite a bit.'

Marty and I and various tourists were on a guided tour of Tredegar House, a mansion just off the main Cardiff–Newport road and former home of the Morgans, one of the greatest of Welsh families. We were on our way to Cwmaman, from where the Stereophonics hail, and the current home of Bernie Davies, a senior member of both the Valley Commandos and of the Firm, Britain's largest criminal organisation. I had last seen Bernie at the Glastonbury Festival, where he had expressed interest in my doing a show at the Cwmaman Institute. I had agreed to visit him the next time I was in Wales.

'He looks a bit like you, Howard. Don't you think so?'

'Who, Marty?'

'Henry Morgan, of course. Look at his eyes and his mouth. Exactly like yours.'

I could vaguely see what Marty meant, but the portrait was of a teenager.

'Excuse me,' said Marty to the woman guide, 'but he was a bit more than just a pirate, wasn't he? I mean he was governor of Jamaica. Let's be fair.'

'Deputy governor only, I think. And he got sacked. And he was imprisoned in the Tower of London for his crimes against king and country. Henry Morgan was a very cruel man. He was a murderer, a drinker, a womaniser and a thief. I don't know why they keep his picture here. If I had my way, it would be thrown away. And he was probably born out of wedlock. The family has had to endure shame for centuries because of Henry Morgan's evil ways and mad behaviour.'

'But he was knighted,' protested Marty, 'and made Sir Henry Morgan.'

'Well, things were different in the seventeenth century, weren't they? All sorts of scallywags were made knights. Anyway, let's not dwell on him, please. On the right there's a picture of Evan Morgan, the last of the family to live here in Tredegar House. Now he was a real character. He would frolic naked in the pool here at weekends with his three best friends, who were none other than H.G. Wells, Aldous Huxley and George Bernard Shaw. He filled the place with wild animals, including an anteater and a boxing kangaroo called Somerset. His mother was even more of an eccentric. She built bigger and bigger bird's nests in the house and ended up living in one of them.'

Marty wasn't about to let the guide get off so easily. 'Was

Henry Morgan born in this house, then? I suppose he must have been if his portrait is here.'

'He certainly was not born here,' answered the guide indignantly.

One of the tour party, an American, suddenly developed an interest in the pirate. 'Where *was* he born? My name is Morgan. I might well be one of his descendants. I've been told my ancestors were Welsh.'

'There's no chance of that, sir, I'm afraid. Henry Morgan had no children, thank God. But if you want to see where he was born, go to Llanrhumney Hall outside Cardiff. You'll have no problem believing he was born there, I can promise you; it's probably the roughest part of Wales. As you are interested, I should add that a BBC Wales team recently went there and decided that he wasn't born there but somewhere up in the valleys. I think it was in Blackwood. I can't see why it matters myself.'

Blackwood was near Cwmaman. Perhaps Bernie Davies would know about this.

In twenty minutes the disappointing tour came to its end. Marty and I decided to visit Henry Morgan's supposed birthplace at Llanrhumney Hall, less than ten miles away. We drove from Tredegar House towards Cardiff on the A48 and came to what we thought was Llanrhumney, but there was no evidence of the name on any newsagent's, pub or post office. Crawling down a hill towards the centre of Cardiff, I noticed a pub called Morgan's. This couldn't be a coincidence. A notice signalled the pub was open all day and served good food, so we parked and walked to the door. It was closed. We knocked hard for several minutes. A large dog ambled up, placed its front paws on the door, and barked repeatedly. Eventually, a young man in slippers and a chef's apron unlocked the door. He yelled at the dog, threatening to kick it, and stared at me and Marty as if we were a couple of bailiffs.

'We're closed, I'm sorry.'

'Closed?' protested Marty. 'How can somewhere advertising hot food all day be closed at lunchtime? We don't want much. A sandwich will do.'

'Like I said, I'm sorry. We would like to open, but we just can't get the staff these days.'

'Can you tell us where Llanrhumney Hall is?' I asked.

'That much I can do for you. Drive back out of here and turn left into the main road. When you come to the Cross Inn, turn left. That's Llanrhumney Avenue. Then turn left into Ball Road and keep going. You can't miss it.'

We followed the landlord's directions and found ourselves in the middle of an inhospitable housing estate. Truanting schoolchildren stared at us menacingly from gardens full of refuse. Most of the homes appeared to have been converted into crack houses.

'I don't believe this, Marty,' I said. 'That landlord must have been winding us up. There's not going to be a stately home in the middle of this lot.'

I wound down the window. 'Where's Llanrhumney Hall?' I asked one of the school skivers.

'You don't want to go there; it's haunted.'

'All the better. Where is it?'

'Just keep going.'

'Thanks. By the way, who's it haunted by?'

'Henry Morgan.'

This was encouraging. 'Oh yeah,' I said. 'Who was he then?'

'He was a no-good criminal that lived there ages ago. They killed him and put his body in the cells under the hall. But people kept hearing his screams, so they chopped his body into little pieces and hid the bits in different parts of the walls. But he still haunts the place and sometimes rides his horse at midnight across the rugby field next door. I've seen him lots of times.'

'Thanks for your help.'

We drove another hundred yards down Ball Road. Next to

a rugby pitch was a magnificent old pub. A sign showed it was the headquarters of Llanrhumney Rugby Club. We parked and walked into a huge cold bar called Morgan's Room. A new pool table dominated, while an old minstrels' gallery served as a lounge bar. Next to the minstrels' gallery was a skittle alley. A barman covered with tattoos came over to serve us.

'A pint of best bitter, please, and what do you want, Marty?'

'A cup of tea, please.'

'We don't do tea or coffee here.'

'A Diet Coke then, please, or some other diet fizzy drink.'

'We don't have any of that either.'

'Pineapple juice?'

'Nor that. You want something non-alcoholic do you?'

'Please.'

'Well there's not much call for that round here. I can get you a small bottle of tomato juice, if you like, but I don't think it's fizzy.'

'That will do. Do you have anything to eat?'

'Plain or cheese and onion?'

Grabbing our crisps and drinks, we sat on stools at the bar. There were two other customers, who glared at us continually. Braving the hostility, I asked the barman, 'Was Henry Morgan the pirate born here?'

'No idea; I've only been here a few years. But some odd people like you do come here looking for him; and I know the previous landlord used to sell Captain Morgan rum.'

We took a walk outside and found a curiously wrought stone which had apparently been uncovered during recent building work. Sculptures of exotic foliage, resembling both marijuana and banana leaves, adorned the surface. We spent a few minutes arguing about which plant's leaves the carvings actually depicted but agreed the leaves were definitely tropical and had probably been brought from the Caribbean by Henry Morgan.

'Let's get out of here, Marty. I don't want to keep Bernie waiting longer any than necessary. It will be dark soon.'

Henry Morgan, son of a scullery maid and a gentleman farmer, was born in 1635 at Llanrhymney Hall. He spent most of his childhood on a farm in Princetown, a small village lying between Merthyr Tydfil and Tredegar, and later moved to his family's estate in Pencarn. An energetic and ambitious young man, Henry embraced pleasure and detested any claims to the moral high ground, especially those made by bigoted Puritans or the Roman Catholic Church. Seeking adventure, fame and fortune, he went to Bristol and spent his time there gambling, brawling and getting into trouble. Sailors were scarce, and if there weren't enough volunteers, the press gangs went to work. There was also great demand for British labour in the plantations of the colonies, much of which was satisfied by indentured servants. Most of these were offenders sentenced to penal servitude overseas, but some were tricked into indentured service by the promise of retirement in a tropical paradise. Whether as an indentured servant or the victim of a press gang, records show that on 3 May 1655 Henry boarded a ship bound for the West Indies.

The road from Tredegar House to Cwmaman wound through valleys that during my childhood had throbbed with coal mines, rain-drenched rugby games, male voice choirs, chapels and pubs. There was little left to remind me of those days – just the rain. Following Bernie's instructions, we arrived at the Falcon, which resembled a Swiss ski lodge with its views of mountains, cascading waterfalls and a furiously flowing river. All that was missing was the snow.

'All right, butt?' Bernie, a gentle mountain of a man covered with tattoos, climbed off his Harley Davidson.

'Fine thanks, Bernie. You?'

'Excellent, butt. Excellent.'

'It's good to see you, Bernie. This is a nice spot.'

'I'm glad you like it. Is it all right if you stay here tonight? I would put you up in my place, but I've got Dave Courtney, Charlie Breaker and that lot coming down sometime tonight or tomorrow morning. I'd better keep them under wraps in my place. Don't want to frighten the locals too much, do we?

'No problem, Bernie. Do the rooms have phones? I've no signal on my mobile.'

'I don't think so. It's not really a hotel; it's the Falcon, like. But you can get a signal just up the hill.'

Marty and I checked into the Falcon. In the crowded bar Bernie and I discussed terms for doing the show. A date was set. I brought up the subject of Henry Morgan.

'Is Tredegar House heavily guarded?'

'I don't know, Bernie. It didn't appear to be. Why do you ask?'

'Well, I'm sure that a lot of people, like you, would rather see a bit more respect given to the old boy's picture. I think it would look great in the Valley Commandos' headquarters, for example. There's no shortage of pirate lovers there.'

'What are you suggesting, Bernie?'

'Nothing at all, butt. Nothing at all.'

'Do you know Blackwood, Bernie?'

'Well, aye, of course I do. It's just over the hill.'

'Do you know anyone from there?'

'Loads. There's one for a start. Old Emrys in the corner there. He's a Blackwood boy, bred and buttered. Come and join us, Emrys.' He brought his pint to our table.

'What do you know about Henry Morgan, Emrys?'

'Only that his family home is in Blackwood. The house used to be a farm called Plas Newydd. A few years ago it changed into a pub. It's called the Monkey Tree now. They do a nice Sunday lunch there, I'm told.'

'Was Henry Morgan born there?'

'I haven't heard that, no. But they say he brought the monkey tree there from Jamaica or somewhere. It's still right in front of the pub. Huge, it is. Amazing how long trees live, isn't it? They also say that Mary Morgan's ghost still haunts the place. Quite a few of the boys from Blackwood have seen her.'

'Who was she?'

'You've got me there. I think his sister, was it? I'm not sure. Bernie, any chance you can buy me a pint? I'll pay you back tomorrow.'

'I'll buy you a pint, Emrys,' I said. 'Don't worry. You won't have to pay me back.'

The next morning Marty and I drove back to Cardiff, where we had arranged to pick up Leroy, who was busy in the City Arms trying to find his long-lost family. 'Shit, mon. Everybody a say no Tiger Bay no dyah agen.'

The Welsh shipping boom began in my grandfather's day in the 1880s as a result of the worldwide demand for Welsh anthracite coal, the best fuel for the ships, factories and railways of the new steam revolution. Cardiff, gateway to the South Wales valleys thick with coalfields and iron mills, was the hub of this maritime expansion. The city briefly became the greatest shipping centre in the world and the site of its only coal exchange, where international prices were fixed by a coal cartel. During the first quarter of the twentieth century people from all over the world were drawn to Cardiff by the work available but the sailors remained chiefly Welsh. The area straddling the docks that housed the seamen between voyages was known as Tiger Bay, the first multiracial community in Britain. Most immigrants were Chinese or Jamaican. As a child, I remember exploring the streets of Tiger Bay, eating my first ever Chinese meal at a restaurant named Dai Hong, and gazing transfixed at groups of Jamaicans playing craps in the street, New Orleans style. Now the streets of houses had been knocked down and replaced with glass and chrome monstrosities peppered with the usual inner-city paraphernalia of shopping malls and expensive coffee bars. The old docks had been converted into marinas of middle-class doll's houses. No wonder Leroy couldn't find his family.

'They're probably around somewhere,' I said, trying to lift Leroy's mood, 'in the suburbs or in little towns up the valleys.'

'Aright. Mi wi come down de agen. Now mi afi go back a London. Mi afi work a night move club tonight as security.'

Marty and I went for a stroll around what was now called Cardiff Bay. Nothing was the same. Even nostalgia refused to return.

During the late 1920s, my father, at the age of sixteen, joined the Reardon Smith Line as an apprentice. It was the largest and longest-lasting of Cardiff's great shipping lines, founded by Irishman Sir William Reardon (O'Riordean) Smith. Within ten years, my father had become the Merchant Navy's youngest captain, and during the Second World War he served as a fleet commodore. I was born the day the war finished, but because of his continuing commitments overseas, I did not see my father until I was two years old. As a reward for his distinguished service, he was allowed to take my mother and me on his subsequent voyages.

My first memories of foreign places were of travelling through first the Suez and then the Panama canals. I was three years old, and my father had been appointed captain of the SS *Bradburn*, a merchant vessel circumnavigating the planet, picking up and discharging cargo wherever it could. I have often wondered why the two canals seared themselves on my memory cells while the other wonders of the world, such as Mount Fuji, the Rock of Gibraltar, ranges of floating icebergs and smoking volcanoes, just passed me by. I think it was due to being in a large vessel moving at what appeared to be a fast speed just inches away from the land.

The idea of linking the Mediterranean and Red Seas was first mooted during the time of the pharaohs, who ordered the digging of a canal through the eastern branch of the Nile Delta. Preventing the canal filling with sand proved to be too difficult. Later the Greeks, followed by the Romans, re-excavated it several times but each time it fell into neglect. The canal was again cleared after the Arab conquest of Egypt. Work continued for scores of years but eventually the canal was again abandoned to the sand. During the mid-nineteenth century the French engineer Ferdinand de Lesseps signed a contract with the Egyptian government to dig a new canal via Suez. France was then at the height of its power, churning out the world's best engineers, architects and scientists. The canal took just over ten years to construct.

Measuring just over a hundred miles, it is easily the longest canal in the world without locks, has several passing bays, and can be widened and deepened when necessary. Apart from the sensation of the ship's apparently rapid progress, my only memories of the journey through the canal are of gazing at a boring flat sandy landscape and being annoyed with my mother for insisting I wear a vest in the stifling heat.

My recollections of the Panama Canal are far more stimulating. I remember big noisy cranes and derricks, colourful, lush and lively landscapes and cascades of water pouring in and out of enormous locks. Why does it need locks? Like the Suez Canal, the Panama Canal links sea level to sea level. While striving to work out the puzzle of these locks, as well as come to terms with the ever-increasing links in my mind between Wales and the Americas, the fated coincidence happened.

'Could I speak to Howard Marks, please?'

'Speaking.'

'It's Jeanette Hyde here, Howard, from the *Observer* travel section. We would like to send you on a trip again.' I'd done a few gigs for the *Observer* and they were always welcome.

'Excellent. Where did you have in mind?'

'Somewhere in South America – Brazil, Panama or Argentina. Take your pick.'

This was wonderful. Here was the opportunity to follow up

my current obsessions with Latin American connections and Welsh rogues. I could research my ancestry as well as recapture my childhood. Brazil was tempting, but a visit there could wait a while; it had been Portuguese and, as far as I knew then, had no strong connections with Wales. Choosing between Panama and Argentina was tricky. I wanted to go to both immediately. It was a toss-up.

'OK, I'll go to Panama.'

Within a week I received my itinerary, and my heart fell. I called Jeanette. 'Jeanette, there's no way I can do this trip. I have to change planes at Miami.'

'So?'

'If I ever set foot in America, I'll be banged up forever.'

'Really! I thought you had served your sentence.'

'Yes, I have, but I'm classified as an aggravated felon, which means I must never enter America, even to change planes. If I do, I am committing an imprisonable offence. Besides, despite having been deported, I am still on parole. Although the US authorities can't enforce parole conditions outside their territory, if I turn up there and they find out I have taken drugs or associated with criminals since my release, I will have to serve the rest of my prison sentence, eighteen and a half years.'

'I see. I'll find an alternative route. It's difficult because there are no direct flights to Panama from Europe. You might have to change in a South or Central American country or the Caribbean.'

'No worries, Jeanette. I can live with that.'

A return ticket arrived in the post. I was changing planes in Jamaica. Fantastic! It was only an overnight stop each way, but it would be long enough to get a taste of rum, an earful of reggae and a lungful of reefer. And it was Henry Morgan's favourite place in the world.

I called Leroy to give him my good news. 'Hey, Leroy, it looks like I'm going to Jamaica next week.'

'Yo na go widout mi, mon. Da place wi eat yo alive.'

'I'm only transiting there, Leroy, on the way to and from Panama.'

'Shit! Hail up Manuel fi mi.'

'Who?'

'Noriega, mon. Yo nu remember im ina Yankee prison?'

I had indeed forgotten the last Panamanian I had met was General Noriega. We were companion inmates of Miami Metropolitan Correctional Center, and our 3.30 a.m. rude awakenings by US marshals to shackle and take us to court sometimes coincided. Trained by former CIA chief George Bush (the old one), Noriega had switched loyalties and begun selling arms to Cuba and trafficking drugs with Colombian cartels. For the first time, the United States adopted the now familiar policy of invading an entire country to capture one opponent. Just months before I met Noriega, the USA had killed thousands of Panamanian nationals and dumped them in mass graves, burned residential neighbourhoods, crushed families in their cars with tanks, and left tens of thousands impoverished and homeless. As a result, Manuel Noriega became the first leader of a country to declare war on the United States since the Second World War.

I was looking forward to my first transatlantic flight since being deported from America, my first visit to Jamaica and my first visit to Panama for over fifty years. I had recently rented myself a bedsit in London's Shepherd's Bush in an attempt to have a life separate from my failing marriage and to lessen the impact of its perpetual emotional and financial haemorrhages. Bedsits are the homes I like best and the rooms, including prison cells, in which I have written most. My books, my sounds, my decks, my drugs and the kettle were close, begging to be used twenty-four hours a day.

I carefully packed, wondered whether I should hide a small piece of Nepalese hashish, decided against it, and scrupulously checked the suitcase to remove all evidence of my habit: no cigarette papers, no clothes with joint burns and no ripped-up pieces of cardboard from which roaches had been fashioned. I threw in a few guidebooks to Central America and the Caribbean, a toilet bag of creams to prevent me burning and itching, my laptop connections and peripherals, and a random selection of shorts, sandals and summer clothes. I locked the door, took the tube to Paddington, tried unsuccessfully again to smoke at the sushi bar, and caught a mid-afternoon Heathrow Express.

I was eager to be off but my excitement swiftly evaporated when I read the notice in bold type on the airline ticket given to me at Terminal Three's Jamaican Airlines check-in desk: 'YOU CAN HELP. Report drug smuggling to U.S. Customs 1-800-etc.' Why, I wondered, should anyone flying non-stop direct from the United Kingdom to Jamaica be requested to consider, let alone blindly assist, enforcing another country's disastrous prohibition policies? But at least the Jamaicans hadn't bothered to reveal the full telephone number. They probably knew that a few dozen goats were more effective and cheaper than US Air Force helicopters in discovering marijuana plantations.

At the security gates passengers were asked to hand in their cigarette lighters. Whether they were considered capable of being used as weapons or whether the airline simply wished to ensure that no one infringed the strict no-smoking rule was not made clear. Every seat was occupied and I was next to a couple of Jamaican children. One of them started playing a game on her mobile phone. A flight attendant asked her to turn it off, reducing her to tears. I wondered how human beings could even consider flying through space at 500 miles per hour in 500 tons of steel machinery which could be disabled by a mere text message.

After twelve hours of sleep, nicotine deprivation and a pathetically small ration of red wine, we landed at Montego Bay. Immigration was friendly but slow. We waited several hours for officials to put meaningless stamps on scraps of paper. Their uniformed colleagues smoked and gazed blankly at the sea of surprisingly contented and patient faces. Everyone was delighted to be here. I was given a six-month visa. I was already beginning to regret I would be there for just one day.

The *Observer* had booked me into a hotel on Treasure Beach, a two-hour drive away. The smiling, dreadlocked hotel driver picked me out immediately, bundled me into the back of the car, and drove like the clappers through the pitch-black Jamaican night.

Swarms of vehicles zigzagged chaotically through laneless streets and alleyways. Laws, a highway code and other means of avoiding danger were entirely absent. 'Drive on the left-hand side of the road' obviously meant do so eventually, that is, make one's way towards the left side. One-way street signs merely suggested that most vehicles should go in the same direction. Driving straight towards or into oncoming traffic was strongly encouraged. Unlit vehicles, arms gesturing randomly out of their windows, tore madly in any direction, emitting clouds of dense black fumes. Drivers changed lanes without slowing or looking, and scraped the road with capsizing bodywork, sending showers of sparks on to pavements crammed with sleeping, eating, TV-watching and trading communities, where the odd death or amputation was not a hindrance to business. People, donkeys and dogs reluctantly ambled off the road, avoiding injury at the last possible moment courtesy of screeching, corroded brakes.

We arrived at Treasure Beach, a string of loosely linked fishing settlements and the site of Jake's Hotel, a ramshackle assembly of wooden cottages, concrete villas, bars, small pools and beach. I had read in the hotel brochure that Jake's is to Treasure Beach as the university is to the city of Oxford, a focus of culture and clowning, but at 10.30 p.m. Jake's was disappointingly dead. The driver took me to my cottage, the only light for miles. There was no wardrobe, no hot water, no telephone. There was, however, a fully stocked fridge, a wooden writing table, an L-shaped stone bench, a large double bed under a rainbow-coloured mosquito net, and a CD player.

I walked out to the veranda, sat in one of the huge armchairs, gazed through almost pitch blackness at outlines of palm trees and shacks, listened to the frothy pounding waves, and sorely wished I'd had the balls to smuggle in enough dope for a smoke. Perhaps it is foolish to take coals to Newcastle, but a Welsh miner can only blame himself for freezing to death if he doesn't. I raided the fridge and read the service directory and the covers of the dozen or so CDs. The music collection was first class. This was no surprise; the hotel is owned by Jason Henzell, son of Perry Henzell, the writer of the first great Jamaican film, *The Harder They Come*, and part of the Island Resorts chain owned by Chris Blackwell, founder of Island records. The hotel is also a personal favourite of Robbie Williams, who according to the hotel brochure wrote his massive hit 'Angels' during one of his stays.

Over a hundred recordings a week are released in Jamaica, a greater output per head than any other country. Jamaican musical rhythm and dance movements derive originally from West Africa, and the songs, including hymns, developed at sugar cane and banana plantations. When slavery was abolished, syncopated rhythm, gyrating hips, bodies dipping forward and bawdy lyrics became the hallmarks of Jamaican muisc and dance. During the early 1900s, calypso, whose greatest star was Jamaican Harry Belafonte, combined with tango and samba to produce mento, a purely Jamaican sound. American rhythm and blues then melded with calypso to produce another uniquely Jamaican rhythm, soca, and with mento to originate the far more popular ska, referred to in the UK as bluebeat. 'My Boy Lollipop', sung by Jamaican Millie Small, arranged by Ernest Ranglin and produced by Chris Blackwell, went to the top of the UK charts in 1964.

Sound systems on wheels began in the 1950s and spawned

the cult of the DJs, known then as toasters. During the 1960s, the ska beat slowed down and a dominant bass line emerged to produce rocksteady, a sound pioneered by Leroy Sibbles and the Heptones and brought to international fame by Desmond Dekker and Jimmy Cliff.

Rastafarian influence resulted in song lyrics expressing black pride and protest. The Jamaican establishment saw this as subversive and the new music was banned from radio stations. However it could still be heard in rum bars and on juke boxes. Reggae emerged, the name derived from rex, the music of Kingston's lion kings. Then came the Jamaican equivalent to the Beatles, the Wailers, a vocal trio comprising Neville 'Bunny' Livingston, Peter 'Tosh' MacIntosh and Robert Nesta Marley. At first they dressed as gangsters, or rude boys, wearing sharp suits and shades, but then found their true style with producer Lee 'Scratch' Perry. To the world, Bob Marley is reggae, but the word was first used by Toots Hibbert, a direct descendant of an anti-slavery activist, in 'Do the Reggay' in 1968. Chris Blackwell's Island Records produced a series of Wailers albums, introducing reggae to a worldwide audience and making Bob Marley the Third World's first superstar. B-sides of popular discs were released with the vocals removed, leaving the heavy bass and drum tracks for toasters to add further instrumentation and their own lyrics, giving birth to the culture of dub poetry.

One of ganja's many marvellous properties is to heighten one's appreciation of tonal resonance and change one's perception of time. This encouraged reggae record producers such as Lee Perry and King Tubby to twiddle their knobs, reverberate, echo, cut up the vocal track, and add snatches of dogs barking, roosters crowing and gunshots. The title track on Peter Tosh's first solo LP *Legalise It* includes a litany of ganja's medicinal uses and a list of those who use it: doctors, nurses, judges and lawyers as well as singers and musicians. The song has become the anthem of pot smokers everywhere.

In Jamaica but dopeless, I listened to a selection of the CDs, thoroughly enjoying my auditory history lesson and reading the biographies of the artists. For the first time I learned that Bob Marley was of mixed race. Feeling slightly ashamed of my ignorance, I read on. According to Jamaica's *Daily Post*, Marley's mother was a Jamaican woman named Ciddy Brooker who married Captain Marley, a British army officer and British West Indian Regiment quartermaster, whose brief was to assist in the colonisation and cultivation of the island. The marriage was a scandal and Marley's family disinherited him. He resigned his commission and took a job in Kingston. Captain Marley's first name was Norval, and he was born in Prestatyn, North Wales. I found it hard to believe what I was reading. Accepting that Elvis was Welsh had been hard enough. I longed to go back to the Royal Oak and catch out Eddie Evans with that snippet of information.

Deeply regretting that I would probably have to leave Jamaica before witnessing a live concert, I fell asleep.

The dawn chorus catapulted me out of bed, but Jake's was still dead. Looking for a telephone outside the hotel, I passed the closed International Communication Centre. Due to either sharp business practice or rural frustration, vandals had disabled all the phone boxes within striking distance. I asked my driver of last night, who was half asleep in his car.

'Cable and Wickedness, mon. Cable and Wickedness. Yo try Jimmy's Seafood place. Im af phone.'

I walked past bars and other flimsy attractions that seemed to serve merely as excuses to design, commission and erect signs. The businesses may go bust in weeks, but the signs live on for years. I came to Jimmy's Seafood. The outside was plastered with notices proclaiming 'Conch puts you in high gear,' 'You get blood from lobsters,' 'God is the highest,' 'When the Devils Says No, God says Yes,' and 'Live by the clock, die by the clock.' It was closed.

Nearby, a bar called Sue's Little Pleasure had just opened.

I walked into a shed twelve foot square with bamboo walls, a pitched zinc roof, concrete floor, solid wooden bar, one framed photograph of Haile Selassie and several unframed photographs and paintings of Welshman Bob Marley. A few awkward stools of different heights stood at the bar; another stool lay on the floor. Several pairs of women's shoes lay for sale on the bar, which also carried a deafening ghetto blaster, badly tuned in to a local radio station. Two crates of Red Stripe and a shelf of rum bottles stood precariously behind the bar. Dozens of small identical bottles of nail varnish sat on another shelf. Behind the bar was sexy Dorothy, who served me a Red Stripe, giggled and disappeared. I took the can to the telephone and called Leroy, who just told me, yet again, to be careful. I sat at one of the outside tables. My driver joined me. We idly watched seven dogs taking turns to penetrate a bitch.

'Yo wa some weed, mon?

I nodded vigorously

'Mek wi go dong a mi bredren farm?'

I nodded even more vigorously.

We drove up into the mountains until we came to a small wooden hut guarded by a heavily armed but amiable local named Shortcut, who smiled, shook my hand and led me to a clearing containing several dozen marijuana plants. Shortcut stoked up a chalice, sucked strongly, puffed out dense clouds of bluish-white smoke, and invited me to do the same. I did my best, sat on the grass, leaned against the wooden hut, and drifted off. The talk of 'mi bredren farm' set me wondering how well the Mr Nice Seedbank plantations were doing in Switzerland.

An unexpected and extraordinary outcome of the success of *Mr Nice* was my acquiring the status of an expert in the cultivation and identification of various strains of marijuana. My rich experience of dealing with the finished product is fully documented, but apart from one abortive effort in the early 1970s I have never tried to grow the cannabis plant and cannot distinguish one strain from another. I hate gardening and do not have much sense of smell or taste; I can merely distinguish marijuana that has a high concentration of THC (tetrahydrocannabinol, cannabis's main psychoactive ingredient) from one that has a low one by how stoned I get smoking it.

My apparent expertise was largely due to a brainwave from Justin Rees of Visual Entertainment, who had produced *Howard Marks – A Video Diary*. Much of the content of the diary was offstage footage of the shows I did for the 1998 Edinburgh Festival, coupled with scenes of me getting stoned in various London clubs. By October 1998, the project was almost in the can. Then Justin called me.

'Howard, I've just had another idea.'

'Great! Your ideas have been first class so far, especially hooking me up with Fatboy Slim at The End last year. I'll never forget that night.'

'This is different, Howard. If we can sort it, would you be prepared to be filmed walking through marijuana plantations, explaining to viewers the differences in the plant strains and techniques involved in their cultivation?'

'I'm up for it in principle; I still smoke it like there's no tomorrow. But my knowledge of horticulture is close to zero.'

'I don't think that matters, Howard.'

'Where are these plantations?'

'We've already talked to people in Holland, Switzerland and Morocco.'

'Morocco! I would love to go there; they make hashish, something I do know a bit about. And I've never run foul of the Moroccan authorities. But Holland and Switzerland might be difficult. I've had problems with them in the past. They might not be keen on me publicly stomping through fields of weed.'

'I'm sure Holland will be OK, Howard. Don't forget all those coffee shops and cannabis cups.'

In the early 1970s Holland decriminalised marijuana consumption and allowed licensed establishments to sell it. Growing marijuana was also permitted, attracting some of the world's finest ganja botanists. Smokers from all over the world swarmed there. In those days, unlike now, smokers smuggled and smugglers smoked, so it didn't take long for Amsterdam to become America, Australia and Europe's favoured location for both wholesale dope dealers to ply their trade and for smugglers to plan their next scams. I jumped on the bandwagon, but in November 1973 was arrested with a joint's worth of hashish (legally bought from a coffee shop) and kept in solitary confinement for a few days by the Dutch police, who then put me on a jet which delivered me into the arms of Her Majesty's Customs & Excise at Heathrow Airport. They promptly charged me with exporting to the United States of America several hundred kilos of hashish hidden in the equipment of rock bands. I skipped bail and went on the run for several years, keeping well clear of Holland. I had a low opinion of the Dutch authorities – they weren't tolerant; they just didn't care. It was no coincidence that double Dutch, Dutch auction, Dutch treat, Dutch bargain, Dutch anchor, Dutch uncle, Dutch captain, Dutch courage, and Dutch cap all carry some meaning of deceit, hypocrisy, or duplicity. Many of my old dealing mates felt differently and kept going back there. They had their phones tapped and were ruthlessly extradited to America. The set-up was obvious to me: Holland was America's hooker, enticing dealers inside through a posture of drug acceptance to spend the rest of their lives in American penitentiaries.

During my fugitive period, 1974–80, the American marijuana magazine *High Times* dramatically increased its circulation. I was convinced it was a United States Drug Enforcement Administration publication. All the British smokers I knew had failed miserably at getting out a well-produced UK dope magazine. They'd not succeeded for two good reasons: they had no money and they were very stoned. So how did the Yanks manage to do it? Something fishy was going on, I thought. It had to be the DEA. If anyone signed up to a subscription for *High Times* or replied to advertisements for bongs and skins, law enforcement would have them tabbed for life.

Once Reagan got into power, however, *High Times* appeared to become sincerely dedicated to serving the needs of the dope-smoking community. It developed a seriously anti-authoritarian attitude but continued to preserve its characteristically American naivety about foreign events. This was typified by its coverage of my 1981 Old Bailey trial, in which I was cleared of importing into Scotland fifteen tons of Colombian marijuana. The evidence against me was formidable: officers from HM Customs & Excise found in my pocket keys that opened doors behind which the same officers had just discovered several tons of the same Colombian marijuana. In my Knightsbridge flat, under my bed, they found £30,000 in used notes, and in my desk there were accounts for the entire operation in my own handwriting. Marty Langford and others had pleaded guilty to working for me. My defence depended on the truth of my claim that I was at the time working for the Mexican secret service to infiltrate Colombian terrorist groups. Although I was acquitted by the jury's majority verdict, I very much doubted if anyone in the courtroom, including the jury, believed my story. The only exception was *High Times*, which in its April 1982 issue carried a report of the nine-week trial and firmly concluded I was an undercover agent working for a number of countries' secret services. It warned dealers to stay away from me for their own safety.

In 1987 *High Times* staff went to Holland to write about marijuana botanists living in Amsterdam. While working on the story, they had the idea of holding competitions related to cannabis. The first few annual contests were for seed companies. Each year the winner was the Seed Bank, the creation of Neville Schoenmaker, an astute Australian botanist who almost single-handedly was responsible for the worldwide spread of home-grown mind-blowing skunk, a powerful hybrid comprising the best qualities of the two main cannabis varieties, *sativa* – from Thailand, South America and Africa – and indica – from the Middle East.

Then the DEA's Operation Green Merchant busted exporters of seeds to America, regardless of how legally they were operating, and Neville Schoenmaker became a fugitive from American injustice. The Seed Bank was incorporated into Sensi Seed Club, resulting in Sensi Seed Bank, run by my old friend Ben Dronkers, who also set up the Cannabis Museum, Cannabis Castle and a bunch of coffee shops. During the late 1980s and early '90s, the *High Times* Cannabis Cup opened up more to the public. Further competitions, for example for best hash, best coffeeshop, best bioweed, best bong and so on, were set up, as were industrial and culinary hemp exhibitions, coffee shop crawls, tours of the Cannabis Castle and Cannabis Museum, and parties with marijuana-influenced music held at Amsterdam's Milky Way. Bob Marley's widow Rita made a surprise trip from Jamaica to join the festivities. Along with Glastonbury, the *High Times* Cannabis Cup had arrived in the social calendar of the hip and cool.

If Holland had allowed all that to happen, surely it wouldn't mind some pictures of me surrounded by dope plants? But I thought I would call a Dutch lawyer first. A couple of weeks and a few hundred pounds later the lawyer discovered that in 1973 I had been charged with exporting hashish from Holland to America. Not only that: in 1975 I had been tried and convicted for the offence in my absence – a strange idea of a fair trial – and sentenced to eight months' imprisonment.

Normally one can be tried only once for any specific criminal act, the principle of double jeopardy. I had now been sentenced three times for smuggling precisely the same load of hashish – by a British court for conspiring in the UK, by a Dutch court for exporting the hashish, and by an American court for importing it. It struck me as a bit unfair. There was, however, some good news: the Dutch judgement was such a long time ago their statute of limitations could be invoked. Unlike those of the United Kingdom, the laws of most European countries and even America incorporate statutes of limitation. Depending on the severity of the offence, judgement can no longer be enforced after a certain time has elapsed. In my case, the limit was fifteen years. As far as the Dutch authorities were concerned I had been at liberty to enter Holland since 1990. I told Justin the good news. Two days later, accompanied by a camera crew, we passed unhindered through Schipol Airport, well in time for the 1998 *High Times* Cannabis Cup.

For my old times' sake, Justin and I checked into the Okura Hotel, where I was staying when first arrested in 1973 and whose hotel records had helped me prove I was an MI6 agent at the time. I walked across the road to the police station in Cornelis Troostplein. Next to it was the Pax Party House, location of the competition. The place was crammed with a cosmopolitan collection of people keen to discover just how much THC the human body could consume and still function on a basic level. Every imaginable hemp product was on display, as was every conceivable accessory, at various noisy and colourful stalls. It was, however, hard to find a decent spliff. I started getting annoyed. Of course it's utterly ridiculous and frighteningly sinister that any society should sacrifice the therapeutic, medicinal and fibrous benefits available from plants because of some mad American-fuelled prohibitionism, but it's equally important to note that 99 per cent of those who buy cannabis are healthy and simply want to smoke (rather than wear) marijuana to get stoned. One of the more impressive stalls belonged to the Sensi Seed Bank. Sitting behind the table was Ben Dronkers.

'Howard, I haven't seen you for centuries. Welcome back to Amsterdam, my friend. It's so good to see you. Try some of this.'

Ben handed me a pungent spliff. I took a big drag and immediately started to spin.

'What the fuck is this, Ben?'

'The best skunk on the planet, in my humble opinion.'

'What's it called?'

'It has no name yet, just a number, G13, with a very interesting history – one that will greatly amuse you, I am sure. Several years ago the DEA started growing cannabis themselves to know what they were fighting against. Obviously, as the American government, they had all the technology, botanical expertise and money they needed, and they succeeded in growing fantastic marijuana. One strain was so strong that even the DEA could not keep it a secret. A woman friend of mine was dating a DEA agent at the time. She managed to get a cutting and smuggle it back to me here, where through careful breeding I have kept its magic alive. I'm going to put the seed on the market this year.'

'That is amusing, Ben. Hilarious, in fact. By the way, this is Justin Rees.'

'Ah yes. We have talked on the phone. You are going to film us at my grow rooms, no? We might as well leave right now, as I have to go there to get more seed stock. It sells like hot cakes at these events. Let us go. I'll show you the G13 plants.'

Ben drove us to the grow rooms, about fifty kilometres from Amsterdam. We smoked weed all the way. Ben had come a long way since we were minor dealers and smugglers in the early 1970s, selling a few kilos of hashish a week. We were doing all right; we knew we were in the right business and would soon be rich. As some of us graduated to selling tens of kilos a week, we laughed at Ben as he went in the other direction and starting selling grams over the counter at Holland's first coffee shop in Rotterdam. Now Ben legally owned and profited from a cannabis seed bank, a hemp factory, his Cannabis Museum and Cannabis Castle, which Easyjet advertises in its inflight magazine. The rest of us have records as long as our arms, and Easynet blocks our websites.

The grow rooms were huge steel vaults. Inside, undulating Rousseau green plants glistened in the disco sunlight. Engulfed in marijuana, I interviewed Ben. My lack of expertise would not show; I just had to ask questions. It worked. Justin was very pleased.

On the way out Ben pulled me aside. 'Would you mind if I called the G13 strain Mr Nice?'

'Of course not; I'd be flattered.'

Ben drove us back to the Pax Party House where the results of the 1998 Cup were about to be announced. Sensi did not do well; almost every prize went to the Greenhouse Seed Company. Ben politely introduced me to the two guys who ran the winning outfit, an Australian named Scott Blakey and a Dutchman called Arjan. I immediately liked Scott and settled down to a long chat with him.

Back at the Okura, in the lobby bar, Justin revealed his next idea: 'Are you OK to do a similar interview in Switzerland tomorrow? You mentioned that at some point you had a problem with the Swiss authorities. Have you been arrested there as well?'

'No, but I did have a Swiss bank account in which I deposited my ill-gotten gains.'

'Do you still have it?'

'I wish. No, the DEA grabbed it once I was convicted of racketeering.'

'I didn't think they could do that. You mean the Swiss authorities handed over funds in your private numbered bank account to the DEA?'

'Justin, the DEA can do whatever the fuck they want whenever and wherever. They have no problem ordering the fucking gnomes of Zurich to do exactly what they wish with any money in their banks. That has been the case since 1972, when Nixon formed the DEA. Only a Nazi with a stash of stolen Jewish loot is safe to bank in Switzerland.'

'You don't like the Swiss, I can tell.'

'I have some good Swiss friends, but most of the population are hypocrites hell-bent on sucking American arse and profiting from the rest of the world's misery. The only good thing about Switzerland is what the Swiss had nothing to do with – the scenery.'

'But are there any outstanding charges against you in Switzerland?'

'No, I don't think so.'

'So you have no objection if I book flights to Zurich tomorrow.'

'No, that's fine.'

'The dope plants, apparently completely legal, are near Zurich. After we do that, I thought we could go down to the Italian border and film you trying to dig up your Mr Nice passport. You buried it there, right? Campione d'Italia wasn't it?'

'You can't believe how much I would love to go back there.'

For most of the 1970s I was a fugitive living under different names all over the world carrying on my dope-smuggling career. At various stages I rented accommodation in the United Kingdom, Eire, Pakistan, Thailand, Hong Kong, New York and Italy. My favourite place was Campione d'Italia, a tiny exquisite village ten kilometres from Lugano. The Romans founded the settlement and named it Campilyeus (Field of Bacchus) because of the profusion of naturally flourishing vines. Although its institutions and the forces of law and order come under Italian authority, Campione d'Italia is surrounded by Swiss territory. Its only access to the rest of

Italy is via a boat ride across Lake Lugano to the truly Italian Ponte Teresa. Telephone, electricity and water services are Swiss. The policemen wear Italian uniforms but drive cars with Swiss number plates. The lavish restaurants and bars happily accept Swiss francs, euros or indeed any other currency. Campione d'Italia's visible economic hub is a casino. Originally built by Mussolini, it once was a haven for spies. Now, enticing personalities from the high echelons of Italian state bureaucracy into rooms sparkling with bright lights and beautiful women, it hosts cultural events, fashion parades and jazz and rock concerts. With a secret tunnel, known to everyone, connecting the casino to the priest's house, it also continues to function as a gambling den. There are just 2,000 residents of Campione d'Italia, most of whom seem wealthy, but tens of thousands of offshore companies are registered within its confines. Both Swiss and Italian tax can be easily evaded. People ask no questions and mind their own lucrative businesses. I loved living there, and did so under the name Mr Nice.

One day during the first few months of 1980 I received information that both the DEA and HM Customs & Excise suspected me of importing marijuana and had a rough idea where I might be living. I ate one more delicious drunken meal at the village's best restaurant, the Taverna, put the Mr Nice passport in my safe, took out another one I had recently acquired, had one last look at the reflection of my apartment in Lake Lugano, and flew unmolested into London's Heathrow Airport. A few days later I sent one of my dealing partners, Jarvis, to empty the apartment of its contents. He buried the Mr Nice passport in Campione d'Italia's public gardens. Although I made a couple of nostalgic visits back in the early 1980s, I kept away from the burial place. During 1983, a fleet of Italian police boats crossed Lake Lugano and invaded Campione d'Italia, arresting several people. There was a blaze of publicity about eradicating the

Mafia. The casino closed down. I had not been back there since.

We rented a car at Zurich airport. Half an hour later, Justin, the cameraman and I were walking up a minor Alp through a large field full of tall marijuana plants. Guiding us was Rolf Schroder, with whom Justin had arranged our visit. Extensive greenhouses crammed with short bushy dope plants bordered the field. Next to the greenhouses was a large outhouse in which several dozen women of apparently Bosnian origin were trimming recently cut buds of high-quality marijuana, laughing and joking as they did so. There were neither security fences nor armed guards. Nearby we could see a motorway. Slightly further away were the spires of the city of Zurich. I had expected some government-sanctioned research centre growing a plant or two, not a full-on plantation. The cameraman pulled out his video, and I began interviewing Rolf.

Swiss law explicitly states that marijuana is prohibited from being cultivated, imported or sold if grown for the production of narcotics. Marijuana not intended for this purpose, however, may be bought, sold and possessed. The plant is not illegal in itself. Even cannabis extract, cannabis tincture, as well as cannabis oil – which often has a THC content close to 90 per cent – are neither illegal nor regulated if not intended for use as narcotics. So, if you cultivate hemp for its seed, its pulp or its essential oil, you do not break Swiss law. I was beginning to warm to the Swiss.

In the early 1990s a farmer friend of Rolf planted one hectare of marijuana. He destroyed all the males, preventing the plants from pollinating themselves, a technique used in the production of marijuana for smoking rather than for industrial purposes, claiming, however, that pulling the males increased the ornamental value as well as the aroma of the flowers. Unsurprisingly, local law enforcement officers were cynical about his motives and ploughed up the whole field, accusing the farmer of narcotics production. He predictably lost his case in the local court and took it to the supreme court, arguing that the police had acted in an arbitrary fashion by assuming his marijuana was intended for illegal purposes while failing to present any proof.

It can take several years to get heard in the Swiss supreme court, so the farmer had to decide whether to continue growing marijuana, risking further harassment and a harsher sentence, or wait until the court ruled. He decided to take the risk and planted another hectare. The police ploughed again, but this time without a valid warrant from a judge.

Meanwhile, the case surrounding the farmer's first crop had reached the supreme court, which to everyone's astonishment found in his favour and ordered the government to compensate him to the tune of almost two million Swiss francs. In another case in Switzerland a marijuana grower was repaid for his confiscated marijuana after proving his crop had been sold to a beer brewing company, thus excluding any possibility of unlawful use.

If cultivating marijuana is legal, it follows that its sale must be equally legal. The problem was finding a marijuana product which could be marketed for legal use but which contained the most psychoactive parts of the plant – the seedless flowers. Another of Rolf's friends, who lived in Zurich, dreamed up the brilliant idea of the aromatherapy pillow, a bag of high-grade marijuana in a pillowcase carrying a stern warning that the buyer must handle the product in strict accordance with national law and not use it as a narcotic nor export it. If the dope was for sniffing rather than smoking it was OK to sell it and buy it.

The first pillows consisted of hemp-fibre bags containing low-to-medium-potency marijuana flowers and sold at rather modest prices. Customers had to show proof of age and agree to use the product legally. As the market evolved, quality and choice increased until eventually one could buy everything from cheap low-potency outdoor weed to high-grade indoor primo bud from a local retailer. Hundreds of kilograms of marijuana and millions of Swiss francs changed hands every day, and nobody seemed bothered. In 1997 Switzerland produced enough high-potency marijuana to supply the entire European market. Each large town in the country had its own marijuana grow shop, while nearby cities in Germany, France and Italy had five or six. Retailers advertised their aroma-bags in clubs and discos.

But the party didn't last forever.

James Blunt of Zurich was the marijuana shop to get serious attention from the media when it was busted. It was selling a wide variety of different-sized aroma-bags and had a reputation for good quality and creative marketing ideas. While others sold their products in hand-labelled Ziplocs from nondescript outlets, James Blunt offered elaborate packaging and a store with an atmosphere comparable to Holland's best coffee shops. James himself provided information about potency and taste on his merchandise, making it obvious that he was not selling marijuana solely for aromatherapy. The prosecutor in Zurich used him as a test case. As expected, he was quickly found guilty, sentenced to several months on probation and ordered to pay a hefty fine. This constituted a major victory for the anti-marijuana establishment, which thereupon declared all grow shops in the canton of Zurich illegal and open to prosecution. The case also provided many other Swiss judges with a precedent to justify prosecutions in their cantons.

Switzerland consists of twenty-five semi-autonomous cantons with powers similar to those of American states. Narcotics law is national, but the various cantons treat the same crime in different ways. While cultivating marijuana has been decreed legal by the highest court in Switzerland, there has been no such ruling on its sale, which leads to contrasting cantonal positions. Geneva and the rest of the French cantons reacted to the Blunt case by closing all the newly opened grow shops immediately. In Zurich and other German cantons reactions were mixed but generally tolerant. The Italian area, including Lugano, where Justin and I were bound later, had hardly reacted at all.

Justin was delighted with the footage. I nicked a few marijuana buds, and we drove over the snow-clad Alps, through the San Gotthard Pass, out of the German part of Switzerland and into Ticino, the only Italian canton of Switzerland. The difference was marked not only by the warmer Mediterranean climate but also by the mainly Latin architecture, language and cuisine.

At Campione d'Italia there is no obvious border; there is not even a shed, just a concrete arch crowned with the Italian flag and a normally vacant lay-by where police and border guards may park if they wish. The three of us checked into the Hotel Campione, which despite its name is not in Campione d'Italia but just the other side of the arch in Switzerland. Freshly showered and clothed, we walked across the border and made our way down to the lake. Nothing much had changed other than the Taverna had halved in size, while the casino had long reopened and was being rebuilt to twenty times its original capacity. We ate at the Taverna, of course. Two of the waiters recognised me from twenty years before. We guardedly caught up on each other's news.

The next morning, under the eye of the video camera and armed with a small trowel, I poked around in Campione d'Italia's public gardens, looking for the Mr Nice passport. I tried to recall every word of Jarvis's instructions, but they did not make sense. I even telephoned Jarvis and asked him to repeat them, but got no further. The gardens must have been relandscaped. The passport was probably buried under what was clearly a recently erected children's playground. What the hell! It had expired fifteen years ago, and was not even mine to begin with.

Several months later, *Howard Marks – A Video Diary* hit the shelves of the audio and video stores. The reviews were favourable, loads of copies sold, and it served to increase the sales of *Mr Nice*, which by now had been translated into Hebrew and German. And then Frank Stefan, a friend of my German publisher, Marcus van der Kolk, telephoned me at my bedsit in Shepherd's Bush.

'Howard, we met briefly in Amsterdam last year. You probably do not remember. Anyway, I bought the rights from Justin Rees to make a German version of your video diary, which I released some time ago. What I would like is to film some extra footage of you which would have special interest for the German market.'

'I'm up for that, Frank.'

'Good. Could you come next weekend to Castrop-Rauxel and be our guest of honour?'

'Where the fuck is Castrop-Rauxel and what's happening there?'

'The CannaBusiness Exhibition. We have a hundred and fifty exhibitors from fourteen nations and expect more then ten thousand people to attend. It would be interesting for you. There will be all the usual paraphernalia on sale, all the growing equipment and new bongs, and I think Marcus will have a stand selling the German *Mr Nice* book. We will pay for your accommodation, and there will be plenty of traditional cannabis use. We just need an excuse.'

I flew to Frankfurt. Marcus, who lived in nearby Darmstadt, met me at the airport. A couple of hours at breakneck speed on the Autobahn, and we neared Castrop-Rauxel, which seemed an extremely boring place. The exhibition hall was its sole landmark. Clouds of dope smoke filled the interior. Hundreds of people smoking cannabis converged on me.

'Howard, you must try this. It is a hybrid of Northern Lights and White Rhino, which we have cultivated in Rotterdam. Please to smoke it in our giant bong.'

I sucked in loads of sweet cloudy fumes and began an

upward ascent.

'This hashish we have made in Germany. Please!'

'Finally, Howard, we have perfected the vaporiser. Made in Berlin. Try.'

Through the crowd I spotted Scott Blakey, who fought his way towards me and rescued me from the onslaught.

'Did Ben ever give you a bag of Mr Nice to smoke?'

'Actually, Scott, he didn't. I just had a drag. What's it like?'

'I've got some here; find out for yourself. It's not too bad.'

I rolled a joint and smoked some. It seemed fine.

'Yeah, it's good.'

'Look, mate, why don't we bring out a whole range of Mr Nice seeds? I've got loads of mind-blowing unreleased strains of dope to run by you. You could sample them slowly and relaxed. We could grade them and name them, then unleash them on the planet.'

'But where can we do it, Scott? It's going to be illegal to grow strong weed in Holland soon, isn't it?'

'Damn right, mate. What about Wales? You must have some pull there. Green green grass of home and all that.'

'Easier said than done, Scott, I'm afraid. What about Jamaica or even Switzerland? I saw a very impressive plantation there earlier this year.'

'The Swiss have clamped down a bit. Certainly in Zurich. No one seems to know what the law actually is there. Apparently, Ticino is OK though. I intend to check it out.'

Frank Stefan suddenly appeared.

'Sit down, Howard, please. I will just switch my camera on. Howard, I have an enormous surprise for you. This is Mefa.'

A man in lederhosen approached me. 'Hello, Mr Nice. I am Mefa from Munich. You have been resurrected. I have found your Mr Nice passport after it lay buried in Campione d'Italia for twenty years. It is in this box.'

Sure enough, there was the Mr Nice passport, battered and

expired, but still the real thing. Crowds gathered, video cameras whirred and reporters took out their notebooks and pens. Frank Stefan had done well with his publicity.

'How did you find it, Mefa?'

'I saw this programme about you on German television. When I looked at the garden where you were digging, something told me where the passport was, so I caught a train from Munich to Lugano, a boat from Lugano to Campione d'Italia, went to the public gardens, and immediately knew where to start digging.'

'Are you a diviner, Mefa?'

'No, I am a construction worker.'

'When did you go to Campione d'Italia?'

'It was precisely August the thirteenth. I have the date on the photographs I took. Can you see?'

'That's my birthday!'

'I had no idea. I have still not read your book.'

It turned out that Mefa's son was called Patrick, as is mine; his mother's name was Ilse, like my first wife; and his father was called Albi, the nickname I used throughout my fugitive years. This was too much to take. I grabbed a bottle of hemp beer, drank it and felt sick. Scott helped me up.

'Well, mate, we can't ignore a sign like that, particularly about burying and regeneration. I'm going to Ticino tomorrow. Coming?'

'I can't, Scott. I'll be in Barcelona. Cañamo have just published my book in Spanish, and I'm going out to promote it.'

A week later I was back in London after completing the Barcelona promotion and Scott called.

'What was the name of the place you used to live in Ticino?'

'Campione d'Italia.'

'It's amazing, isn't it? I've never seen anything like it in my life.'

'I think the same. You spent a couple of days there, yeah?'

'Not only that, I've rented a flat here. I'm still waiting to sign the lease. And I've had a look at the mountains. It's perfect for what we want to do. We're opening Mr Nice Seedbank right here, right where he was buried all those years ago. You're the seed, mate. Neville Schoenmaker wants to join us. Between Neville and me, we have produced almost all the winning entries in the *High Times* Cannabis Cup since 1990. There's no stopping us now.'

Mr Nice Seedbank began producing and selling seeds during 2000. Everything was done legally and with the full knowledge of the Ticino cantonal authorities, who sent round teams of inspectors at regular intervals. Meanwhile, home-grown marijuana production in Europe soared to unprecedented levels. By 2001, in the United Kingdom more than half the marijuana consumed resulted from the efforts of home growers using seeds produced by Mr Nice Seedbank and several other seed companies which had followed its lead and set up in Ticino. It seemed too good to be true.

'Which weed a di best, mon?'

The images dancing in front of my eyes changed from marijuana plants on the Alps to marijuana plants on the Caribbean hills.

'Yo a sleep, mon. Must be di jet lag. Yo neva try di Jamaican gum?' asked Shortcut.

I knew that 'gum' was the Jamaican word for locally produced hashish, but I had never tried it and was certainly interested in doing so.

'No, I haven't, Shortcut. Have you got any here?'

'Next time wen yo come back, mi wi mek sure yo get some.'

As I had been daydreaming of Swiss mountains, even Jamaican time had marched on. I had to think about my plans. I was leaving for Panama in a few hours, flying first from Montego Bay to Kingston's Norman Manley International Airport, the other side of Jamaica, then after a few hours stopover catching another plane to Panama City. I did not intend to leave Jamaica without paying my respects to Henry Morgan.

The driver took me back to Jake's Hotel. During the short trip we arranged that for fifty dollars he would drive me to Montego Bay, making small detours on the way to see what my guidebook said were former hang-outs of Henry Morgan. We left Treasure Beach after a late and nourishing breakfast of salt fish, ackee – a fruit, most of which is poisonous but the rest of which is a delicacy – and various members of the banana family. In less than an hour we had arrived at Black River; we then hugged the coast west until we came to Belmont, the birth and burial place of Peter Tosh. Ironically, his success in depicting truth from a ghetto perspective had led to a barrage of demands from old friends, needy causes and shady characters. Tosh began to display signs of paranoia, believing himself both to be the victim of an establishment plot and haunted by ghosts. In 1987, on 11 September, Tosh's fears were realised when hired killers opened fire in his living room, killing him and two of his friends. We drew up alongside a small red, gold and green mausoleum, decorated with cobwebs, stained glass, and press cuttings. A fine old lady, Peter Tosh's mother, stood outside.

'Were you a friend of Peter?'

'No ma'am, I wasn't. Unfortunately, I never even met your son. However, I am a strong admirer and champion his cause. Legalise it.'

'God bless you, my dear.'

Belmont merges subtly into Bluefields, where Henry Morgan thought of the brilliant idea of invading Panama, and from where he and his men set sail to fulfil his idea.

Whoever transported Henry Morgan from Bristol dropped him at Barbados and put him to work on a sugar plantation. He led a revolt, escaped, captured a boat and became a pirate, a tough and dangerous career. Disease was rife, and a hacksaw the only surgical instrument available. Psychologically, Morgan displayed most symptoms of bipolarity and managed his oscillations of temperament with ample quantities of rum. His sailors, a gang of sea thieves, rogues and vagabonds, were also dependent on rum to function in conditions of peril, fearful storms, poisonous insects, deadly diseases and unexplored hostile territory.

Although piracy was contrary to the law of all seafaring nations, Britain, when at war against Spain, found it hard to disapprove of Spanish galleons being looted. British Caribbean governors issued letters of marque, which legalised attacks on Spanish galleons provided a percentage went to the crown. Pirates became known by the more respectable name of privateers, and as long as they confined their antics to the sea, were not breaking the law. Henry Morgan seized Spanish galleons, but his real interest lay in the cities that held South American precious metals before they were exported to Spain. His eyes were on Panama, the biggest bank in the world. While swigging rum at his place in Bluefields he reasoned that even if it was illegal to sack Spanish settlements, the British authorities, especially those thousands of miles away, would turn a blind eye to any such attack.

Leaving my driver to have a snooze in his car, I walked around Bluefields looking for traces of Henry Morgan's abode. The only significant building was the largely derelict Bluefields House, next to the police station. It looked promising at first, but there was no mention of Morgan. I asked the resident caretaker, but he had never heard of him. Instead, he took me through the wild gardens to a breadfruit tree, the first in Jamaica. Captain Bligh had planted it from seedlings brought from Tahiti.

We then headed inland towards Montego Bay, arriving in time for me to catch my flight to Kingston. The plane flew over the spectacular Blue Mountains, source of the world's best coffee, and landed at Kingston, where I discovered the flight to Panama had been cancelled; there wouldn't be another for a couple of days. I was not perturbed; Jamaica had plenty to offer. Reluctantly, the airline provided accommodation at the Pelican Hotel in downtown Kingston. I checked in and telephoned Leroy in London.

'Leroy, what's a good nightspot in downtown Kingston?'

'Yo crazy, mon. Yo stay in a di hotel until sun come up. Yo hear mi.'

'But I've been to all sorts of places today. The people have been really kind and friendly. There's been no danger of any kind – the opposite, in fact.'

'Kingston a no place fi play with, mon. Yo stay in a di hotel.'

I was not used to arguing with Leroy. I stayed in the hotel.

I checked my emails. One was from a woman called Tina: 'Dear Howard, I know this must come as a huge surprise to you, but I am your daughter. My mother is Susan Malone. I'm living near her in Swansea. She told me all about the day in the chapel. I've known for ages. I tried to see you in Brixton Prison in 1980, but the guards would have none of it. Since then, I've been too shy to approach you. If you were any old Joe Bloggs, I would have. But you're the local hero down here. I'm happy to have a DNA test if you want.'

I was overwhelmed with both the joy of having another child and the sorrow of not knowing her. I had heard of love children suddenly appearing in people's lives, but it hadn't happened to any friends of mine. Henry Morgan and the *Observer* would have to wait; I was flying home to see my new daughter.

Four

SEEDS

Flying from Kingston to Gatwick, I thought of 1963, the year I met Susan Malone, the year when just about everything that could happen did happen. The world's first disco, Whisky A Go-Go, opened in Los Angeles; satellites and rockets careered through space; the Pope, the most immortal of mortals, died; President Kennedy, the world's most powerful person, was assassinated; and Martin Luther King voiced his dream of racial harmony. The world was changing faster than ever before. The British Conservative party went as far right as it could by choosing a grouse-killing peer of the realm (Alec Douglas-Hume) as its leader and the Prime Minister but the Tories were on their way out. Hugh Gaitskell, leader of the Labour party, died, leaving the way clear for Harold Wilson to rise to the top, and Labour were on their way in. But most of my memories of that year are of sitting as close as I could to a raging coal fire to protect myself against the coldest winter of my life.

I had a choice of three pastimes – watching television, studying for my A levels or braving the dark, lonely streets to slip into a pub for some serious underage drinking. The most entertaining television programmes of that black-and-white era were the first weekly broadcasts of *Doctor Who* and *That Was the Week that Was,* an insolent satirical review of everything. *That Was the Week that Was* relied shamelessly on such sagas as the Profumo Scandal, the continuing tale of the penetration of the British elite by the Russian KGB, who used hookers and West Indian playboys as their means of entry. Tabloids carried photographs and cartoons of sexy prostitutes fawning over cabinet ministers and of Caribbean immigrants smoking marijuana in west London's illegal shebeens. *From Russia with Love,* 1963's big box-office hit, was happening in London. James Bond was real – and British.

Until 1963 I had thought of crime as violent, cruel, a bit silly and necessarily wrong. The Great Train Robbery, during which £2.3 million – equivalent to £40 million today – in used banknotes was stolen from a Royal Mail train, changed that. The gang fitted the Hollywood image, with each member providing a particular skill. Buster Edwards, a small-time thief, fraudster and ex-boxer, helped out. Bruce Reynolds, an antique dealer, was the brains and meticulous mastermind; Gordon Goody was the muscle. Charlie Wilson was the well-connected underworld crook; John Wheater, a public-school-educated solicitor, was the respectable front man. And Ronnie Biggs recruited a driver for the hijacked train.

At 3.00 a.m., in the grey light of an August morning, the mail train pulled to a stop at false signals erected in the remote Buckinghamshire countryside, and a group posing as railway workers wearing uniform blue overalls appeared on the tracks and quietly took 120 sacks of loot to a nearby rented farmhouse. The plan was for no violence – the gang wanted a victimless crime – but for reasons best known to himself the driver of the train decided to take them on and ended up receiving a thump with an iron bar.

The media jumped on this to demonstrate that the robbers were nothing more than sordid men of violence, but we weren't fooled. The train robbers were romantic daredevils who had made a mockery of the foolish and out-of-touch Tory government. They showed what could be done. They were heroes. We loved the reports of how they played Monopoly with real money as they lay low in the farmhouse. I dreamed of one day meeting Bruce Reynolds.

The police closed in and the train robbers scattered. Forensic experts found fingerprints on the Monopoly set. Gang members fled to all corners of the globe. Possible sightings of the fugitives filled tabloid front pages. Occasionally, one of them would be caught and locked up; we would go to the pub and commiserate. Then another would escape from prison; we would go out and celebrate. We were proud to be British. We had the world's best criminals.

At the time I was completely unaware of any Welsh–English hostility or problem. Neither my parents nor other adults with whom I came into contact taught me that England was anything other than a friendly and powerful parent country. In school we had learned how in the early years of the fifteenth century Owain Glyndwr had failed to drive the Anglo-Norman conquerors from Welsh soil, but since then the two nations had been joined in indivisible union. Wales had no capital city until 1955. Road signs and official forms were in English. The Welsh were just western English. England was no enemy; that epithet applied to the Germans and the Japanese; the hangover from the Second World War continuing to manifest itself in ration books, comics and boys' games.

There were differences, of course. The Welsh could sing better, but not the songs that I liked. The English had glamour and sex, while the Welsh had chapels and sheep. The English were better footballers; Wales had just four teams in the four football divisions and only one player of note, John Charles, who quickly left Cardiff to play for Leeds. The Welsh were good at rugby union, and it was important to beat England at least in this sport. Although tempers occasionally flared both on and off the field, such as when my grandfather beat the radio to bits with his hobnail boots when Wales missed an easy penalty, it was just good sports-field rivalry. In 1952, Wales had won the Grand Slam, trouncing Scotland, Ireland, France and England, but that year we joined the English in their mourning of the death of King George VI. His grandson would be the next prince of Wales, the first since the future Edward VIII took the title in 1910. We seemed pleased, and the next year queued outside the few houses that had television to watch the coronation of Queen Elizabeth II.

Knowing and understanding little more Welsh history than that, I remember sitting down with Marty at the Moulders Arms, a rough and ready pub in Cardiff city centre near the edge of Tiger Bay. The Four Seasons' 'Walk Like a Man' belted out of the jukebox. We silently mouthed the lyrics, showing off our knowledge of modern music. Although intending to celebrate prematurely our eighteenth birthdays, we were also drinking in an attempt to cheer up. Wales hadn't won the Grand Slam or Triple Crown for over ten years, and hopes for any turn in the losing tide had just been dashed by losing 6–13 to England at Cardiff. Welsh heavyweight boxers Joe Erskine and Dick Richardson had lost their British empire and European titles. In ten years there had been only four Welsh singers in the top twenty: Shirley Bassey, Petula Clark, Maureen Evans – who sang cover versions for Woolworth's Embassy label – and Ricky Valance ('Tell Laura I Love Her'). To add to our depression, Wales was enduring the worst of British winters, now known as the Big Freeze of 1963.

'Marty, I think Liverpool should have been made capital of Wales. There's probably more Welshmen there than in Cardiff, and a lot more happening with music and football. There's nothing here – it's dead. I'm going to London for a university interview soon. I can't wait.'

Marty leaned over to whisper, 'I agree with you, but I wouldn't say how great Liverpool is in too loud a voice. Liverpool council have drowned the Tryweryn Valley just to get cheap water. Loads of families lost their homes. They were just told to bugger off and live somewhere else. There's a lot of bad feeling about it, especially round here.'

Marty's warning came too late – I had been overheard.

'So you're an English-lover, are you?' asked a red-headed bloke with arms of pure muscle.

'I've nothing against them.'

'And you call yourself Welsh?'

'I am Welsh and probably speak the language better than you do.'

Welsh was my first language; I learned English at the age of four. At the same time my father, recently retired from the Merchant Navy, began to learn Welsh. I was quicker so we conversed in English while my mother and I continued to speak to each other in Welsh. A year later my sister was born, and both my parents and I spoke to her in Welsh. My father and mother talked English to each other. I attended an English-speaking primary school where fewer than 5 per cent of the pupils spoke Welsh and quickly became more articulate in English than Welsh.

'All the more reason for you to hate the fucking English then. Have you got any idea what they've done to us?'

'Yes, but that was hundreds of years ago,' I said.

'Was it indeed? Hundreds of years ago? Time you learned something other than the words of English pop songs.'

'American, actually. That was the Four Seasons.'

'Same fucking thing. The English might suck up to the Yanks; fucked if I will. Hundreds of years ago? When did the English charge us for using our roads? When did the English physically force us to stop speaking Welsh by putting Welsh Nots around our necks? When did they rape our country by turning it into a heap of slag? When did they send starving Welsh children down the pits so they could steal our coal, our tin, our lead and even our gold? When did they flood our valleys to steal our water? Hundreds of years ago? I don't

Wish You Were Here

UK Anti-drugs Co-ordinator
Also known as 'Drugs Czar'

IN CONFIDENCE

You should complete this form and return it to Recruitment & Assessment Services, Innovation Court, New Street, Basingstoke, Hants, RG21 7JB by **5 September 1997**.

If you request an acknowledgement but do not receive one within ten days, please inform us.

PLEASE USE BLACK INK AS THIS FORM MAY BE PHOTOCOPIED

Surname *(BLOCK LETTERS)*	MARKS	Permanent address *(BLOCK LETTERS)* — 30 WAUNBANT ROAD, KENFIG HILL, MID-GLAMORGAN
Forenames *(in full)*	DENNIS HOWARD	
Title *(Dr, Mr, Mrs, Miss, Ms etc)*	MR	
Any other names by which you have been known	MR NICE	
Date of birth	AUGUST 13th, 1945	
Age	52	Postcode — CF33 6DE
Place of birth	KENFIG HILL, MID-GLAMORGAN	Telephone number — 01656-740649
Nationality at birth	BRITISH	I have lived there since *(year)* — 1945
Present nationality	BRITISH	Address for letters *(if different from above)*
Have you ever possessed any other nationality or citizenship? *(Tick appropriate box)*	Yes ☐ No ☒	
If YES, give full details with dates		
Are you subject to immigration control?	Yes ☐ No ☒	Postcode
If so, do you have an unrestricted entitlement to take up employment in the UK?	Yes ☐ No ☐	Telephone number or number where a message may be left — 0468-076856
		Fax Number — +34-71-799518

EDUCATION, PROFESSIONAL QUALIFICATIONS, OTHER TRAINING

Name of University, College or other institution	Dates From	Dates To	Course details	Qualifications obtained, (including grades) membership of professional institution etc
Balliol College, Oxford	1964	1967	Natural Science (Physics)	B.A. (Oxon)
University of London	1967	1968	Physics	Grad.Inst P.
Balliol College, Oxford	1968	1969	History and Philosophy	Dip.H.Ph.Sc.
University of Sussex	1969	1970	Philosophy of Science	M.A. (Oxon)
United States Federal Penitentiary, Terre Haute	1991	1993	General Education	G.E.D.
English Language Centre	1994		English as a foreign language	T.O.E.F.L. London

From Drug Baron to Drug Czar

Who wants to lock YOU up?

and who are YOU going to vote for?

HOWARD MARKS ☒

Legalise Cannabis Party

29, St. Augustines Street, Norwich

Who to Vote For

Eddie Bunker. Mr Blue and Mr Nice

Dave Courtney, Tel Currie, Freddie Foreman

Bruce Reynolds, Robert Sabbag

Notting Hill Carnival 2005

Sleeping Police.
If you snooze you lose

Leroy Sibbles and Claudette Finnegan

Ernest Ranglin

Ken Boothe

Jamaica Beachbum

fucking think so. It happened during our parents' time. It's happening now, and wankers like you just sit back and watch them take the piss out of us, silence us, and starve us to death while they use our money to build bloody Polaris submarines. You may as well fuck off to Liverpool or London; you're no fucking use here, you groveller.'

Marty stood up. 'Come on, Howard, let's get out of here.'

'Go on, you English-loving yellow-bellied chicken. Go and pollute some other pub.'

Marty and I scarpered. We knew we didn't stand a chance.

'What was all that Welsh Not stuff about?' I asked Marty.

'Haven't you heard of that? I thought you were doing A levels this summer.'

'I am, but in science and maths not Welsh history.'

Marty patiently explained that a hundred-odd years ago, when popular disturbances and riots were common in Wales, MPs had asked in Westminster why the Welsh people were so prone to lawlessness. Parliament decided the Welsh language was the problem: Welsh was not an official language and simply wasn't a suitable medium for education. The moral and material condition of the Welsh could only be improved by force-feeding them English. To accomplish this piece of cultural oppression, schools introduced the Welsh Not. Any child heard speaking Welsh during school was given a plaque to be handed on to whoever next spoke the language. At the end of lessons, the child left with the Not was punished.

'But that stuff doesn't happen now, Marty.'

'I know, but it wasn't that long ago, not hundreds of years ago. That hard nut in the pub did have a point, as he did about the mines. Don't forget the English poured into the Welsh coal mining areas and tipped the language balance forever.'

'They weren't trying to destroy the Welsh language; they were just looking for work.'

'I'm not saying it's the workers' fault,' protested Marty. 'The English fat cats never came to the mines; they just owned them and packed people off to work there. They didn't care what was happening to the Welsh language and culture. The Welsh cared, all right, but no one listened. There's still plenty of resentment against English domination; you've just experienced some of it.'

Less than a week later a professionally made gelignite bomb blew up a transformer at the Tryweryn Valley dam site. Other blasts followed. Mudiad Amddyffyn Cymru, the Movement for the Defence of Wales, had dramatically announced its existence and purpose. Plaid Cymru, the largely ineffectual forty-year-old Welsh nationalist party, quickly distanced itself from the attacks, preferring to carry on whining. The police quickly caught the bombers but English-owned cottages in Wales started to go up in flames and Welsh language societies mounted demonstrations tinged with confrontation. Some of the protesters carried placards bearing the slogan 'Free Wales Army' and sported the emblem of a white eagle in tribute to the legendary White Eagles of Snowdon, who from their lofty crags would swoop down on any invaders. A militant Welsh terrorist group had briefly overtaken the IRA as a thorn in England's side. There would be no more grovelling to the English. Welsh patriotism was no longer safely consigned to history. The Welsh had the most beautiful flag in the world, the most stirring national anthem and one of the oldest living languages. Wales, with its vast resources, could become the envy of the world's independent nations. I would never again forget I was Welsh.

Despite these distractions, I managed to do enough revision to get three grade As in my A Levels. I celebrated by going to see the Everly Brothers' midweek concert in Cardiff. Unfortunately, one of the brothers was ill, but the solo performance was excellent. After the show, special buses took us back to the valleys. I sat next to a beautiful girl who smiled shyly.

'Great show, wasn't it?' I said.

'Yes, but I wish both the brothers had been there. I love them.'

'Where are you from?'

'Ireland, but my family have just moved to Kenfig Hill.'

'That's where I live,' I said with unconcealed excitement.

'I know. I've seen you a few times waiting for the school bus in the morning when my dad drives me to my job. I work in the council offices. You're called Howard, aren't you?' Her smile broadened at the look of pleasure on my face. 'My name is Susan.'

'Any chance of a date?'

'OK, but I can't come out until Friday. Dad doesn't like me going out in the week much. I could only come to the concert tonight if I promised to stay in until then.'

'Let's make it Friday then.'

'OK, but where shall we meet?'

'Elim Chapel Youth Club. I'll be there from eight o'clock.'

'OK, my dad will drop me off there. Look out for me won't you?'

Now, almost forty years later, I was on my way back to Britain to meet for the first time the outcome of that chance meeting, my daughter.

I already had four children. Four years ago Myfanwy, now thirty-two, had provided me with a delightful grandson and was living on a farm in Devon studying to become a Rudolf Steiner teacher. She had been just one year old when I left her and her mother Rosie for life on the run as a fugitive, but we never lost our love for each other and still spent wonderful times together. Amber, my first of three children with Judy, was twenty-seven and a brilliant barrister who would go on to work for the Court of Criminal Appeals. Francesca, twenty-three, had qualified as a yoga teacher and would soon gain a philosophy degree from Trinity College, Dublin. Patrick,

sixteen, was convalescing from a number of serious and
lengthy surgical operations on his back.

He had been born with scoliosis, a helical twist of the spine,
and had aggravated his condition by jumping off a roof,
breaking both his legs, when four years old. Despite Judy's
unceasing efforts to improve his condition through treatments
other than surgery, nothing worked. Mustering more courage
than I had ever had to, Patrick submitted himself to the
surgeon's knife. The operations worked, and he is now a tall
proud teenager with a will and a spine of steel.

The pride I have for each of my children continues to make
my life the most precious joy, but it wasn't all happy families.
My relationship with Judy did not outlast the seven years of
separation caused by my imprisonment. Survival in prison
forces you to abandon, or at least significantly reduce,
emotional attachments to those outside. Failure to do so is a
prescription for vulnerability and continuous psychological
pain. I left the penitentiary with emotions and ideals hardened
to the limits. Judy had kept the family and family house
together without the children calling someone else 'Daddy' and
I am certain that had the positions been reversed I would not
have been a model loyal husband. However, I found it
impossible to accept her admitted infidelities as insignificant,
had no intention of being faithful myself, and found the prospect of renewed marriage vows a restriction on the precious
freedom I had regained on my release from prison. So I had got
my bedsit in Shepherd's Bush and was seeking a divorce.

At Gatwick the immigration queues doubled back on one
another several times. Mobile phones beeped despite the
notices commanding them to be turned off. Two-way mirrors
gave distorted reflections, and several hundred CCTV
cameras swept every inch of airport space. I wondered how
difficult drug smuggling must be these days. Passing through
passport control, I picked up my bag and strolled through the

green channel. A dog with brown and white patches slightly resembling a spaniel ran its snotty nose over my luggage, emitted a machine-gun burst of hard sniffs and winked knowingly at its handler.

'Where have you just come from, sir?' asked an officer of Her Majesty's Customs & Excise.

'Jamaica.'

'Holiday?'

'No. I'm writing a travel piece for the *Observer*.'

'Are you carrying any marijuana or other prohibited goods?'

'No.'

'Did you smoke marijuana while you were in Jamaica?'

'Yes, I did. I think your dog picked that up from my clothes.'

'Are you Howard Marks?'

I nodded and gave a smile.

'I enjoyed your book, Mr Marks. Thank you. Have a good day.'

Maybe smuggling wouldn't be that hard.

It was mid-morning. I took the Gatwick Express to Victoria and a cab from there to my bedsit. I telephoned the number Tina had given me. A strong Welsh accent answered. 'Hello. Who's speaking please?'

'Can I speak to Tina? It's Howard.'

There was a short but definite pause then, 'This is Tina.'

A long silence followed.

'Rather than try to talk now, perhaps we should just arrange to meet somewhere soon,' she suggested, trying to break the impasse. 'Are you still living in Majorca?'

'No, I live in London these days. What about you?'

'Gowerton, just outside Swansea, not far from Kenfig Hill. Do you ever go back there?'

'Yes, sometimes, to see a few close friends. Do you ever come to London?'

'Once in a blue moon, but I can come up for the day pretty

much when I feel like it. In fact, I would rather see you alone the first time, so we can have a private chat. You can meet the children later.'

'Children? How many do you have?'

'Three – two sons in their early teens and a daughter doing her A levels next year.'

I was only just getting used to having one baby grandchild and suddenly I had three teenage grandchildren, the oldest older than my son. I felt strangely disorientated about my decades of ignorance; I had no idea how to deal with it.

'We could meet halfway,' I said, aware of my words awkwardly stumbling over one another. Why was I treating this next meeting as a business appointment, politely trying to reduce any inconvenience to her?

'That's an excellent idea,' she said. 'I could see you in Bristol, I have to take a train there anyway in the next few days to pick up some medical results. When would suit you best?'

'What about tomorrow, Tina?'

'Tomorrow's fine. I can be there by two o'clock. Or is that too early for you? You can make it later if you want.'

'No, two o'clock is perfect. I'll meet you at Temple Meads on the platform where the trains from South Wales stop, and we'll have some lunch. How will I recognise you?'

'Don't worry, I'll recognise you easily enough. I've got books and books of photographs of you.'

Twenty-four hours later I was on a busy station platform watching hundreds of people getting off the Swansea train and trying to identify a daughter I had never met and of whose existence I had been aware for less than a week. A beautiful blue-eyed smiling face shone from the crowd and headed towards me. Still behaving as if I was a travelling salesman meeting a new client, I shook her hand and kissed her lightly on each cheek. I was slightly taller than her. She was slim with soft skin and a reddish tinge in her dark hair. Was this from her mother's Irish ancestry or was it dyed? I couldn't tell. Why did it matter?

'What do you fancy for lunch?' I stammered.

It was two thirty, and most places were closing for the afternoon; an upmarket Chinese restaurant was the only visible exception. Tina and I shuffled in and ordered some instantly forgotten food and a bottle of red wine. The ice of our embarrassment began to thaw as she summarised her life story.

Susan Malone had no idea she was pregnant when, in the summer of 1963, her family left Kenfig Hill to live in the Swansea area, where her father had secured a good job. Susan met another man, who also had no idea she was pregnant. They married and Tina was born, far too soon for the new husband's liking. Knowing Tina was not his daughter, he left to seek another life. During her early years Tina thought her real father had abandoned both her and her mother the moment she was born. I felt intensely sorry for both her and Susan's husband, and I felt angry with her mother.

'But why didn't Susan tell me she was pregnant with my child?' I asked incredulously. 'She knew where I lived in Kenfig Hill. She could have easily come to see me or at least written a letter.'

'You can imagine how many times I've asked my mother that,' said Tina, 'and her answer has always been the same. She heard that you had got into Oxford and didn't want to ruin your life by saddling you with me. Not that she's always that saintly, mind, especially these days.'

'That's a hell of a sacrifice. Are you sure her husband wasn't a better catch – like very rich?'

'Positive. And my mother said that after she left Kenfig Hill you started going out with her best friend, Mavis. She didn't like that much,' said Tina with a disapproving look on her face.

'But I wouldn't have if I'd known Susan was pregnant with my child,' I protested.

'I know that now,' said Tina, 'but I honestly don't think my mother did then.'

'So when did Susan tell you I was your father?'

'When you were arrested in 1980 for bringing in all those tons of marijuana into Scotland and the newspapers were full of you being an MI6 agent with connections to the IRA, *Mafia*, CIA and God knows who else, my mother said, "That's your dad."'

'So, until then you thought Susan's husband was your father?' I asked.

'No. My mother told me when I was about twelve that my real father had left her before I was born. She just never told me your name. Once I found out, I tried to see you. You were on remand in Brixton prison. The prison guards just laughed at me and said I wasn't on your list of family members. I asked if I could see you anyway, and they said you were too high a security risk for that sort of visit. So that was that. I was gutted.'

'But why didn't you write to me? I would have arranged for us to see each other.'

'Look, Howard . . .'

I had been wondering whether she would call me Dad or Howard. I was relieved she had chosen Howard.

'Look, Howard, it took a lot of courage for me to go to Brixton and do that. My mother really didn't want me to. And when I was refused I felt rejected and felt I had done wrong by trying to get to know you. Maybe your family – or should I say families – would also reject me. I couldn't take the risk. I was too scared. When I had plucked up enough courage to try again you had been caught in Spain doing some even bigger dope deal and were being extradited to America never to return. Then when you surprised everyone and did come back you became a bloody superstar, and I was just too shy and nervous to contact you. I was worried you would think I was after your money.'

'I haven't got any.'

'Really? Everyone thinks you're loaded, what with money in Swiss bank accounts from the old days and writing two best-sellers and touring up and down the country doing shows.'

'I know people think that, but I promise you I'm skint.'

'Well I'm glad that you know that I know. That means you'll know for sure I'm not after your money. I haven't cost you anything so far, and I never will. I just want to know you and us to be friends.'

Her eyes welled up. I caught hold of her hand.

'What do you do, Tina?'

'I look after old people. I have to pick up some medical reports today. The three children don't leave me too many spare hours in a week, so I'm only working part-time. I'll go full-time when I can. I love the work. The children's father and I split up ages ago – I'm alone now. I prefer it, to be honest.'

Tina was caring and good. I noticed how her hands were the same shape as mine. This was the first physical likeness between us I had discovered.

'You're looking at our hands, aren't you? Shall we have a DNA test?'

'No,' I said without thinking for a split second.

'What! You are that sure you're my father?'

'I didn't say that.'

'You mean you're one hundred per cent sure you are not my father?'

'I didn't say that either. No one could be sure—'

'You would be if we took a DNA test.'

'Tina, I'm saying no one could be sure given just what I know now. Anyway, what would be the point of a DNA test?'

'You would know whether you're my father.'

'Would there really be any point in knowing that? You and I can't have a normal father–daughter relationship – it's too late for that. We could be close friends. I'm sure we will be, and I don't want our relationship to depend on some biological connection. I want us to be friends whether you're my daughter or not. Don't you?'

'Of course I do, Howard. I see what you mean. OK, let's forget the DNA test. I know: we can take it if we end up not being friends.'

My main reason for not wanting to have a DNA test was my lack of certainty as to whether Tina was actually my daughter. Having my doubts confirmed would deprive her of the shaky security of knowing that she could, at least, identify her father even if he had not fulfilled a single paternal duty. But in thinking the way I was, perhaps I was being fatherly. It was confusing.

Mr Nice had now been translated into five languages – Hebrew, German, Spanish, French and Italian. The Italian edition was on the point of being distributed and the publishers, Edizioni Socrates – who had also published Italian translations of Wim Wenders and Alexander Trocchi – had asked if I would come to Italy to help with promotion. Apart from my visit to Campione d'Italia, I had not been to Italy for almost twenty years. The country and the people had always captivated me. My first schoolboy history interest had been the Romans, their amphitheatres and their debauchery. Pythagoras and Archimedes – who spent their lives in what is now Italy, not Greece – were my first scientific heroes; Roman Catholicism provided my first religious enigmas; Sophia Loren, Gina Lollobrigida and Claudia Cardinale were my first pin-ups. Much of my postgraduate work at Oxford in the late 1960s involved Galileo and other Renaissance heavyweights while some of my first hashish smuggling ventures during the early 1970s took place in Italy. Shortly afterwards, when I first went on the run from the forces of injustice, I lived in Genoa. My favourite wine is Brunello di Montalcino and my youngest daughter's name is Francesca. My most profitable period of dope smuggling was the late 1970s, when I was airfreighting tons of Pakistani hashish and Thai marijuana on Alitalia

planes destined for New York's Kennedy Airport, where the
Gambino crime family made sure the shipments got through.
(I of course made sure they got well paid.) During the years I
spent imprisoned in the United States I became good friends
with members of the Genovese, Colombo, Bonnano and
Lucchese crime families. On my release, they – who will never
be released – begged me to step on Italian soil and pass on
their prayers to their native land, a country which has always
ruled the world – through its food, fashion, culture, ancient
armies, religion or criminal organisations. It would now give
me great pleasure to do so. During the same trip I could visit
Scott Blakey in Lugano and see how the Mr Nice Seedbank
plantations were progressing.

Edizioni Socrates wanted me to visit Rome for some press
and television interviews and Milan, a few days later, to give a
talk. I planned my itinerary. I would fly to Rome, stay two
nights, fly to Sicily for a couple of days to pass on a hello (or
goodbye) from my *Mafia* friends, fly to Milan for one night to
give the talk, and the next day take the train to Lugano to look
at marijuana plants. It looked like being an interesting week.

A few days later I offered my passport to an Italian
immigration officer at Rome airport. He snatched it from my
hand, stuck it under a light and signalled to two armed
policemen standing nearby. They frogmarched me into a
holding room and motioned me to sit down. Familiar feelings
flooded in. I had been in this situation countless times, but I
usually knew why. This time I had no idea. The immigration
officer's behaviour suggested my name was on a hot list. How
could I possibly be wanted by the Italian authorities? I hadn't
set foot in the country since the 1980s, and apart from the
consumption of drugs had not broken any country's laws since
my arrest by Spanish and American authorities in 1988. There
was only one explanation: I was going to be arrested for my
activities during the 1970s. Perhaps Italian law also had no
statute of limitations.

However, the unwritten policy adopted by most countries lacking statute of limitations legislation is not to prosecute if the offender of long ago seems rehabilitated, reformed and unlikely to reoffend. As I had spent nine years in prison since breaking Italian law and was making my income through writing and performing, I should clearly fall into this category. But one never knows. Italy, with its passion for dictators, had recently moved to the right by electing the country's richest man, Silvio Berlusconi, as its prime minister. He was fiercely anti-drugs, a strong ally of President Bush and a personal friend of Tony Blair – who took summer holidays at his home. Berlusconi liked to make a big deal of being tough on criminals, past and present. Although *Mr Nice* does not set out to glamorise crime, Berlusconi's cronies might not agree. I was a perfect target.

On the other hand, perhaps the Italian authorities simply wanted to treat me as persona non grata and send me back to the UK – as had happened to me when I tried to enter Hong Kong three years earlier. I could handle that; Italy's attractions were beginning to wear thin.

The immigration officer who had taken my passport marched noisily into the room. 'You English?' he barked.

'No, I'm Welsh. I'm British.'

'You speak English?'

'Yes, of course.'

'What is this?' he asked, brandishing my passport.

'It's my passport.'

'I don't mean the passport,' he bellowed. 'I mean this other document.'

My passport was in a holder which also contained a few credit cards, my driving licence and a laminated colour photocopy of my Spanish *Residencia*, a document showing I had the right to live in Spain. I had been advised to carry a copy with me while travelling but to leave the original in Spain as it would be costly and time-consuming to replace.

'It shows I am allowed to live in Spain.'

'It's false.'

'It's not false; it's a copy of the real one.'

'It's false. You should not carry false documents into our country. It is illegal.'

'I also have a photocopy of my passport in my briefcase. Is that illegal, too?'

He began to look sheepish and a bit flustered. Now was the time to strike. 'Excuse me, officer, but I am not required by law to have my original Spanish *Residencia* on me to enter Italy. I am not even legally bound to carry a valid passport. I merely have to provide you with proof of my identity. I have presented you with my valid British passport, a valid driving licence and some credit cards. It doesn't matter what photocopies I am also carrying. That is not your concern. If you are not satisfied I am who I say I am, then please contact your superior, the British embassy, or the Spanish embassy. And please do it quickly. I have a busy day ahead. Also, there are several people from the Italian media waiting for me at the airport here, and I am sure they will soon want to know why I'm being detained.'

'I'm just doing my job.'

'Me too. Now can we please get on with it?'

He threw my documents on the floor and stormed out, followed by the two policemen. One of them winked at me as he left. I picked up my documents and began the long walk to the baggage carousels. I rammed a cigarette into my mouth – the experience had been nerve-racking. Two other armed officers wearing different uniforms ran up to me. 'No smoking,' one of them said aggressively. 'Put it out now. Next time we arrest you.' Italy had changed.

My suitcase was the only one left on the carousel. I picked it up and headed for the green channel, fully expecting to be stopped and searched by more armed officials wearing yet another style of uniform, but they ignored me. They'd had plenty of time to search my case. It did contain a little piece of hashish, but I had hidden it well in a partially used toothpaste tube. Fuck them.

My poor opinion of today's Italy improved markedly as soon as I met my publishers, most of whom were young and beautiful. They were furious at the treatment dished out to me by the immigration officer and treated me royally. Time was scarce, and I was whisked away to the Spanish Steps for an alfresco interview. The questions were stricter than usual.

'Mr Marks, can you honestly say that cannabis is completely harmless?'

'It might well adversely affect a small minority, and I am sure it is a totally inappropriate drug for many others. I would advise such people not to take it.'

'So you admit it's harmful?'

'Yes, but a lot less harmful than other recreational drugs, including tobacco and coffee.'

'But why, Mr Marks, do you want to legalise something you admit might be harmful to those who take it?'

'Many harmful things are legal, such as cars and kitchen knives. Some people have died from eating carrots or peanuts. My point is that cannabis would be less harmful to society if legalised and controlled rather than left to gangsters like me to hawk outside schools.'

'But, Mr Marks, the same argument could be used to legalise cocaine, ecstasy even heroin.'

'I know.'

'So you think all drugs should be legalised?'

'All the ones that I've taken, for sure. And that includes cocaine, ecstasy and heroin, and God knows what else. Each one of them would be safer if not prohibited. I suppose one has to allow for the possibility of one day someone discovering or synthesising a drug that when taken produces the wilful desire to murder, maim and rape. In which case, it should be illegal.

But I have never come across such a drug. The only one that gets close is this one, alcohol.'

I raised my glass in a toast to Rome. So did everyone else.

The interview was followed by a long lunch, which in turn was followed, almost immediately, by an even longer dinner. My good memories of life in Italy returned

The next day the publishers and I scoured the newspapers over our coffee and sweet pastries. The headlines were predictable: 'Oxford Professor Says "Legalise heroin"' and 'British Secret Service Agent Sells Drugs to Schoolchildren', or words to that effect. We weren't bothered; we knew as far as publicity was concerned the criterion of success was the space devoted to the topic, not what was written.

I flew to Palermo, stronghold of the world's greatest criminal organisation, and checked into the Villa Igiea, a castle-shaped art nouveau villa originally belonging to the Florio family, the first people ever to put tuna in cans. With a sweeping view of the Bay of Palermo and jasmine-laden terraced gardens, it was the favourite Palermo hotel of *Mafia* boss Lucky Luciano. I had stayed there during my first brief visit to Sicily in 1982. The enormous American bar was empty but open. I drank as much grappa, my favourite Italian spirit, as I could.

At the buffet breakfast the next morning the formally dressed waiters discomfited me by staring at my unmanicured nails, dishevelled hair and clothes adorned with unknown labels. After a swim in the hotel pool – situated next to an ancient temple – I wandered into town, ogled unashamedly the beauties sporting the latest Milanese and Florentine fashions, dodged the Vespas and the baby buggies, and bought some cigarettes at an exquisite *tabaccherìa*. I walked inside *il cattedrale* – which displays St Agatha's arm and Mary Magdalene's foot – and offered prayers from my imprisoned Italian friends. I had to eat lunch at the Grande Albergo e delle Palme, where *Mafia* leaders met in October 1957 to organise the world's drug trade; my fellow inmate Antonio Aiello,

sentenced to life imprisonment for his role in the Pizza
Connection, had pleaded with me to do so. He used to eat
there every day. After a bottle of Brunello di Montalcino, I
began to think of my days with the Mob.

Although there is at least one alternative theory – that *mafia*
derives from the Arabic mu'afah meaning refuge or protection
– it is widely thought that *mafia* is an acronym of *Morte ai
Francesi Italiani allarme* (Death to all French threatened by the
Italians), the rallying cry of the Sicilian Vespers, a thirteenth-
century insurrection again French rule. The French gave way
to Spanish and then Austrian despots and even Garibaldi's
nineteenth-century unification fell far short of Sicilian
expectations: the island was still ruled by remote and uncaring
bureaucrats, only now from Rome. By this time the *Mafia* was
a significant presence in Sicilian society and political life.

Organised crime can be spawned by irrational and unjust
laws. During the early years of the twentieth century the
United States government told hundreds of thousands of its
new Italian citizens they could no longer continue their
traditional customs of drinking a glass of wine and buying a
lottery ticket. Prohibition and eliminating numbers rackets
were the orders of the day. The *Mafia* saw its opportunity.
Legal and illegal economies intertwined, as did criminal
organisations, social institutions and political bodies. This
mixture of illegal and legal, criminal and institutional is at
the heart of the *Mafia*, which traditionally regards violence
and illegality as acceptable ways to survive and gain a social
role when the legal economy is too weak to offer opportunities.
Government and institutions are distant, foreign and
approachable only through mediating *Mafiosi*. For the *Mafia*,
rights do not exist; there are only favours bestowed within a
sinister network of common interests.

While Prohibition was eventually repealed in the USA, life
had got rougher back in Sicily and Mussolini had driven the

Mafia deeper underground. Popular discontent continued to be displayed through banditry and its accompanying *omertà* – law of silence – an attitude deeply rooted in romantic law-breaking and criminal nepotism. The United States seemed a far more sympathetic home than Italy, so much so that the *Mafia*, through Lucky Luciano, facilitated the Anglo-American invasion of Sicily and Italy in 1943. Sicilians obviously expected some proper reward for their unconventional wartime services, such as annexation to the United States or membership of the British empire or full independence. Instead, anarchy, hunger and a problematic regional assembly followed the Second World War. Corruption was rife, and the island became littered with half-finished building projects – evidence of *Mafia* involvement.

I took a taxi for the thirty-minute drive to Corleone, the celluloid home of the *Mafia*. I saw nothing to suggest the presence of a criminal organisation or reminiscent of a Hollywood movie. The same taxi took me back. Some believe the drug-dealing *Mafia* is the creation of pulp-thriller writers, a legend fostered by a sensationalist press and fuelled by Italian and United States governments eager for scapegoats. Mario Puzo claimed that his choice for the birthplace and nursery of the mythical Corleone crime family was random; Corleone could, he said, just as well have been any of a thousand other tiny Sicilian villages. However, when *il capo dei tutti capi*, the boss of all bosses, Salvatore Riina was arrested in 1993 it was revealed that he had lived there undisturbed for over twenty years with his children registered at the local school and hospital. Perhaps Riina had moved there after seeing *The Godfather*. Perhaps all the *Mafiosi* were in Palermo's Ucciardone prison, collaborating with the warders to secure good food in return for no escapes. Or is the *Mafia* still as invisible as it is ineradicable? I spent the evening sending postcards to United States penitentiaries.

The next morning, a Saturday, I flew to Milan to be met by the same glamorous team of publishers and publicity agents, now accompanied by a group of men wearing a mixture of punk and biker clothes and holding tightly on to the leads of large ferocious dogs. One of the men approached me and held out his hand.

'*Buongiorno. Signore Nice. Benvenuto a Milano. Sono Alberto de Ya Basta. Andiamo per favore.*'

Alberto drove; I sat next to him, and an Alsatian covered the back seat. After about forty minutes we arrived outside a huge fortress-like building covered in murals and surrounded by parked cars. A sign showed we were at the Centro Sociale Leoncavallo, the venue for my evening talk.

Italian social centres are based in abandoned buildings – warehouses, factories, military forts, schools – occupied by squatters and transformed into cultural and political hubs explicitly free from state control. This revolutionary culture has developed out of need. Politicians of all persuasions are continually caught up in corruption scandals, and large numbers of Italians have understandably inferred that it is power itself that corrupts. Spearheaded by the well-disciplined Ya Basta (Enough is Enough) of Milan, the social centre network is a parallel political framework serving the needs of the community around each centre and providing alternative services, such as child-care and advocacy for refugees. It also confronts the state through direct action. In the centres culture and politics mix; a meeting about unionising fast-food workers could easily finish as a rave. Italy has three or four hundred autonomous social centres and the Leoncavallo in Milan is the oldest and biggest. Keeping the same name and upholding its role as an anarchist urban guerilla anti-fascist collective, it has changed its location several times. The last was in 1994, when Ya Basta mobilised 20,000 people to reclaim the current site from the authorities.

Alberto, I and his dog walked into the Leoncavallo

complex, which comprises a concert hall, conference room, skateboard ramp, cinema, several indoor and outdoor bars and restaurants, a children's area, art exhibition halls, bookshops and masses of workshop space. Several posters advertised that evening's line-up of speakers. One was talking about the Arab–Israeli conflict, another about raising ecological awareness. There was a debate about Iraq and a forum on how to curb the state's unconstitutional excesses in countering terrorism. I was speaking about the need to legalise cannabis.

My speech emphasised the dismal failure of prohibition – people were taking more drugs than ever. I outlined the new dangers provided by such policies: honest people were being made into criminals (bringing the rule of law into disrepute), unchecked poisons were flooding the streets, and various criminal and terrorist organisations were being provided with a ready means of funding their operations. Then I pointed out the irrationality and futility of trying to legislate against those wishing to change their states of mind by ingesting natural substances and ended with my well-rehearsed conclusion: 'Prohibition is not control and should not be equated with control. It is the abrogation of control leading to unregulated peddling of adulterated substances outside the reach of the law. It would be difficult to frame, even if one deliberately contrived so to do, a policy more physically dangerous, more individually criminalising, or more socially destructive. Prohibition is an extremely dangerous social experiment and should be dismantled as soon as possible.'

The audience applauded. The marijuana smoke enveloping the auditorium suggested I was preaching to the converted. I invited questions.

'Which political party do you think should and will dismantle prohibition?'

'Either the extreme right based on individual privacy or the extreme left based on harm reduction. It doesn't matter. I think everyone has the right to get stoned. I don't think politics need to come into it.'

'But you formed a political party and stood at the 1997 British general election. How can you say that politics is unimportant?'

'I did that merely to draw attention to the legalisation issue. I would hate to be a politician. Most of the ones I have met have been lying, insincere wankers. As far as I'm concerned, I would always vote for the party with the most liberal drug policy, even if it was the Nazis.'

Uncomfortable shuffles and murmurs of disapproval convinced me I was being far too flippant with my answers to this politically hypersensitive audience. I tried to rescue myself.

'Let me make myself clear. I spent the first nineteen years of my life in a socially and economically depressed mining community in South Wales. If a pig had stood for election against a member of the Tory or any other right-wing party, we would, without exception, have voted for the pig.'

A few cackles of laughter replaced the mutterings of discontent.

'How can you justify, Mr Marks, supporting the legalisation of cannabis and socialist policies when you made millions out of its illegality?'

'In the same way that doctors welcome the discovery of effective cures despite making their living from disease. Would a wealthy funeral director have to be a hit man to be consistent?'

A few dissenting voices came from various sections of the audience, but now they were arguing with one another, not me. I could handle that.

'I hear you have a seed bank in Switzerland selling cannabis seeds around the world. Does this not make you a capitalist?'

'It's not my seed company; I don't own any part of it; and it pays me no money.'

'But it is called Mr Nice Seedbank, is it not? I have here an Italian magazine with an article about it.'

'Mr Nice is not my name.'

'But a photograph of your face is on the front of every packet. Why have you allowed this if you have no interest in the company?'

'It's a photograph of the front cover of my book. I don't own the copyright of the photograph and have no control over its use. I said I did not own any part of Mr Nice Seedbank; I did not say I had no interest. I am interested. A close friend of mine owns the company; I approve of people being able to grow their own marijuana; and the use of the name and cover of my book might increase its sales.'

'So you are a capitalist, Mr Marks?'

'If being paid for writing books makes me partly capitalist, so be it. Incidentally, copies are being offered for sale here and I'll happily sign them afterwards. Goodnight and thank you.'

Heated but good-natured arguments were taking place throughout the auditorium as Alberto escorted me off the stage. Outside, people had set up stalls. Sound checks were taking place and bars beginning to open. Roughly 10,000 people swarmed in, mainly young local people coming to dance to European DJs playing in the room I had just left. Other bars hosted rappers and samba drumming. The canteen and art gallery were full of people. There was no security, no bouncers, no dress control and no hostility.

The party continued all night. It was pointless checking into a hotel for a couple of hours sleep, so I decided to keep moving. Alberto and his dog kindly drove me to Milan station, where I took an old-fashioned train for Lugano and sat in an otherwise empty compartment with bench seats and pictures of the Italian lakes. At the Swiss border town of Chiasso two Italian customs officers, uniformed, heavily armed and with a large Alsatian, boarded the train and made a beeline for my compartment. On entering, the dog went instantly berserk, displaying symptoms of both St Vitus's dance and epilepsy. It repeatedly jumped on and off my holdall and bit random parts of it, slobbering and barking as if the bag were full of cats. My now smaller piece of hashish was still hidden in the toothpaste tube; surely the dog couldn't smell that? The officers asked me to wait outside the compartment while they continued the search.

Although the train was stationary, I dismissed thoughts of doing a runner. I imagined the Alsatian bringing me down and going for my throat. I had seen more than enough of that in prison. One of the customs officers stepped out of the compartment and waved me towards him. I was dreading the sight of the dog chewing away at my toothpaste tube, but it was obvious nothing had been found. Clearly, the holdall had merely absorbed a few whiffs of marijuana smoke while being stored at Leoncavallo. The two men and the dog left.

I needed a drink so I decided to leave the train and take the next one on to Lugano. The Swiss border guards politely waved me through without even examining my passport. The first shop I saw outside Chiasso station was a grow shop. Inside were marijuana magazines, pipes, bongs, large rolling papers, herb grinders, nutrient solutions and indoor growing lights. The staff were smoking joints and offered me one as soon as I entered. I bought a small bag of skunk. Had Switzerland finally legalised cannabis? Passing another three grow shops, I went into a bar, drank a large grappa, and telephoned Scott Blakey to advise him I would be in Lugano station within the hour. He met me off the train.

'All right, mate?' I hadn't seen Scott for well over a year. He looked fit with his suntan and waist-length hair.

'Fine thanks, Scott. What's been happening here? I must have seen at least ten grow shops in Chiasso.'

'There's that many in Lugano,' said Scott. 'Chiasso must have more than twenty. You've seen nothing yet, mate. Come with me – I'll show you something special.'

We drove towards Bellinzona, the provincial capital of Ticino, and stopped outside a three- or four-storey building. Scott led the way inside into a maze of rooms in which marijuana was growing under strong lights. In other rooms people were cutting and cleaning buds. Several offices rang, buzzed and whirred with telephones, computer printers and faxes. Laboratories tested samples of weed. Two local government officials were wandering around the building ensuring that fire regulations, hygiene standards and employee conditions conformed to legal requirements. Beautiful women were placing seeds in packets with my face on the front. Mr Nice Seedbank catalogues proclaiming twelve new Mr Nice strains were piled up ready for mailing.

'This is amazing, Scott, absolutely amazing. And this is all legal?'

'Obviously, mate. But you've still seen nothing yet.'

We left the extraordinary building and drove a few miles up a mountain to a large area cordoned off by high electronic fences festooned with sophisticated security devices. Scott pressed a few buttons on his zapper, a section of fence opened, and we drove in.

'Take a look.'

Spread in front of us were several acres of almost fully grown marijuana plants.

'Jesus!' I could say nothing else; I was speechless. For several seconds both of us gazed at this wonderful sight. I had seen nothing like it since the days I'd spent in the Himalayas in the 1980s.

'You're telling me this is legal, too, Scott?'

'Of course. I have no interest in breaking any country's laws. I never have done, other than smoke dope.'

'How much marijuana are we looking at?'

'Once it's been harvested and cleaned a bit, I would think about five or six tons at least.'

'What's going to be done with it?'

'We're going to make oil with our new distillation equipment. We will get about a litre from every ton. Then we'll take all the THC out of the oil and sell it in America.'

'What! Who the fuck is going to buy THC in America?'

'Nobody. The Americans buy what's left after the THC has been taken out of it. They use it for making perfume.'

'So what happens to the THC?'

'It doesn't survive the chemical process of—' Scott burst out laughing before he could finish the sentence; the look of astonishment on my face was too much for him. One of the reasons *Mr Nice* had been a successful book was because it was about smuggling good-quality marijuana and hashish that got many people, particularly Americans, stoned. That's why Scott chose the name for his seeds. Now the same name was also being used for an operation to remove from marijuana the ingredient that got you high. This was irony on a grand scale.

Cannabis is a dioecious annual herb, that is, it has the male and female reproductive organs in separate plants. The female produces seeds after being pollinated by a male. If the female plant is not pollinated it will produce mature flowers that are seedless (sinsemilla). Such plants have high levels of over 600 identifiable different cannabinoids (psychoactive molecular acids) in their flowers, stems and leaves. The highest concentrations occur in the mature female flower. In mammals psychoactive cannabinoids produce euphoria, enhancement of sensory perception, pain relief and variations in concentration and memory. They also have anti-convulsive, anti-anxiety, anti-psychotic, anti-nausea, anti-rheumatoid-arthritic and pain-relieving properties. Delta9-tetrahydrocannabinol (THC) is the primary active cannabinoid, with cannabidiol (CBD) and cannabigerol (CBG) playing significant roles. The particular effects of any cannabis plant are determined by the varying amounts of different cannabinoids in its composition, rather than merely the percentage of THC present.

Some countries, including the United States, have made

cannabis seeds illegal to possess, import or attempt to acquire. Most other countries, including the United Kingdom, base their drug legislation on the chemicals contained in the substance concerned and treat cannabis seeds as legal because they contain negligible amounts of THC. Collecting cannabis seeds, therefore, is in some countries a legal way of storing the genetic material of various strains. Scott wanted to produce seeds with high-quality, easily identifiable characteristics that were reliable and constant. Mr Nice Seedbank produced genetically identical seeds by keeping and cloning the original male and female parent plants.

In Switzerland the production of cannabis seeds for non-recreational purposes such as preserving genetic characteristics or cooking or producing birdseed was legal. Scott, as a foreigner, was unable to get a Swiss work permit but could own, invest in or consult for a Swiss company. Accordingly, Ticino business people had incorporated and staffed a Swiss company, Gene Bank Technology, to buy the rights to produce some Mr Nice Seedbank strains and, with the benefit of Scott's expert consultancy, to grow them. Gene Bank Technology had recently contracted a respected and well-established Ticino firm of flower growers, Martinelli Bros, to produce Mr Nice strains. Several farms interested in cannabis production had sought advice from Gene Bank Technology, which quickly gained a first-class reputation for honesty, reliability and promptness with delivery of clones. Demand soon exceeded supply. Gene Bank Technology's operations in Ticino supported otherwise-failing vegetable farmers and enabled them to make their livelihoods from a profitable product easily adapted to the local climate. Italian and Swiss cosmetic firms had contracted Gene Bank Technology to produce high-quality cannabis-flower oil. Accordingly, Gene Bank Technology had set up the marijuana plantation now in front of our eyes. In a few weeks the plantation's yield of cannabis oil – modified so it couldn't get anyone high – would be exported to the United States of America.

Trading cannabis seeds within Switzerland, however, was illegal unless one could prove the seeds had been bought from non-recreationally motivated producers and could further prove they would not be sold to companies that might resell them for recreational use – an impossible task. In Holland the production of cannabis seeds, although previously legal, was now illegal. Importing or trading cannabis seeds within the country, however, was legal, wherever they were produced. This apparent inconsistency is a result of the peculiarly Dutch concept of *gedogen*, which roughly translates as 'toleration'. This is not passive toleration – turning a blind eye – it's an active and open-eyed government policy that officially tolerates what is officially prohibited. If there is a social problem that does not have a straightforward solution, the Dutch will *gedogen* it. Typical examples are prostitution and the use of soft drugs. The Dutch know these are never going to go away so eradication is not the goal. In response to these two national approaches Mr Nice Seedbank had evolved its strategy: the seeds were produced in Switzerland and imported into Holland from where it was sold worldwide.

Scott and I drove away from the marijuana plantation to eat and get drunk at what is still my favourite restaurant after all these years, Campione d'Italia's Taverna.

On returning the next day to my bedsit in Shepherd's Bush I was greeted by an invitation to speak at the Hay-on-Wye book festival. The fee, a case of champagne and free accommodation, was acceptable. I telephoned Tina and asked if she wanted to attend the festival and meet me there. She was delighted.

After arranging to fly to Panama in a few days, I caught an early-afternoon train from London to Hereford, where I met

Tina. We took a cab together to Hay. Literati superstars and culture seekers sauntered through the small town's guest houses, bars, bookshops and restaurants. We saw politicians Mo Mowlam and Roy Hattersley talking to media heavyweights Harold Evans and Rosie Boycott. We had a drink at the Old Black Lion, where poets Roger McGough and James Fenton were sharing jokes with writers Louis de Bernières and Edna O'Brien.

At 9 o'clock at the Gerrard Marquee I did a half-hour extract from my regular show to a packed auditorium. Tina was suitably impressed. The *Guardian* had invited me to their festival party later that evening, so we went along. I was introduced to a bearded man about my age. He was dressed all in black including his boots and a cowboy hat. His name was Paulo Coelho. It was obvious that neither of us had heard of the other. We had a few seconds chat about something instantly forgotten, and then he excused himself to go out to the garden for a smoke. Tina and I circulated. I introduced her to Ian McEwan, Christopher Hitchens and some other authors I knew. After a while we too went out for a smoke. Paulo Coelho was still there, alone and sitting at a trestle table. A copy of his book *The Alchemist* lay on the table. I introduced him to Tina.

'So, Howard, I hear you are a celebrity. I must admit I have not read your latest book. What is it called? *Nice Guy* or something?'

'*Mr Nice*, actually. I must confess to not having read yours, *The Alchemist*.' I felt pleased at being able to say the name of his book, which was staring right at me, while he had forgotten the name of mine.

'I have,' said Tina, surprising me rather. 'It's bloody great. It's a bit short, mind. I read it all on the train coming up here from Swansea.'

'That's the best compliment an author can hope for,' said Paulo. 'His book was too short. Would you agree, Howard?'

'In an obvious sense, yes, of course I do. And I think mine was too long—'

'You're right,' interrupted Tina. 'It did go on a bit in parts.'

'Mine was too long,' I continued, a bit pissed off with Tina, 'but I suppose the real compliment is the size of the book sales.'

'How many books have you sold, Howard?'

'I suppose about a million,' I said proudly, 'if you count the different languages and the sales of my new book, *Dope Stories*. How about you?'

'Counting all the languages, about sixty-five million.'

Tina looked at the floor trying not to laugh. Paulo sensed my embarrassment. 'Howard, please take my card. If you are ever in Brazil, look me up. Have you been there?'

'Thanks. No, I haven't. I would love to, of course. I'll be close, Panama, in a few days, then back to Jamaica.'

'A writing trip?'

'Yes, a travel piece for the *Observer*, and I'm doing some research for my next book.'

'What's that about?'

'Another autobiography really, but it will cover Wales and South American connections, such as Henry Morgan, the Welsh colony in Patagonia and the visits to South America made by Welshmen long before other Europeans.'

'Then, Howard, you must definitely come to Brazil as part of your research. I have incomplete but vivid memories of learning as a child about the discovery in the Brazilian forest of a tribe who had remained there isolated for seven hundred years and spoke only ancient Welsh. It was so long ago that I don't know now if it was a fairy story or history, but it has stayed with me forever.'

I took his card, and we shook hands.

'Sorry for embarrassing you there – I didn't realise you didn't recognise him,' said Tina as we walked away from the party.

'I'd never heard of him before, but I was really interested in what he was saying about that tribe.'

'What! You're kidding. You'd never heard of Paulo Coelho, one of the world's biggest-selling authors ever. I don't believe it. I honestly don't believe it.'

'Tina, there's no end of gaps in both my memory and my knowledge. There's loads of stuff which I'm totally ignorant of.'

'Tell me about it; I was part of that stuff.'

Tina and I had become friends. We remain friends. We haven't had a DNA test.

Five

PANAMA

Panama City and its airport lie on the Pacific coast. European explorers were familiar with the Atlantic northern coast long before Balboa discovered the country's Pacific southern coast and declared all the lands it touched to be the property of Spain. I decided I would get to know the country in the same order.

The sun dazzled me with its welcome as I got off the plane and walked the few steps to the bright and airy arrivals hall. Invisible speakers emitted Latin American rhythms, increasing the holiday atmosphere. A young clean-shaven immigration officer dealt efficiently with the arriving passengers. He smiled broadly as he stamped each passport after just a cursory glance at the holder. I handed mine to him. He took one look at the name, turned bright red and pressed a button under his desk. Another fresh-faced immigration officer joined us and took my passport.

'Sir, would you come this way, please.'

Severely brought down, I followed him to a stark windowless office with a metal desk, two upright plastic chairs and a large CCTV camera.

'Wait here, please.'

He disappeared with my passport and closed the door.

The usual thoughts raced through my head. I had never been here before. Why were the Panamanian authorities interested in me? Some other country must have advised them I was coming. Was there an international arrest warrant for me, an all-points bulletin to lock me up wherever I was found? Had I inadvertently left something suspicious in my luggage before I checked it in? Had Panama suddenly become the fifty-first state of America?

The door opened. In walked someone I first believed to be Craig Lovato, the DEA agent who had arrested me in 1988. My mind disintegrated. No, it wasn't Lovato, it was the great Brazilian footballer Rivelino. Or was it Cheech, or Chong? He carried an expensive leather briefcase and wore an immaculate grey uniform covered with medals, tassels, stripes and insignia. Was he a Mexican about to bust me for telling an Old Bailey jury in 1981 that I worked for his secret service? He put his briefcase on the desk and opened it. A pair of handcuffs fell out. My heart sank. Then he smiled broadly and pulled out a copy of the Spanish translation of *Mr Nice*.

'Ah, Señor Nice. We study your book in our police college. Would you be so kind as to sign it for me?'

'Of course. I'd be glad to.'

'Thank you, Señor Nice. I am sorry to have delayed you.'

'It's no problem at all. I have to wait here at the airport to catch my next flight, so there is no inconvenience whatsoever. In fact, I'm very flattered that you want my autograph.'

'My colleagues and I love your book, Señor Nice. It is very good. To which place are you flying?'

'Bocas del Toro.'

'You will enjoy it there. The flight leaves in about two hours, I believe. Would you like to wait in the VIP lounge? It is very easy for me to arrange.'

'That's very kind of you. Thank you.'

After passing through the friendliest possible immigration

and customs checks and downing half a bottle of tequila in the
VIP lounge, I caught a domestic flight to Bocas del Toro on
the island of Colón, where tales of wrecks and buried treasure
are commonplace. As the name suggests, it was a favourite
spot of Columbus (Cristóbal Colón), who had tarried there
when searching for a sea channel between Cuba – which he
thought was eastern Asia – and South America. On the plane
I remembered a grey-haired history teacher telling us that
Columbus discovered the world to be round and that
previously sailors had been paranoid about sailing off the edge.
Yet when I was about five years old my father had taken me up
to the 'ton' of Kenfig Hill and pointed out a ship coming over
the horizon. At first we could only see the top of the ship's
mast, and then slowly the rest came into view. My father
explained the curvature of the earth made me see the top of the
boat first. If the world were flat, we would have seen both top
and bottom at the same time. The world could only be round.
Many years later I found out that ancient Greek philosopher
Eratothsenes had accurately calculated the circumference of
the earth as long ago as 600 BC.

Millions of years before that, archipelagos of unconnected
volcanic islands had surfaced between the separate land
masses of North and South America and eventually spewed up
enough lava to link and form an S-shaped isthmus. Plants and
terrestrial animals could now move between the top and
bottom of the world across this wasp-waist of the Americas.
The coexistence and mingling of previously isolated species
caused new land creatures to evolve. Conversely, the new
feature provided an insurmountable barrier for fish and other
marine organisms in the now divided Atlantic and Pacific. It
also redirected the flow of the world's oceans, gave rise to the
Gulf Stream, and radically altered global climates. Densely
folded mountain ranges bisect the isthmus, causing differing
weather patterns on the Pacific and Atlantic coasts.

A few minutes water-ferry ride from Costa Rica and a short

flight from the high-tech international banking centre of Panama City, Bocas del Toro has no muggers, no miles of tropical swamp and no mosquitoes. Everything moves on water: water taxis move people from island to island; big boats arrive with city goods and passengers, and little ones leave with fish, coconuts and bananas. It seemed an ideal place in which to relax and read up on Panama for my *Observer* article and on Henry Morgan for my own mad projects, so I carefully studied the hotel information offered at the airport and chose Punta Caracol Acqua Lodge, a complex of cabins on stilts with palm-leaf roofs. Solar panels provided the electricity while biodigesters debugged the drinking water. A complimentary glass-bottomed water taxi took me to a small complex of wooden gangways connecting guest rooms with restaurants and shops, all above a natural aquarium full of manta rays, barracuda and squid.

The hotel bar was still open after I had checked in so I ordered a Seco, sugar-cane rum and milk, known as a *baja panties* – panty lowerer – and listened to the sounds of nature competing with the dishes and glasses being washed and stacked. Nearby, playful dolphins ignored the impressive sunset.

An exquisite woman with gold rings in her ears and nose and coloured beads on her forearms and calves sat in the corner and smiled at me. She wore a pirate headscarf over her straight black hair, a bright cloth around her waist and a blouse printed with psychedelic symbols. I smiled back at her. She smiled again and left. She was at breakfast the next morning, this time in a denim mini-skirt and black bikini top. I sat facing her just one small table away.

The hotel restaurant stood on a floating wooden platform surrounded by coral atolls and hidden by mangroves in an inlet where dolphins ate jellyfish, gave birth to their young and popped up to greet children paddling canoes on their way to school. Cuddly two- and three-toed sloths hung from mangrove branches. Nearby, later in the day, turtles would crawl out of the sea and lay their eggs on the beach. A little farther away were playful manatees, the rare sea cows that sailors once believed to be mermaids. A friendly but mildly disturbing pelican swooped out of what might have been sea mist or dewy fog, perched on the back of a nearby chair and looked longingly at my plate of fried sausages and banana poppadoms. The beautiful woman started laughing. So did I.

'Do you speak English?'

'Sure,' she drawled.

'Sorry, I didn't realise you were American,' I said with obvious disappointment.

'I hope you mean South American.'

'Sorry again. I didn't,' I said with equally obvious relief, 'but let me introduce myself. I'm Howard.'

'Hi, Howard. I'm Rosa. You're British, right?'

'Right. You look as if you might be from round here but sound like you're from New York.'

'That's where I learned my English, went to university and lived for a while, but you'll find most Panamanians speak English with an American accent. Actually, I am of mixed race, part Kuna, one of our country's seven indigenous peoples. We have always been here. Shall we sit at the same table?'

The pelican seemed slightly disconcerted by her presence but stood its ground.

'Isn't it beautiful? You know we have almost a thousand separate species of bird in our country.'

As it happened, I did know. There were also over a hundred species of cockroach and countless different butterflies, as well as miniature red frogs with venomous skin, golden toads with luminous skin, and square trees. I smiled and nodded. The pelican gave up and shot away across the clear blue water.

'There are even more fish. I can tell you don't like North

Americans. Don't worry; no one will hold that against you in Panama.'

For almost a century American troops had occupied and controlled the country, packing it full of military, air and naval bases. United States forces used it as a base to invade other countries, to hit drug barons and to train soldiers to fight against enemies real and imaginary.

But now the GIs have gone. Fort Grant, once the most powerful defence complex in the world, is now a route for joggers and strollers. Fort Sherman, former US Army jungle training camp, is an ecological showcase. Fort Clayton, the old headquarters of US Army South, has been converted into the City of Knowledge, an academic community and technological park. Canopy Tower, once a US military radar post, is a birdwatching platform. Fort Davis and other buildings that once housed munitions and armaments now accommodate light industry and factories. Abandoned construction cranes have become tools in pioneering studies of the ecosystem of the dry tropical forest canopy. Military bases are now tourist centres in a classic transformation of swords into ploughshares. The country runs itself. What happened?

'Howard, you seem deep in thought.'

'I'm here to write a travel article on Panama and was wondering why its tourist industry seems in some ways to have only just started.'

'I guess we never needed tourism. Millions of people have always visited Panama but for other reasons. Don't forget we were Uncle Sam's favourite nephew. Now we have to survive alone, but our government is not investing enough in tourism; it simply doesn't realise the potential. The exception is the cruise ship industry, which thanks to al-Qaeda is the fastest-growing tourist market. Until recently cruise ships made no stop at Panama; they just went through it. Now they stop at ports or anchor for the day in the middle of the canal's lakes.'

★

Despite the country having miles of beautiful shell-covered beaches on two oceans and cheap high-quality hotels with excellent service and every conceivable water toy, there is no Panamanian tourist office outside the country. The weather is warm throughout the year, and the country exudes cheerful hospitality, extravagant scenery, the world's best drinking water, an overdose of flora and fauna, a rich historical and cultural patrimony and several autonomous Indian communities upholding their customs and traditions, including hunting for supper with blowpipes. Hurricanes don't get close, earthquakes and volcanic eruptions stopped long ago and tourists are almost impossible to find, while ecological awareness has reduced visitors' potential for doing serious damage.

Panama has a rich Pre-Columbian heritage of peoples whose presence stretches back over 12,000 years. At the time of the European conquest the population of the isthmus numbered at least a million. Fewer than 500 years ago, Spaniards Balboa and Pedrarias (the Cruel) Davila discovered and founded Old Panama, the Native American meaning of which is 'good fishing'. When the Spanish torched the small village's huts and built a new city, they kept the old name and spread in all directions, capturing the Mayan cities of Central America and the Inca strongholds of Peru, plundering gold, silver, pearls and other priceless treasures. Old Panama, the oldest non-indigenous settlement in the New World, became the jumping-off point for further conquests north and south, its Renaissance-style architecture serving as the model for the other Central and South American cities built by the Spanish colonists.

Mule trains took plunder across the isthmus to Portobelo on the Atlantic coast, where galleons bound for Spain waited. Soon other merchant ships brought silks and spices from Spanish colonies in Asia for trans-shipment through this bullion pipeline. Old Panama became the metropolis of the Pacific.

After slaying most of the Indians, the Spanish imported

slaves from Africa. Some ran away to the jungle or to the still largely deserted Caribbean coast and set up still-surviving communities, such as that of Bocas del Toro, where tourism has evolved without a local authority plan or multi-million-dollar investment.

'Do you just write about travel?'

'No, I write about all sorts of things, mainly drugs. I used to be a marijuana smuggler. When I was released from prison, I wrote a book about my exploits.'

'A drug smuggler? Fantastic! Do you have a copy of your book with you?'

I did. A firm believer in blatant self-promotion, I always carry copies of *Mr Nice* to donate to hotel libraries and give to likeable strangers I meet on my travels. I reached into my plastic bag of history books, guidebooks and tourist brochures and pulled out two copies of *Mr Nice*, one in English and one in Spanish.

'Take your pick, Rosa. I'll be back in a few minutes. I'm just going to get my laundry together and bring it down to reception.'

When I returned, Rosa was engrossed in the English version. Her black eyes fluttered at me as her body language changed from mildly curious to flirtatious.

'So you have met General Manuel Noriega. He was not as bad as the gringos make out and did a lot for Panama. We do not subscribe to the propaganda that gringos invaded our country to stop the naughty general from selling cocaine to Uncle Sam. They did it to smash the Panamanian army and economy and remind us we are not really a country, just a canal. Were you as big a smuggler as he was? The DEA seemed to think you were.'

'Nothing like. Noriega smuggled cocaine, I only did marijuana. I smuggled greater quantities than he did, but they were worth much less.'

'I love cocaine.'

'I didn't say I didn't take it. Do you have any?'

'Not here, Howard. It's too dangerous. You never know who is watching. I don't like to take it outside Panama City. That's where I live now most of the time. By the way, where are you heading after here?'

'I was thinking I would visit Portobelo. We have a Portobello Road in London. I lived there during the 1960s, when it was the centre of London's hippy community. Few people are aware of how it got its name, so I thought I would mention it in my travel piece.'

Until the 1870s the houses and shops of Notting Hill extended only to Elgin Crescent. Between there and the village of Kensal Green were corn fields, meadows and a few farm buildings. Portobello Road was a rough country track leading to Portobello Farm, which had been named in honour of Admiral Vernon's capture of the city from the Spaniards in 1739.

'Portobelo is a beautiful part of our Atlantic Caribbean coast, which is much gentler than the Pacific coast, where the tides are tremendous. But there is nothing in Portobelo now, just a few remnants of old forts. What the pirates didn't destroy, the gringos did.'

'Wasn't Sir Francis Drake buried there? I'm sure I read something about his body being put into a lead coffin and dropped into the sea.'

'Yes. Gringos are still trying to find it.'

'I also understand that my hero, Henry Morgan, made a name for himself in Portobelo.'

'Ah, Henry Morgan, the English pirate.'

'Welsh, actually. Confusing the Welsh with the English is as bad as treating South America as North America. And Henry was much more than just a pirate.'

'But he was bad, no?'

'If you were a Spanish colonist, yes.'

*

Spain and Portugal, with the blessing of the pope, divided the
New World between them. At the end of the sixteenth
century, Sir Francis Drake, with his partly Welsh crew, circled
the world, on his way capturing Spanish galleons, burning the
odd Caribbean settlement, and relieving whoever he came
across of their treasures. In the following century fear of
Britain grew in the New World, as Barbados and Jamaica were
colonised by British gamblers, touts, pimps and dissenters
who had come to own land, not work it. Demand for labour
increased, and the Dutch and Portuguese slave ships could not
move black flesh fast enough to satisfy it. Felons were paroled
out of British prisons, and vagrants and beggars were lifted
from London's streets to be sent to work in the plantations. In
this way Britain could profit from the human freight it fed,
clothed and hanged. The Dutch and French followed suit and
Caribbean islands constantly changed hands in repeated bouts
of naval warfare. Peace treaties between the European nations
were made and broken; the need for able fighting sailors
increased, as did the job security offered by piracy. Easy-to-
forge letters of marque flew out of the competing countries'
naval bureaucracies.

The lure of freedom and wealth turned indentured
servants into pirates, but for many their harsh seafaring lives
yielded scant reward. With no loyalty to their countries, their
shared adversity bonded them into an autonomous power.
Headquartered on the usually French but sometimes
Spanish possession of Île de la Tortue off the north-west
coast of present-day Haiti, they lived by raiding Spanish
treasure ships and capturing animals for their leather,
cooking their meat over smoking (*boucan*) fires, so earning
the name of buccaneers. In 1640 they formed the Brethren of
the Coast.

To join this democratic fraternity, a man had to subscribe to
the Custom of the Coast, which took precedence over national

laws and specified members' wages and compensation for those maimed or wounded in service. A third of the Brethren of the Coast comprised fugitive black slaves, who had the same rights as white members in voting and sharing booty. The Brethren of the Coast was the first great international criminal organisation, the forerunner of Meyer Lansky's International Crime Syndicate. Ethics more meaningful than blind patriotism and religious persuasion united the Brethren. No Brother stole from another. No Brother cheated another at gambling, hid knowledge of treasure or tried to get the better of any other Brother. Even crews of different ships on different raids would not swindle one another when declaring their spoils. Henry Morgan's achievements as a Caribbean pirate soon came to the attention of the Brethren, who enrolled him as a member. In a few years he became their leader – the admiral of the Brethren of the Coast, the most powerful criminal in the world.

Henry Morgan had high cheekbones, a firm chin, sensual lips and smoky blue eyes. Commanding awe and respect through his deep-throated oratory, he walked like a tiger, swore like a trooper, spoke fluent French and kept his Welsh accent. He wore a scarlet bandana, matted his hair with marigold paste and was never without his pistol and cutlass. Women found him irresistible. He thrived on tropical heat and seemed to be immune to deadly fevers. Although a natural liar, Henry Morgan always kept his word.

'The Spanish weren't as bad to us indigenous Panamanians as they were to the people of the other South American colonies, although I think that is because they discovered no gold here. But I don't approve of colonialists, whether Spanish, British or American. They are just criminals to me. Shit! Sorry, Howard, I didn't mean to offend you. I'm not intending to imply you are a criminal.'

'I'm not a criminal any more, but I used to be, obviously.

And I have much respect for some criminal communities and their morals.'

'The honour among thieves thing, you mean?'

'Yes, stuff like that.'

'But I don't regard smuggling as a crime, Howard. Most people don't.'

'Henry Morgan didn't regard ripping off the Spaniards' plundered treasure as a crime.'

Morgan's exploits had also impressed the British administrators of Jamaica, who gladly accepted his donations of plunder. In 1662 there was so much looted silver and gold in Jamaica the British government planned to set up a mint. The governor of Jamaica began to issue Morgan with letters of marque which allowed him to plunder cities as well as boats. Morgan thereupon attacked Puerto Principe, Cuba, which threatened Jamaica, and proposed attacking Portobelo, which after Havana and Cartagena was the most strongly fortified city in the Americas.

The Spanish colonists sold their treasure at crowded fairs, the biggest of which was at Portobelo. With the galleons on their way from Europe, traders at the fair were desperate to secure as much gold from Peru, pearls and tobacco from Venezuela, and emeralds from New Granada – Colombia – as they could. At the same time, the port's merchants and gentry were accumulating funds to buy the European-made luxuries the fleet would bring from Spain. It was the logical time to strike. In June 1668 eight disreputable vessels carrying 400 desperate characters followed Morgan's flagship out of Jamaica's Port Royal across the Caribbean to a sheltered cove three miles south of Portobelo. Protecting the narrow entrance to the harbour were the strongest fortresses in the New World. Against incredible odds, Morgan attacked and won.

The fall of Portobelo was a disgrace. Its inhabitants could have defended the town had they armed themselves at once instead of running to hide their valuables and money. Instead it was a rout. Morgan detailed squads to rush the monasteries and churches so the priests and nuns could not hide their treasures and with a flash of diabolical inspiration, decided to use them to storm the citadel. He knew the reverence Roman Catholics had for their clergy and shielded his attacking column with them. The pirates remained in Portobelo for two weeks, raiding, burning, torturing, raping and pillaging, and left behind them a ruined city, gutted of its valuables and defences. Henry Morgan had made the richest haul in history.

'Have you ever tried marijuana from Panama? I can get you a little if you want.'

'I would love some.'

'Then let's go and see my friend Living Stone. He lives nearby. You will love him, I know.'

Rosa and I took a boat to town. Apart from a few female Scandinavian backpackers and a couple of Canadian surfers abiding by their international dress code, the streets were full of locals. Everything and everyone seemed festive. Bocas del Toro is Panama's rainiest province, accounting for its massive production of bananas – 'green gold' – and the consequent presence of Chiquita Brands International Inc., the United States's giant banana corporation. West Indians migrated here to work on banana plantations; Graham Greene referred to it as 'an island of prosperity in a sea of poverty'.

We walked along the beach to where an enormous black man was sleeping in a hammock. Although the ends of the hammock were strong and high enough to keep the man's head and feet off the ground, the middle was no match for his weight. Most of him lay on the ground.

'That's Living Stone,' said Rosa, seeing the smile on my face. 'He loves it here. He is an extremely rich man who could have his holidays in any part of the world in a five-star hotel, but he prefers here.'

Living Stone woke up, rubbed his face and broke into a smile.

'Hello, Rosa and Rosa's friend. I am Living Stone.'

Rosa explained who I was and what I was doing in Panama. They spoke in the local dialect, Guari-Guari, Jamaican patois embellished with Spanish and indigenous Indian words. I went to get some drinks from a kiosk.

'Hey, Howard, you look like Henry Morgan; no wonder you're researching him. Are you going to look for his treasure? You might find you have a rightful claim. Let's go for a walk.'

Henry Morgan's next project after Portbelo was to sack Old Panama. The Spanish-controlled Pacific Ocean on one side and the fortifications and flooded plains dissuaded any would-be attackers who managed to cut their way through the thick jungle of the isthmus that separated the city from the Atlantic coast. It was considered impregnable; no sane man could even dream of the conquest of Old Panama.

Nevertheless, Henry Morgan's messengers spread the word of potential riches: there would be gold, jewels, food, wine and women. Too shrewd to mention Old Panama for fear of alerting the Spanish, Henry Morgan asked those interested to assemble on the Île de la Tortue. Forty ships carrying 3,000 reckless men of all nationalities swarmed to the island rendezvous. European pirates and escaped slaves then waited along the coast in palm-thatched huts, canvas shelters and dingy tents waiting for their orders.

The route was via Santa Catalina and Providencia, Spanish-owned islands 500 miles to the north of the Colombian coast. Although originally colonized in the seventeenth century by English Puritans and Jamaican woodcutters, the islands now belong to Colombia and are a favoured intermediate point for cocaine smuggling from there to Jamaica.

Arriving on the isthmus, resistance to Morgan's attack was initially negligible. He now planned to row up the Rio Chagres in small boats and then march overland using Indian trails to Old Panama. The Chagres is a river which displays no respect for the regular business of rivers – that of getting to the ocean with as little bother as possible. Although its source is just a few miles from the Pacific Ocean, it meanders about and avoids any chance of a short cut. Thick jungle rolls to the river's edge and suddenly stops like a frozen green wave. Both river and overland trips would be taxing and hazardous.

The buccaneers learned by interrogating prisoners that the Spaniards had known for three weeks about their imminent arrival. Ambushes lined the proposed route to Old Panama, and a formidable army was waiting for them outside the city.

Expecting to live off the country through which they would pass, Morgan and his men took no supplies and crowded into the inadequate number of canoes and rowing boats brought by the fleet. The trip was a nightmare of discouragement and hardship. The river was full of rapids, whirlpools and hidden sandbanks, which meant the overloaded boats were in constant danger of capsizing in the alligator-infested water. All day under the tropical sun the men cursed and sweated at their oars, tormented by hunger. Spotted giant cats watched the men with curiosity. Great snakes floated in the water, wary of the convoy, while clans of chattering monkeys dashed through the vines and treetops. The few villages they passed were desolate and empty; the Spaniards had burned or destroyed everything when they fled before the buccaneers' approach and had cut trees and set them in the river to impede progress. Deserted farms and empty granaries taunted the starving buccaneers and Indian bowmen lay in ambush.

Occasionally, the buccaneers left their boats and slashed their way through the jungle, dragging their cannon and heavy equipment. Fighting for breath in the stifling heat and constantly tormented by swarms of stinging insects, they struggled forward until the swamps forced them back into the river. Gnawing twigs and leaves, they frantically turned over stones, tore bark from rotting logs, and dug into heaps of natural compost, looking for grubs and worms to eat. They caught and roasted stray dogs, monkeys, snakes. At one of the deserted settlements they found a few leather bags, which they beat with stones, cut into strips and chewed. Finally, the buccaneers abandoned their boats for the mule trail, which led over the continental divide and down the Pacific slope.

After nine days the pirates staggered to the top of a small hill and saw the Pacific gleaming in the distance. Below them lay rolling expanse of fertile farmland where fat cattle grazed in the lush grass. Hacking chunks from the cattle, the buccaneers ate the raw meat like famished wolves. Bestial, filthy but content, they slept like tired dogs with the tower of the cathedral of Old Panama silhouetted against the moonlit shimmering bay.

The next day the Spanish infantry, cavalry and artillery waited confidently. They gathered 2,000 wild bulls to drive at the buccaneers and trample them to death. Stampeded by shouting, yelling cowboys, the bulls came bellowing across the field towards the pirates. Morgan's expert shooters knelt and fired quickly. Those bulls not killed or crippled smelt the blood and stampeded back into the Spanish ranks. The buccaneers charged in the wake of the bulls. The battle turned into a shambles of yelling, cursing and dying men. The Spaniards finally threw away their weapons and scattered into the jungle, where they hid until found and tortured.

Henry Morgan, once described as a pox-ridden bundle of vices, had terrorised the conquistadores. With a mere handful of desperadoes as his army, Henry had taken the main Spanish Caribbean ports, crossed the isthmus to the Pacific, sacked Old Panama and cut the main trade route between Spain and her American colonies. He had damaged the prestige of Spain, the richest and most powerful country in the world, to such an extent that it soon faded as a global power. Spain went into mourning, and the queen regent spent hours on her knees praying to the Virgin to send a thunderbolt to strike down Henry Morgan. Unwittingly, he had pioneered the finest form of British imperialism, buccaneering, the seed of the British empire.

Leaving Rosa at the hammock, Living Stone and I walked to an empty stretch of the beach. He pulled out a joint and handed it to me.

'It's not the best, Howard, but it will work.'

It did.

'So are you really looking for Morgan's treasure, or have you come to do some business. Rosa seemed confused when she talked to me about you.'

'I just wanted some weed to smoke, Living Stone. I don't smuggle dope any longer. It's not that I have reformed; I'm just too well known to risk getting back into that game. And I've never thought of looking for anyone's buried treasure, to be honest. But if you know of any, I'll smuggle it to Europe for you.'

Living Stone laughed.

'I'm just so used to smugglers in the Caribbean pretending to be looking for treasure ships. I see them all come through here. I jump to conclusions. I'm sorry. My family come from Darien, where everyone is either a smuggler or a liar.'

Bordering Colombia, the Panamanian province of Darien is one of the wildest, least-known parts of the planet. Its population is descended from bands of renegade African slaves – *cimarrónes*, later called Maroons – pirates and independent indigenous Indian tribes and currently comprises Colombian Marxist guerrillas, paramilitary bandits, abducted missionaries and cocaine traffickers. The hundred-mile Darien Gap is the only break in the otherwise continuous Pan-American Highway stretching 20,000 miles from Circle, Alaska to the southernmost tip of Chile. It is thought that completing the road link would facilitate the spread of drugs and disease from Colombia.

'But I can get you some weed, no problem. Have this on me.'

Living Stone produced a matchbox full of small bright-rusty-coloured buds with a strong aroma of fresh-tilled earth combined with red clay, a strong hashish smell.

'Is this Panama Red?'

'It is. It's grown in the mountains just here, and it's the best. You'll enjoy it. Anyway, Henry Morgan's treasure won't be in Panama; it will be on some remote island. Panama held bad memories for him.'

To deprive Morgan of his loot, its Spanish defenders had set fire to Old Panama. Morgan lost not only the valuable contents and fittings of its wealthy homes, but also the advantage of being able to threaten to torch the city if ransoms were not paid. Even worse, Morgan learned from prisoners that a galleon had left Old Panama for Peru carrying half of Old Panama's wealth, including a pure gold crucifix that weighed more than a ton, as well as members of its richest families. Portobelo had yielded 250,000 dollars in plundered goods alone. Old Panama would have produced a dozen times that much had it not been for the disasters of the ship escaping and the fire. Now it had yielded less.

A caravan of underladen pack mules and sullen buccaneers accompanied Morgan on the gruelling march back across the isthmus. Morgan was not to blame but he was increasingly met with sullen looks, neglect of discipline and outright defiance. Although each of his men had sought him out, begged him for employment and offered undying loyalty, and although Morgan had led them to inconceivable riches, been scrupulously fair in his payments and had several times risked his life and freedom to save theirs, their fantasies had not been realised.

When Morgan discovered that some of the men were

plotting his death, he called a secret meeting of the small group who remained loyal to him. Delaying dividing the loot, he appointed his cronies to sort and classify the spoils and quietly prepared three of his most seaworthy ships for departure. The next day Morgan announced the loot would be divided the following morning and that this night would be a grand celebration. Morgan opened the first keg and proposed a toast to the spoils of Old Panama and to their next adventure. The buccaneers drank themselves unconscious, and the chests of jewels, coins and bullion were quietly got aboard the ships. As soon as the cargo was safely loaded, the vessels were cut loose, the sails unfurled, and the trade winds speeded the ships to Port Royal, Jamaica. Morgan neither knew nor cared what happened to the men left behind. From now on he would devote his life to hedonism, his faith in human nature wrecked beyond repair. His buccaneering days were over. The brave beautiful boastful Welsh child had died.

'You must be referring to when he lost the loyalty of his men?'

'No,' said Living Stone, 'I mean when he lost the only woman he loved. Haven't you read about her?'

'I haven't yet. There's still a lot for me to find out.'

'You will. Then you'll see what I mean.'

We walked back to the hammock where Rosa was sunbathing. She and I said goodbye to Living Stone and caught a boat back to the Punta Caracol. We arranged to meet in a couple of hours at the bar to have a drink. In my room I looked through my bag of books and pamphlets on Henry Morgan.

We arrived at the bar at precisely the same time. Rosa, now wearing a flimsy, flowery black and white dress, noticed my book.

'Great! You're a John Steinbeck fan. I think *The Grapes of Wrath* is the best book ever written. I did a course on him at university. What's that one?

'It's called *Cup of Gold*.'

'Must have missed it.'

'It's the first book he wrote.'

'You're kidding! Was it published under another name?'

'No, but it was originally subtitled, *A Life of Sir Henry Morgan, Buccaneer, with Occasional Reference to History*. It's really interesting. Steinbeck had the inspiration to write it after he visited Panama, but it was a failure when it came out. Later, he claimed to be embarrassed by its immaturity.'

'I've brought my interesting book, too.'

Rosa pulled her copy of *Mr Nice* out of her handbag. She opened it, looking at me, pretending to be shy. I opened my Steinbeck, pretending to read it, looking at her. I watched intently as her seductive eyes moved left and right across the pages and occasionally up at me. A nearby electric fan blew her hair in all directions. Rosa reached for her handbag, took out her pirate scarf and tied it around her head. She caught me looking at her legs and smiled.

'Shall we have a drink, Howard? I need a stiff one.'

I called the waiter and asked for two extra-strong Mojitos. Rosa resumed reading *Mr Nice*; I monitored every reaction and fantasised. The waiter brought the drinks. Rosa and I sucked our straws.

'I can see why you are obsessed with Henry Morgan, Howard; he was probably one of your previous lives, no? I feel I'm reading about him, not you.'

The rum kicked in, and I tried to work out how I could stop Rosa reading my fucking book and get her to come to my room. I became conscious I was leering at her so started reading about Henry Morgan, thinking I was reading about myself.

Henry Morgan shagged thousands of women. Rather than pledge himself to a jealous tropical beauty who might cramp his style, Henry married his cousin, whom he had known since childhood, and carried on with his promiscuity. At the time reputedly the most beautiful woman in the world lived in Old

Panama. Steinbeck gives her name as Ysobel, but historical sources name her as Maria Eleanora Lopez y Ganero. The Brethren of the Coast were well aware of Maria's existence but had never seen her. She was the object of everyone's desire, the delirium in every buccaneer's mind.

After the sack of the city Morgan's men captured Maria and brought her to him. He had expected a young woman with pink skin and angelic blue eyes which would drop under his stare, but Maria's skin was as white as snow, and her eyes just laughed at him, making light of the situation. He shut his eyes and once more saw the young woman of his preconceptions. He had come here because he was sure he would love her; he must continue to love her. Henry banished his wife from his mind and asked Maria to marry him. Maria said she was already married, as was he. Henry persevered as black sparks of ridicule lurked under her eyelids.

'So you're a family man, Howard,' said Rosa with a hint of mockery. 'I would never have guessed. I like the good life far too much to get married again.'

'Well, so do I really. I live alone, but I have quite a few children,' I said lamely.

'So I can see. There's a photograph here of you cutting a birthday cake. You're wearing a paper hat. That's so cute.'

Slightly embarrassed, I went back to Steinbeck.

Maria launched into Henry and told him his chat-up lines were worse than the Spaniards', who at least had the suave gestures to accompany their words. She said how much she had been looking forward to meeting him, how she had thought he was the only realist in a world of dreamers, a dark and bold force, how she had lusted after his brutal sexuality, the crush of his hard muscles, the delicious pain of little hurts.

'I don't believe this. You worked for the British secret service? MI6. Is that the same one James Bond worked for?'

'Yes, it is, but I didn't have a licence to kill, and I never drink Martinis.'

'Did you make love to beautiful foreign spies? I bet you did.'
Rosa put down her copy of *Mr Nice* and moved closer. Her
breath smelt sweet.

'They did once ask me to seduce a Czechoslovakian
secretary whom they suspected of working for the KGB, but
nothing came of it. MI6 is not as glamorous as it's made out.'

'How long did you work for them?'

'Less than a year. They realised they had made a stupid
choice.'

Rosa resumed reading. So did I.

But now, Maria explained, she could see Henry in his true
light. He was a clumsy babbler, a bungling romancer, a bitter
disappointment. Henry offered her money. She said she was
an heiress and didn't need any. Henry threatened to take her
by force. She said he didn't have the guts; his attempt would
make her laugh. Everyone knew Henry Morgan disapproved
of rape and public lovemaking; he preferred to seduce in
private. Henry called his men to take Maria away.

'What's a Welsh wanker, for Christ's sake?' asked Rosa.

'Wanking means jacking off.'

'So why is this Irish guy McCann calling you that? You've
got children.'

' "Wanker" is a general insult. Actually, it comes from the
Spanish name Juan Carlos. When England was at war with
Spain, anyone deserving criticism was a Juan Carlos, a
wanker.'

'Did I tell you I had Spanish blood?'

'No, you just said you had mixed blood.'

'You've really got a hang-up about the Spanish, haven't
you? Is it because they arrested you and handed you over to
the gringos? Are you getting your own back by pretending to
be Henry Morgan?'

I knew then I had blown my chances.

'No, Rosa, I like the Spanish, I promise you. I lived in Spain
for years.'

'Well, I'm exhausted, and my eyes are shutting. I'm off to bed. Can I hold on to the book a little longer? I'll finish it soon.'

'Of course. You can keep it if you want. Goodnight, Rosa.'

Henry was filled with shame. How could he face his men after this humiliation, this rejection, this slur on his manhood? He paced the room for an age before sending scouts to find Maria's husband. They soon returned with him. Henry released him from his chains, took him to Maria's cell and let them spend the night together. The next day Henry demanded an enormous ransom from the husband for the release of them both, which was duly paid. The buccaneers assumed that Henry had made love to her and decided to exchange her for some more loot. Henry had kept his face but not his pride. Never again would he allow himself to be in thrall to a woman; he would carry on being unfaithful to his wife.

Many years later, he was asked, 'Is it true, Sir Henry, that you have never been defeated?'

'No, Duchess, I was once defeated by a prisoner in Panama, a woman who resisted my requests and turned down my sincere affection. That beautiful lady defeated me.'

'And was she really that beautiful, Sir Henry?'

'Incredibly beautiful, Milady. Her eyes and face outshined the sun and the star. Only she, only she defeated me.'

I didn't see Rosa the next day, but the day after as I was checking out of the Punta Caracol, she appeared.

'Enjoy the rest of Panama. Where are you going to?'

'I'm flying to Colón, visiting Portobelo, then going to Panama City. Which is the best hotel to stay in there?'

'Without a doubt the Miramar Intercontinental, where Mick Jagger stayed. I'll be there myself in a couple of days. I'll look you up.'

Maybe I hadn't blown it.

The short Aeroperlas flight from Bocas del Toro to Colón

began its descent near the northern entrance to the Panama
Canal, where the huge Gatún Locks raise southbound ships
from the Caribbean waters of the Atlantic. I reminded myself
I still had to figure out why locks were needed to join sea level
to sea level. We flew over a walled area, the Colón Free Trade
Zone, which the United States made into the biggest duty-free
zone in the western hemisphere. Ship-fuelling services,
maritime training centres, cargo storage and distribution areas
and ship-repair yards were surrounded by the offices of
international dredging companies, experts in the construction
and maintenance of harbours and waterways, and specialists
in land reclamation, coastal defence and riverbank protection.

Portobelo was a short bus ride from the airport. Rosa had
been correct: there was nothing. There were no places to stay,
no bank and no tourist office, although a tattered notice stated
that one would be opening soon. The customs house that once
had stored priceless plunder was now a museum. It was
closed. Rusty cannons still pointed out to sea, but the castle of
San Felipe was no more. The Americans had dismantled it to
use the stone for construction. Food stands and booths
offering boat trips to Drake Island stood among ruined
military buildings half-heartedly offering their goods and
services. Portobelo is now a sleepy little town that sits amid the
decay of empire, slipping into tropical indolence. The bus took
me back to Colón airport.

On arrival at Panama City's airport, I took a taxi to the
Hotel Miramar Intercontinental. It was rush hour, so we took
a short cut through the park, a small tropical rainforest known
as the Lung of Panama. Monkeys and owls gazed at the
crawling traffic. Banking, insurance, shipping, offshore
businesses and financial services boosted by drug dollars all
contribute to Panama City's atmosphere. Kids sell flowers and
food to commuters, sandwich boards offer mortgages and
furniture, gorgeous secretaries giggle on every corner, and
women in orange jumpsuits gather leaves and other litter.

Lottery tickets, tax-free casinos and cockpits satisfy the inhabitants' gambling urges, while arms dealers offload as many weapons as they can to anyone who can afford them. Like Hong Kong, Panama City is pivotal in world trade. It keeps its gaze on the outside and pays little attention to its own hinterland. The city's cluster of skyscrapers, like all money-laundering centres, is a hive of intrigue with its numerous empty apartments let to fictitious occupants for astronomical rents.

At the heart of the Bay of Panama, the Miramar Inter-continental had every leisure facility from Turkish baths to a dance club. Two porters escorted me to my enormous room, one wall of which was a fully equipped office workstation. Pausing only long enough to change and hoping to see some tribute to Henry Morgan's achievements, I took a taxi a few miles east to Old Panama. There was no statue of him – there isn't anywhere, yet – but Henry had obviously done a good job: a few scattered ruins of walls and churches, occasionally serving as backdrops for weddings and raves, and a museum was all there was. When Henry retired from the city, the Spanish had salvaged what they could and moved a few miles west to found a well-fortified replacement city.

From Old Panama I took a *diablo rojo*, one of the buses that decorate the streets with their colourful paintwork and pictures of superstars, to Paseo de las Bovedas and walked on the high sea wall built by the Spanish to protect them against the likes of Henry Morgan. Ships' horns moaned as the vessels waited to use the world's greatest short cut. Below the wall dungeons had been converted to restaurants and art galleries. I strolled through cobbled alleyways of crumbling colonial churches and along red-bricked streets. Paint peeled off multicoloured rotting walls. I came across the Parque Bolívar, where Simón Bolívar first urged the union of the former Spanish colonites. Panama declared independence in 1821 and immediately decided to join the loose confederation of nations led by Bolívar, who had envisaged it as the centre of this peaceful progressive union. He had succeeded in freeing Bolivia, Colombia, Ecuador, Peru and Venezuela from Spanish rule and said of Panama, 'If the world had to choose a capital, the Isthmus of Panama would be the obvious place for that high destiny.' His dreams came to nothing, and Panama declined into a neglected province of Colombia. The old city still had the filth and elegance of seventeenth-century Spain but now also vibrated to the sounds of restoration. Hammers and saws echoed from inside gutted buildings with facades like film sets. A brass band in white uniforms and gloves played Strauss waltzers.

Although dusk was falling, the Museo del Interoceanico was still open. I walked in and learned everything about the Panama Canal.

World commerce, travel and naval warfare have always focused on the only two isthmuses which both link continents and separate oceans – Suez and Panama. King Carlos V of Spain in 1534 saw the sense of digging through Panama to transport the gold of Peru to Spain directly by sea but settled instead for a network of cobbled mule trails. Centuries later, gold was again the catalyst: a carpenter from New Jersey saw something shiny in Coloma, California and the rush was on. A trans-Panamanian railroad was shrewdly opened, and the miners now had three routes from the populated East Coast of the United States to the empty new El Dorado of California: 'the Plains across, the Horn around, or the Isthmus over'. Those who wished to avoid shipwreck, seasickness or donating their scalps to the Apaches chose the isthmus. Thousands stopped at Panama for a new suit, good fare, lodgings, whimsical shopping needs and a few nights of debauchery. Indian merchants, Chinese laundries, brothels and bars made Panama rich, cosmopolitan, decadent and cool. A canal could only make it better.

During the nineteenth century French technical schools

were the finest in the world. Ferdinand de Lesseps had just built the Suez Canal and with Alexandre Eiffel as part of his team had little problem raising the readies for a Panama venture. The French peacefully took over Panama – whose Colombian masters had ruined its trade and involved it in endless civil wars – and built hospitals, offices, dock facilities, living quarters and machine shops. Panama thrived, but in their enthusiasm the French had overlooked a crucial point: digging through mountainous rock formations clad with dense jungle and enmeshed in massive sinuous muddy rivers was a lot harder than channelling through the flat sandy beaches of the Mediterranean and Red Sea. Storms that turned air into instant liquid, smothering humidity, forbidding jungle twilight, flash floods and freak earthquakes didn't help. Equipment instantly rusted and clothes were permanently wet. The ditch was a bitch, an expensive one.

Panama boasted the world's most deadly vermin, insects and reptiles, as well as vampire bats, pumas and jaguars. Tropical diseases included dysentery, dengue fever, yellow fever, cholera and smallpox. It was here that French biologists discovered mosquitoes were the cause of malaria, rather than bad air as its name (*mal aria*) suggests. So many nameless labourers died that a trade developed, shipping cadavers pickled in large barrels to hospitals and medical schools all over the world. Eventually, the French ran out of money and gave up.

Meanwhile, the United States began to take up the white man's burden from the British. The USA colonised the Philippines, absorbed Hawaii, Puerto Rico and Guam, and appropriated a naval base at Cuba's Guantanamo Bay. A canal through the isthmus would facilitate American supremacy at sea, so the United States encouraged Panama's bid for independence from Colombia with money, guns and the odd warship. Panama gained its autonomy and some badly needed loot, and the US got the sovereignty of the Canal Zone, a ten-mile-wide strip of land running through the middle of the country from the Pacific to the Atlantic coasts, plus the right to intervene in Panama should the situation threaten canal movements. The United States bought the concessions and equipment the French had abandoned but did not continue where the French had left off. Instead, the Americans dammed the Rio Chagres, creating the world's biggest artificial lake eighty-five feet above sea level, and built a series of locks from the lake to the two oceans. Now I knew why the Panama Canal had locks. Taking ten years and with the world's biggest locks, gates and concrete structures, at the time it was the largest, most costly single peacetime project mounted anywhere on earth – the biggest experiment ever done with nature. Running from north-west to south-east, the canal is fifty miles long and reduces trade routes by up to 8,000 miles.

The Museo del Interoceanico closed, and I went back to the Miramar to indulge myself in several-star luxury for twenty-four hours, by which time Rosa should have got in touch.

The phone eventually rang. 'Howard, it's Rosa. Have you been to the Union Club of Panama?'

I had heard of the Union, one of the most exclusive clubs in the world. For many years Panamanian politics had remained a mere competition among members of the club.

'Let's meet there tonight at eleven o'clock. Just mention my name, Rosa Guerrero, at the door.'

I changed into the smartest clothes I had. It was a long walk to the Union Club of Panama, but I felt in the mood. Before leaving, I telephoned Leroy in London. His sister answered and said he had left some hours ago for Gatwick and Jamaica. I left her my Panama number.

I left the hotel's private marina and headed away from the shore into the city. Shop windows displayed electronics, designer fashions and jewellery at prices cheaper than any-where else in the world. Aromas of all sorts of cuisines diluted the night smells of luscious flowers and ship oil. Bars became bawdier, and three-hour hotels draped in bougainvillea promised to satisfy any sexual urge. The street bent back towards the waterfront, and I could see the outline of the Union Club.

'I'm a guest of Rosa Guerrero,' I said to one of an army of broad shoulders in chauffeurs' suits and identity tags. He led me through a mirrored-ceiling lobby of stockbrokers calling their mistresses on mobiles and up a green-carpeted slipway to a balcony drenched in smoke, costly scent and beat music. Directed towards a teak throne next to a table of sparkling glasses and scrolled silver cutlery, I took a seat. A white-gloved waiter brought an ice bucket containing a bottle of Bollinger, which I quickly emptied; the night sea air had made me thirsty. I listened to the conversation at the next table. Some women were ridiculing receding male hairlines and support stockings. The men were discussing the rule of the white arses. Resentment of United States control is still the dominant theme of Panamanian politics and national identity. The waiter brought another bottle of champagne and a sealed white envelope. It was not the bill but a fax from Rosa: 'I'm so sorry, Howard, but I just can't make it tonight. Enjoy the Union Club. The tab's on me. I know we will meet again. I've written down my email and other details. Living Stone says hello. You can get in touch with him through me. He says, "Don't sell Panama down the canal." Bye. Rosa.'

I was too drunk to feel disappointed. I left the Union Club, accepting the management's offer of a limousine back to the Miramar. The telephone rang as soon as I fell asleep. It was Leroy.

'Mi dyah now, mon. Get yo arse over hyah. Now yo a go see di real Jamaica.'

Six

JAMAICA

I noticed we were driving away from Kingston. 'Where are we going?'

'Mi a go where yo always want fi go, mon, Port Royal. Wait until yo see di name a di hotel.'

Leroy suddenly stopped the car, got out, looked at the last of the swiftly setting red sun, walked a few yards, called someone on his mobile and walked back.

'Mi bredren Prescot a di hotel manager. Im soon come pick yo up and take care a yo. Mi afi go ina Kingston now an mi see yo tomorrow, mon.'

Leroy took my case out and left me, surprised and confused, on the empty road. I supposed he must have had his reasons. I had learned on my last visit that 'Soon come' is Jamaica's equivalent of *mañana*. Arriving early might suggest mental instability or a deliberate attempt to antagonise, while turning up on time might suggest an overzealous and indecent ploy to flummox, unless it's for a cricket match. Ten minutes late is anally punctual, while fifteen minutes late displays rare efficiency. Jamaicans have to be at least one hour late before they feel the need to excuse or explain. Prepared for a considerable wait, I decided to wheel my case towards Port

Royal. The road appeared to be on a dyke, the open Caribbean Sea on my left and Kingston Harbour, the world's seventh largest, on my right. Around the first bend, a lonely stone monument commemorated Jamaica's first coconut tree. I was wondering whether the tree had grown from a coconut washed ashore or had been deliberately planted when a black Isuzu travelling in the opposite direction slowed down, screeched through a U-turn and pulled up alongside.

'Niceman?'

'You Leroy's friend?'

'Ah huh. I'm Prescot. I work for the hotel. Please get in, Niceman.'

Prescot was wearing dark brown plastic-framed spectacles, black polyester trousers, polished brogues, a white shirt with a pocketful of different-coloured ballpoint pens and high-lighters, and a yacht club tie. He spoke precise and perfect American English. After a few hundred yards, he turned right into a driveway.

'Are we here, Prescot?'

'Indeed we are, Niceman. You are welcome.'

'Why didn't Leroy bring me all the way here? It's so close to where he dropped me.'

'Apparently, he had something important to do in Kingston. You know Leroy.'

My concern lifted as I saw the name of the hotel, Morgan's Harbour Hotel and Beach Club. At last there was some acknowledgement of the great man's presence in the Caribbean. A large picture of Henry Morgan dominated reception. Ripples of excitement tickled my stomach.

'We have a special room for you, Niceman – Room 105.' Prescott took my case and escorted me to the room. 'Recognise it?'

'Not so far, no.'

'Have you seen the film *Dr No*?'

'Of course, but decades ago. Why?'

'This is the room where the large spider attacked James Bond. Much of the film was made in this hotel. Downstairs at the bar James Bond tumbled among the crates of Red Stripe. You must remember that scene, Niceman?'

I didn't.

'Well, enjoy your stay. Here is my card. Call me if you need anything.'

Morgan's Harbour Hotel and Beach Club stands on several acres of flat seashore studded with rocks and boasts a large but quiet marina where snorkelling, diving and wreck exploration excursions tempt hotel guests and passers-by. A breezy waterfront restaurant and salt-licked open-air bar, empty apart from a table of three, tempted me. I sat at the bar and ordered a Front-end Loader, a rum concoction guaranteed to liven up your libido. Night had fallen. Boat bells rang and lamps and fairy lights wavered through the wind. Some napkins flew off the tables. Two of the three other customers were clearly Colombian, complete with Bogota airport duty-free carrier bags, the third Jamaican. They spoke in hushed but confident tones. I assumed they were dope smugglers. Nothing wrong with that. Prescot was suddenly at my side.

'Good evening, Niceman. If you wish to eat, I suggest you use Sir Henry's Restaurant inside. It is getting windy out here. It usually does this time of night.'

Prescot motioned to the Jamaican diner, who quickly abandoned the Colombians and bopped, rather than walked, to join us. 'Niceman, this is Beano.'

'Peace, mon. You is Leroy's bredren, yeah?' said Beano in a monotonous gravelly whisper.

Displaying a set of gold-capped teeth, one with a sparkling emerald, and still bopping, he held out his fist, giving it the Jamaican twist. I did the same while touching his. He slipped me some ganja. Those years in the penitentiary occasionally came in handy. Wearing an army jacket with epaulettes, green army pants held up by a Rasta belt, leather shoes, no socks, a leather military cap and a woollen jumper under his long grey shirt, Beano was the stereotypical Jamaican ganja baron. A gold watch, rings on every finger, a thick gold bracelet, mirror shades, several knife scars, a smoking joint and a rag hanging from his back pocket filled in the gaps.

Prescot led me away from the bar. Beano bopped back to the Colombians.

'Beano is a good man. He is a member of our police force and a respected reggae concert promoter. He lives in Ocho Rios but is often here.'

Shows how wrong one can be, or how right. I guess police and politicians have to work with the ganja barons, whose generosity probably enables their offspring to attend the better schools.

Inside Sir Henry's I asked for a plain lobster and any rum drink. The waiter brought over another Loader, compliments of the house. I drank it like water and ordered a third. A Front-end Loader comprises overproof rum, pimento liquor, molasses, clear syrup and various roots with names such as cock-stiff, strong back and genital root. Overproof rum is an integral part of Jamaica's pharmacopoeia and serves as an antiseptic. It also cures colds and fevers and was used by Henry Morgan as a virility aid.

Henry Morgan was ceremoniously welcomed when he sailed into Port Royal with his treasure, but he had broken the 1670 Treaty of Madrid by which England and Spain had agreed to respect each other's territories in the Americas. This had been signed just before he sacked Old Panama and Spain demanded the death penalty. Despite Henry suffering from a heavy fever, the authorities arrested him and put him on a leaky ship bound for London to face charges of treason. On arrival in England, he was immediately released on bail. At his trial there was no judge or jury, nor a single witness. Henry proved he could not have known about the peace treaty with

Spain, apologised for his ignorance and left the court a free man.

Henry Morgan drank at the inns, smoked tobacco in the coffee houses, gambled at the races, attended the theatre and journeyed to Wales. Nobility welcomed him at their homes, where he entertained them with swashbuckling tales of adventure and romance. King Charles II and Henry became great friends. The king assisted Henry's wenching with court beauties, while Henry's street credibility enabled the king to engage in clandestine orgies at dockside taverns, grog shops and brothels. Henry introduced the king to His Majesty's best-known mistress, the Welsh actress Nell Gwyn. Henry's health improved and he begged the king to let him return to Jamaica, the island he loved. Charles II responded by knighting Henry and appointing him lieutenant-governor of Jamaica.

On his return to Port Royal, Henry formed his own political party, and became judge-admiral of the customs, dishing out fines and confiscating selected spoils. He was the official first citizen of Port Royal and was acting governor – effectively dictator – of Jamaica for two years.

Port Royal was now the richest city in the world, and dedicated to the disposal of plunder and providing a good time. Wearing London fashion as they strolled down paved walkways, residents lived in luxuriously furnished cut-stone homes with fully stocked wine cellars, tiled roofs and sash windows. A synagogue, Quaker meeting house, Roman Catholic chapel, Presbyterian and Anglican churches evidenced Port Royal's toleration of all religions.

It was also the wickedest city in the world, whatever criterion you used. There were more taverns per head, more brothels per square yard and more stolen goods than anywhere else before or since. Along the dockside narrow alleys were lined with dirty houses offering every brand of vice ever invented. Rations were frugal aboard ship, so their clients ate like horses and drank like fish. Gamblers engaged in cockfighting, bull- and bear-baiting, dominoes and games of billiards. Taverns burned to the ground during orgies of dancing, swordplay and nakedness. Fornicating took place on an unprecedented scale, encouraged by the 'House of Correction for Lazy Strumpets' situated at the water's edge. Tales of Port Royal's decadence, drunkenness and wantonness circulated the world, and prophets warned of the town being razed by God as punishment for its wickedness.

Highly sexed, Henry had his own harem and saw nothing immoral in taking full advantage of attractive young women of all races, preferably virgins. As for buccaneering, although he made secret deals with pirates and occasionally got them out of trouble, Henry didn't join their escapades. His offices ruled out undertaking any piracy, privateering or aggression against Spain. Deprived of Morgan's leadership, the Brethren of the Coast were giving way to a new breed of pirate – rogues, cutthroats and other seafaring trash. Henry had no time for them. They had shown him their true colours in Panama: they were scum who couldn't take losses or show gratitude for sharing in someone else's good fortune. Henry was now getting into real crime by running a colony with the help of his mate the king of England. He took it easy and lay in his hammock on one of his plantations, drinking rum and inventing more cocktails.

One Front-end Loader might make you horny, but three or four just gets you blind pissed. I staggered drunkenly from Sir Henry's Restaurant through reception, where Henry's face smiled down at me, mocking my drunken gait, and went to my room. I lay on the bed listening to an orchestra of flies playing a symphony of boredom as they described labyrinthine circles and engaged in intricate airy dance formations, occasionally flying into my flushed face and cannoning off. In my alcoholic haze the flies seemed to dart and wheel around, performing three-dimensional figures which turned into thin black lines, crossing and recrossing in every direction. I lit up Beano's spliff, and the flies' collective mind started writing a series of strange characters in the air, forming an elusive sentence – the secret of all secrets. Feeling like I had been sliced in two with only one half of me present, looking for something that did not exist, I fell asleep dreaming of James Bond's spider and the last days of Henry Morgan.

Henry stamped out the use of Jamaica as a base for pirates and buccaneers, closing Port Royal to illegal craft, whether foreign or British, and imposed stringent checks on ships flying the flags of potential enemies of Great Britain. He issued an ultimatum to captains: seek pardon for your previous misdemeanours, promise never to indulge in such practices again, and buy cheap land in Jamaica – as he had done. Believing that Henry Morgan would take such a course only if there was money to be made by it, the pirates became plantation owners, Jamaica's landed gentry. Roman Catholic James II succeeded Protestant Charles II. Despite James's affection for Spain, he was an avid fan of Henry and continued to support him. A Dutch attempt to discredit Henry by exposing him as a former criminal ended, as Eddie Evans had pointed out in Kenfig Hill, with Henry Morgan the first person ever to be awarded monetary damages in a libel case. He had now reached the peak of his power but the challenges had run out. The thrill had gone. He developed swollen legs, a huge paunch, puffy eyes and yellow skin. He lost his appetite. Age brought nothing with it but a restless waiting, a wish for peace and a dull expectancy of a state that could not be imagined. On 25 August 1685, Henry Morgan died of alcoholic poisoning and tuberculosis.

My sleep lasted only a few hours. I woke up feeling more disoriented than ever before in my life. The wind had risen and was now accompanied by high-pitched howls. I opened the wooden shutters and confronted a grey disc with black lines like spokes radiating from a beak which snapped and clicked. Two wide-open bright orange eyes studded a wheel-like face.

The eyes blazed with wrath and a tail spread out like a fan.

The owl, symbol of wisdom in the West, symbol of foolishness in the East, and an omen of evil and portent of family death in the Caribbean, screeched horribly and flapped away above the choppy harbour water. Bats flitted in the dark, gnashing their tiny teeth. Mice and rats screamed and glared at me from their obscurity with small mean eyes. A pale luminous exhalation rose from the sea, assumed a human shape, floated slowly towards the hotel and roamed about the great trees. Terrified, I went downstairs into the garden. I gazed at the huge deep harbour, collected my thoughts and concentrated on its past.

On 7 June 1692, dawn penetrated Port Royal's hot and sultry atmosphere. There was no wind, and the sea lay unruffled, flat like oil, clogged with weed. Ships filled the harbour, ready to unload their cargoes into the already overflowing storehouses. Revellers with heads throbbing from rum were ending a night of carousing and staggering to their beds. To them, dawn was the end of the day, not the beginning.

A thunderous noise sounded from the mountains to the north, and three shocks increasing in severity rocked the port. The land tilted, wharves and warehouses crumbled, a church collapsed to the ground, its bells jangling madly, and the cemetery, including Henry Morgan's grave, slipped into the sea. People slipped from upper storeys and were crushed beneath tons of falling masonry. Trapped beneath falling walls and beams, they were suffocated by dense clouds of dust. Others fell into chasms that suddenly yawned out of the ground and were squeezed to death as the cracks closed like the pincers of a giant crab. Dogs ate the flesh of the faces of the partially swallowed, leaving shiny skulls grinning at the sky. Blood-spattered and broken-boned people crawled out of disappearing buildings. Looting started immediately. Slaves thanked providence or God and began killing their white masters. Gigantic waves tore vessels from their moorings and swept them over the sunken ruins, masts mingling with roofs. One ship ended up perched on houses like Noah's Ark.

In two minutes 2,000 people had died, rivers had changed their courses, old springs had vanished and new ones appeared, hills had slid into valleys burying plantations, and mountains had been distorted and bared. One of the earth's biggest quakes had wiped out Henry's Sodom and Gomorrah and taken his body away.

An event such as this is bound to leave a paranormal hangover. If Port Royal had no ghosts, then they didn't exist anywhere. Calmed by my cold rationalisation of the irrational, I sat on an overturned boat, relit my spliff, and without any fear watched several more apparitions of smoke and vapour spout from the depths, hearing African, Spanish and Welsh whispers until dawn broke and swallowed them all. A thick silence hung in the salty air.

I walked out of the hotel, turned right and found myself in Port Royal's deserted main square. A gleaming white church stood in the corner. The gates were locked, but most of the cemetery's graves were clearly visible. One housed the body of one Lewis Galdy, a Huguenot born in Montpellier who fled from France to Jamaica to escape religious persecution. He became a successful Port Royal merchant and cockfight promoter. On the day of the earthquake Galdy ran out of his office as it keeled over and sank into the ground in clouds of dust, powdered lime and mortar. A great hole opened under his feet, swallowed him and closed. A minute later a second quake catapulted him out of the ground. Galdy soared through the air like a cannonball and splashed into the sea, from where he was rescued by a passing boat. His experience was unique and remains so. Predictably, Lewis Galdy became more religious and spent the rest of his days as a churchwarden.

Beyond the church was an old parade ground lined with barrack buildings and the historic Fort Charles, once commanded by Nelson. After an hour's walking through streets with names such as Gaol Alley and Love Lane, I had visited every corner of today's Port Royal, a tranquil fishing community. But there are two Port Royals: this diminished community and the city that slid beneath the sea. It is not easy to escape this other city, which preserves a sometimes tangible presence. Fishermen listen above the sound of the sea for the whispering chimes of church bells, some of which have been recovered and rest in Jamaica's museums. The tops of buildings are visible above the seabed. Treasure seekers continually bring up bottles, tiles, pipes, wheels, pewter spoons, brass candlesticks, ceramics, guns and pieces of eight. Divers claim to have walked through the submerged streets of the old city and seen skeletons holding tankards sitting on stools around tables. There is a report of a cathedral with a mound of treasure on its altar, guarded by a ten-foot giant crab.

The noise of people preparing breakfast and coughing outboard motors mingled with reggae tunes as I walked back into the bar of Morgan's Harbour Hotel and Beach Club. I drank a jug of freezing fruit juice. Prescot, every bit as well-dressed as the night before, joined me.

'Sleep well, Niceman?'

'A bit disturbed. I think the buccaneers must still be around. Has anyone else felt haunted here?'

'Ah huh. I don't think there's anyone who has been here who hasn't. Now you know why Leroy will never stay the night here. The place is full of duppies. Nothing else can scare that brother. He just called me to say he will be here in an hour or so.'

'Duppy' is a Bantu word meaning ghost. Duppies are part of everyday Jamaican life, and their reality is not questioned. Each person has two souls after death; one goes to heaven while the other, the duppy, stays on earth. Spanish colonists sometimes supposedly hid valuables and money in pottery jars buried under roots of trees. The African slave who dug the hole was killed, and his duppy would stay on guard for eternity. Obeah, the belief that spirits can be used to harm the living by using spells and amulets, accords with the belief in duppies. Henry Morgan regularly consulted obeah practitioners during his dying days.

I ordered a breakfast of ackee and saltfish, finishing it just as Leroy walked up to my table.

'Sleep good, mon?'

'Sure. I'm not scared of duppies.'

'Yo afi be careful round dem duppies, yah. Dem can control yo body and yo mind.'

'Do they only come out at night?'

'Dem duppy come out anytime dem feel like. Dem live ina cotton tree and look like man or animal. An dem laugh like witch and talk ina dem nose. Dem only count to three. When duppy ride donkey, dem sidown backway.'

This was too much. I started laughing.

Leroy gave me a look intended to kill. I could sense his blood boiling so changed the subject.

'So what's the plan for today, Big Man?'

'Wi ago dong a Trench Town, den wi a go Nine Mile. Yo afi go pay respect to Bob Marley pilgrimage. Yo shoulda listen Bob Marley album, *Duppy Conqueror*. Dat wi teach yo someting. Learn about Old Hige Annie Palmer, white witch of Rosehall who leave her skin anight and drink baby blood. Learn about Rolling Calf – dat is when a butcher dead, im turn ina Rolling Calf. Dat is de worse duppy yo wan fi deal with. Learn about di Three-Foot Horse, and di Whistling Cowboy. Yo wa fi talk an laugh about more duppy. Den wi ago look fi where Henry Morgan im live. A di same part a di island. Wi no af a whole heap of time if yo ago leave Jamaica tomorrow.'

'How the hell do you know I am leaving tomorrow?' I had told no one of my travel plans.

'Mi know wen yo come and go. A fi mi town dis. Mi know everyting wa go on in a dis country. Mi friend dem always keep mi up to date. Mi af connection everywhere, mon, in a di police, an custom, an Air Jamaica, you name it. Mi hav it. If mi no know it, mi know a man who can.'

'Cool.'

Leroy deliberately placed the car's no smoking sign in a more prominent position and sporadically polished the dashboard as we drove on the Palasidoes back towards Michael Manley International Airport and Kingston.

'Look de si di smoke over deso, mon?'

On the right-hand side, between us and the sea, police were watching and feeding a bonfire. White smoke rose into the sky.

'A deso dem bun di weed that dem tek from people.'

'They burn all of it?'

'Shit! No.' Leroy laughed.

We were soon in the centre of Kingston, then in Trench Town, so named because of a large sewer trench from Old Kingston running through it to the sea.

'Dis where everyting start, from di ghetto. Now reggae music cover di world from man like Bob Marley, Toots Hibbert, Bunny Wailer, Peter Tosh, Ken Booth, Leroy Sibbles, the Heptones and Jimmy Cliff.'

We passed the Queen's Theatre where Bob Marley – known locally as Tuff Gong – and the Wailers first played. The streets smelled of piss. People were living in shipping crates, fish barrels, oil drums and on the ground. Pit latrines provided less than basic sanitation, and collective yard kitchens produced the food. There was little evidence of plumbing or electricity, and the area reeked of overpopulation, disease, malnutrition and infant mortality. Bob Marley and Elvis Presley might share many qualities, but this place could never become Graceland. Just minutes away by car lay tropical paradises, beaches and cliffs, waterfalls spouting out of hills, clear streams and organic free food on trees everywhere. It made no sense.

Three miles from Trench Town at 55 Hope Road is the Bob Marley Museum, a wooden plantation house bought by Chris Blackwell – who was once saved by a Rasta from a near-fatal boating accident – as a home for Bob Marley. Tour buses crammed the recently paved parking lot. Leroy stayed in the car while I went for the guided tour. Marijuana plants grew in the herb garden; a rehearsal room sported holes from bullets meant for Bob.

Despite being feared by the government for his influence and militance, and his promotion of black pride, Bob Marley has become part of the collective consciousness of the nation. Of mixed parentage, he was acceptable to both races and could speak about exploitation from the moral high ground. His life was short and bright.

We left Kingston and drove west on the Sir Alexander Bustamente Highway through Spanish Town to May Pen, where Leroy stopped at a coconut stall.

'Cold jelly, mon.'

Cold jelly is chilled coconut. The stallholder trimmed two coconut shells with a machete, deftly opening a hole at the top of each. The milk was instantly refreshing and tasted healthy. When we had finished drinking, the coconut man hacked out a scoop from each shell and broke the nuts in two. We used the scoops to dig out the soft coconut flesh.

At May Pen we headed inland through Morgans, Morgans Pass and Arthur's Seat.

'Leroy, this is one of the places where Henry Morgan must have lived. Can we get out and have a look round?'

'Noting no de, yah, mon. Believe mi, mi check everyting and knock pon every door ask a whole heap of questions just two day ago.'

A quick drive around confirmed Leroy's description. We carried on inland to the Bob Marley Mausoleum, a tasteful extension of Marley's birthplace, at Nine Mile, where I dutifully paid my respects while Leroy again stayed in the car

park. When I returned, he had been joined on a bench by a
Rasta whom he obviously knew. I smiled at the Rasta. He
smiled at me, took two joints from his pocket and gave me
one.

'Peace, Niceman. Mi name Mo.'

Mo and I simultaneously lit our joints and took slow
deliberate lungfuls of ganja. I could tell that Mo, like me, was
marvelling at a herb that could make you feel so good about
yourself and others with just one breath. We held the precious
breath inside us. Mo breathed out, sighing 'Jah' with
reverence. I did the same. We both felt the warmth and
fullness of our open hearts and surrendered control.

Reggae, ganja and Rastafarianism are tightly interwoven in
today's Jamaica, but their beginnings were independent. Back
in around 1,000 BC wise King Solomon lived with 700 wives
and made love to a further 400 queens and 600 concubines.
His sexual skills and spiritual strength attracted beautiful
women from all over the Middle East and Africa, including
Makeda, the Queen of Sheba, who bore Solomon his favourite
son, Menelik. For many years father and son lived in
Jerusalem, where Solomon built the First Temple to house the
Ark of the Covenant, the holy of holies which has inspired so
many religious poets and Hollywood film directors. Almost all
accounts agree the Ark contained the original stone tablets of
the Ten Commandments as given by God to Moses as well as
some manna from heaven. It is believed to be the resting-place
of the spirit of God and to exist simultaneously both in heaven
and on earth.

Believing his father was promiscuous and misusing his
sexual energy, Menelik stole the Ark of the Covenant from the
Temple of Jerusalem and took it to the ancient Ethiopian city
of Aksum, 400 miles north of today's Addis Ababa. The Ark,
it is claimed, now rests inside the city's Church of St Mary Our
Lady of Zion, which was built on the site of Ethiopia's oldest
Christian church. Near Aksum in the Ethiopian highlands

there was a community of African Jews called Falashas who claim descent from Solomon and adhere to a form of primitive Judaism based on the Torah, the first five books of the Old Testament, written by Moses. Now all living in Israel, they observe the sabbath, practise circumcision, worship in synagogues and abide by Jewish dietary laws.

Born in Jamaica in 1887, Marcus Mosiah Garvey envisaged a free Negro race and believed that the descendants of slaves should return to Africa to set up their own nation state. Organising strikes and riots in Kingston, he quickly gained a reputation for his powerful oratory. Rural black Jamaicans did not adapt well to working in urban environments and learned to survive by street scams picked up from the hoodlums and freed prisoners who continued to arrive in Trench Town and other West Kingston ghettos. Gradually the area turned into a battlefield for the often corrupt politicians raging against the injustices of the establishment. Garvey had prophesied that a black king, crowned in Africa, would rise to lead all Africans, wherever they might be, out of bondage, and in 1930 Emperor Haile Selassie I, known as Ras Tafari – the feared prince – was elected the 225th monarch of Ethiopia. Garvey saw Ethiopia, the oldest monarchy in the world, as a symbol of freedom, sovereignty and African spirituality, and kick-started Rastafarianism, the spiritual nationality of Jamaica and the island's most compelling cultural force.

Jamaicans now had an ideology that recognised their ancestry and respected the dignity of Africa. Many acclaimed Haile Selassie as the living God and saw Marcus Mosiah Garvey, whose middle name was a combination of Moses and Messiah, as a prophet and the forerunner of Haile Selassie, as John the Baptist had been to Jesus. They identified with the Jews, who had spent generations in captivity and slavery and who had been forcibly scattered throughout the world. Jamaicans were the lost tribes of Israel who had been sold into slavery in Babylon, which is not a place but the sum of all the institutions and thinking that keep people economically, politically, mentally and spiritually enslaved.

The pioneer of Rastafarianism in Jamaica was Leonard Percival Howell. Despite his surname and having a son named Cardiff, I could find no other Welsh connection. In 1940 Howell and Joseph Hibbert, ardent believers in the divinity of Haile Selassie, set up Pinnacle, the first Rasta commune. African music was played continually to the 4,000 formerly homeless members, who lived on the productive land in thatched huts. Howell based his sermons to the early Rastas on the Old Testament, particularly Psalms and Proverbs, teaching that if God was any colour, he was black, and that the first human beings were Ethiopians. In defiance of materialistic values and vanity, the Rastas wore torn clothes and began wearing dreadlocks, which, following the biblical precept 'for no razor shall touch the heads of the righteous', are washed but not combed, brushed or cut. Dreadlocks remind them of God and connect them more directly with him. Wearing matted or twisted locks of hair is widespread in Africa. The Masai of Kenya and groups in Somalia, Ghana, Senegal, Gambia and of course Ethiopia, have all worn them.

The Rastas eschewed meat and shellfish for 'I-tal' food – grains, fruit, roots and vegetables – and shunned alcohol, nicotine, cocaine, caffeine, sugar, processed foods and the use of pesticides or fertilisers. Many believed themselves to be the true Jews and began wearing the Star of David. They also expropriated the colours of the Ethiopian flag: red symbolising blood spilled; gold, hope for victory; and green, the fertile land. The Rastas beat their drums, sang about love and freedom, and quoted from the Bible. Although each family was responsible for itself, a programme of unpaid communal work ensured social benefits to the community. Strictly apolitical, they refused to pay taxes to the government. Pinnacle survived several brutal British raids during which the authorities locked up the Rastas, and cut off their dreads. It was finally destroyed in the late 1950s. The Rastas, with nowhere else to go, fled to West Kingston, where they found their soulmates in the Burru people, who shared the same passion for drumming and Africa.

Neither Haile Selassie nor any members of the Falashas nor the Ethiopian Christians smoked ganja. Marcus Garvey described it as a harmful weed and regarded Rastafarians, particularly Leonard Percival Howell, as crazy fanatics. Stemming from a multiplicity of beliefs, Rastafarianism is fraught with troubling paradoxes. Not all Rastas have dreads or are vegetarians or read the Bible or are faithful to their women or approve of reggae. Rastafarianism has no churches and is not legally recognised as a religion in Jamaica. It is a state of mind and soul arrived at through spiritual growth and awareness of inner divinity. A devout Christian, Garvey never believed in the divinity of Haile Selassie – neither had Haile Selassie – and in later life became critical of him. In 1935, Mussolini's Italy invaded Ethiopia, occupying it for five years while Haile Selassie endured comfortable exile in England. In Garvey's opinion Haile Selassie had betrayed his people to fascists and opted for a life of personal luxury. His dream was shattered and he died a sad man. But all this had little or no effect on Jamaica's growing numbers of Rastafarian devotees, who continued to revere Haile Selassie as the living God and to smoke ganja in his honour. When Haile Selassie first visited Jamaica in 1966 at the invitation of Mortimo Planno – later Bob Marley's manager – his aeroplane was greeted by over 100 Rastafarians, some wearing white robes and chanting, 'Hosanna to the Son of David.' They threw large spliffs at the emperor's feet. Haile Selassie was so astonished, he had to retreat to his plane for a while to recover.

The blame or, rather, credit for Rastafarian ganja can safely be given to Howell, one of the finest growers of marijuana the world has known. For over a decade, Pinnacle's cash crop had been ganja, the Indian word for marijuana. After the British abolition of slavery in 1834, the plantation owners had no one to work the fields, and ships from India brought workers to British Guyana, Trinidad and Jamaica. They were regular users of marijuana and introduced the plant to Jamaica, where it became popular among fishermen and farmers. There was no connection with Ethiopia.

Howell constantly praised the virtues of the herb. It was the sacrament, 'the healing of the nations'. By smoking it, a Rasta could arrive at the spiritual plane of consciousness. Ganja smoking heightened intellectual powers, speeded up focused thinking and prepared the user for meditation, prayer, the gaining of wisdom and communal harmony with others. Spliffs helped people forgive, relax, be calm and forget. Howell quoted numerous Biblical passages to support his enthusiasm for the herb: 'He causeth the grass to grow for the cattle and herb for the service of man' (Psalm 104:14), 'Smoke went up from His nostrils' (Psalm 18:8) and made much of reports that ganja had been found growing on King Solomon's grave. Howell referred to ganja as 'wisdom weed', an elixir of divine origin.

Ganja grown in Pinnacle quickly found its way into the Kingston ghettos, where the most prolific users were musicians. When the Rastas were eventually forced out of the security of their commune, they moved into the same impoverished neighbourhood. Sharing a love for African rhythms and ganja, they collaborated.

Music and ganja are the archetypal tools of communication: each brings about similar physical responses in different people at the same time; each draws groups together; and each creates a sense of unity, enabling people to bond and resonate with one another. Ganja fosters musical creativity and heightens the enjoyment of listening. The most inspired, innovative and pleasurable music of the last century was created by stoners, be they jazz-age swingers, cool beboppers, cosmic hippies or Trench Town roots rockers. The effect of ganja on music appreciation and creativity is almost universal and does not fade with repetition.

Having given this matter much thought, I think there are two explanations: so-called short-term memory loss and time deceleration. When I am stoned, time seems to slow down. In other words, my thinking speeds up. Musical events pass by me at a much more leisurely rate, enabling me to appreciate details and delights I would miss during a straight audition. As for making music when stoned, improvisational jazz has depended on short-term memory for its evolution. When I am stoned, my memory is quickly re-established, suggesting that what has happened is not a loss of short-term memory or a damaging of the brain mediating it, but a different manner of using it. I merely lose track of trains of ideas that are normally being recorded in short-term memory because my perceptions need far more attention than they normally do. My consciousness is heavily involved with matters far removed from mere utilitarian attention to continuity of logical or linguistic thought processes. My experience is so interesting and attention-consuming that I ignore, not lose, my short-term memories. When the virtuoso performer abandons his calculated intents, the result is not nonsense but often his finest creation. Forgetfulness is the catalytic germ of spontaneous creativity.

Feeling happy and blessed, Leroy and I said goodbye to Mo, who gave me another spliff for the road. We drove towards Jamaica's north-east coast on a series of secondary roads through Friendship, Clapham, Lucky Hill, Windsor Castle, Montreal, and other strangely named places. At Show Meself Corner, I decided to light Mo's spliff. Leroy shot me a slightly disapproving glance. I made sure the ash and smoke went out of the window. A few miles from the shore, Leroy stopped the car on a deserted main road.

'Llanrhumney, mon.'

The countryside was green and beautiful with gentle hills

and meadows, reminiscent of certain parts of Wales, but unlike the Cardiff suburb whose name it shared.

'Are you sure, Leroy? There doesn't seem to be anything here either. There's not even a sign saying it's Llanrhumney.'

'Mi one hundred per cent sure, Mon. One hundred per cent sure. Believe mi.'

'Have you checked it out and knocked on all the doors? I assume there are some around here.'

'De is one, just one, an' belong to di house by di wood. Mi stop de yesterday and mi chat to Marvin, di caretaker. Im know bout Henry Morgan an im know where Henry Morgan treasure buried. Mi just call im from Tuff Gong place. Im a wait fi wi over de.'

We walked over to a building half of which was a ruin and half of which had been recently renovated. Marvin, smiling broadly and wearing just a pair of jeans and a baseball cap, was sitting on his tractor, which he started as soon as we had shaken hands. Leroy immediately jumped on to the back of the tractor and, with one hand, pulled me up alongside him. The tractor lurched forward and sped towards the wood. Leroy leaned over, pulled out two machetes and gave me one of them. Sharp and lethal, it gleamed in the sun.

'What the fuck do I need this for?'

'Just follow mi, mon, and do what mi do.'

Reaching its cruising speed, the tractor tore into the wood. Without warning, Leroy raised his machete into the air and took aim at Marvin's head.

Leroy was going to kill him! I couldn't stop him – he was too big. His killer eyes glared into mine, commanding me to raise my machete. I had seen those eyes before in the exercise yards of maximum-security penitentiaries. Leroy had led riots against guards and stopped fellow Jamaicans from carving one another to bits. He was one heavy motherfucker. There was no way I was going to slice off Marvin's head, but if I didn't, I might lose mine. I might lose mine anyway. I had obviously got caught up in some vicious posse feud and had unwittingly provided Leroy with the means of getting his target alone, unarmed, in the middle of nowhere with two machetes behind him. Obviously, Leroy would kill me next, and anyone who subsequently discovered the carnage would reasonably infer Marvin and I had killed each other in a machete fight while squabbling over Henry Morgan's treasure. Leroy had been a senior police officer and would know all about presenting the right clues. No wonder he had found out exactly how long I was staying and which flight I was meant to catch back tomorrow. All my friends had told me I shouldn't bother with people I had befriended in prison; they were all bad. Why hadn't I listened? Never mind, it would soon be over. I might meet some nice angels.

The machete flashed down, whistled through the air and chopped through a cluster of branches.

'Come on, mon. Help mi chop down di bush. If wi don't, di tractor stop, and wi stuck ina di mud.'

More relieved than is imaginable, I slashed away at the over-hanging vegetation, helping Marvin's tractor to get through.

'Leroy, I thought you were going to kill me and Marvin – chop our heads off.'

'Yo is stoned, mon, too fucking stoned. Mi tell yo dat de Rasta weed too strong fi yo.'

'But I saw that murder look in your eyes, in your face. You were going to kill.'

'Dat ano me, mon. Yo just see a duppy. Now yo af learn your lesson.'

'I don't believe in fucking duppies.'

'Shit! So yo woulda rather believe mi, yo big friend, woulda kill yo. Mi, who save yo arse all di time ina di Yankee prison woulda kill yo ina Jamaica. If mi ever see yo a come fi kill mi, mi know it woulda be a duppy. Shoulda be di same fi yo.'

'All right, maybe I am a bit stoned. And a bit jet-lagged. I

didn't sleep that well last night and the tractor is making me
feel slightly sick.'

Leroy stared hard into my face. There was no need for him
to say a word.

'All right, I've seen a duppy.'

Despite our efforts, the tractor stopped in a few inches of
mud halfway across a narrow river. Marvin reversed the
tractor out of the river for a few yards and then drove down
into it again, but stuck at exactly the same place. Marvin asked
us to get off and repeated the procedure, charging in with full
revs. This time he made it. Leroy and I waded through, got
back on the tractor, and motored slowly up a slight grassy
incline. Near the top the hill got steeper, and we abandoned
the tractor and walked to the summit, which was covered with
stone walls reduced to ruins a few feet high with some old
cannon and other rusty bits and pieces. There were several
small caves with boarded-up entrances. Marvin motioned me
to follow him. Large red letters stood out from one the walls.
C-A-R-T-R-E-F spelt the Welsh word for home. I felt weird.

Leroy went for a walk as Marvin explained to me how this
had been Henry Morgan's main home in Jamaica. The land
was well irrigated and fertile, and the summit served as an
excellent lookout. The boarded-up tunnels supposedly went
in labyrinthine fashion all the way to the sea, and still housed
plenty of precious artefacts, but they were hard to find and
even harder to transport, as many of the caves had collapsed,
and there were more than a few duppies down there to keep
people away. The treasure was all there and would remain so.
Leroy returned with a chocolate pod and some fleshy red pear-
shaped apples which tasted of delicate flowers.

The tractor trip back was much easier and thankfully,
uneventful. Marvin passed out some welcome Red Stripes,
and Leroy discreetly gave him some money before we got
back into the car and drove away from Llanrhumney. Dusk
was stealing into the hilly creases, filling them with purple

haze. The sun cut itself on a sharp hill and bled into the valleys. Long shadows of hilltops flew into the fields like stalking owls.

I had expected to be thrilled by the experience of following in Henry Morgan's footsteps and visiting the land in Jamaica he had chosen to remind him of his Welsh birthplace, let alone discovering the possible whereabouts of his treasure. I know expectations are rarely fulfilled, and when they are tend to be anticlimactic, but perhaps my unease was because Henry had lived there during his dotage, his period of disillusionment and paranoia, when he was surrounded by the ghosts of vanished thrills. He should have spent his last years in Wales, where the blood of his ancestors had soaked the soil to keep it Welsh for always. Or perhaps my unease was because of the duppy assassin who looked just like Leroy.

After driving for fifteen minutes, we saw the sea and came across a sign for Oracabessa.

'Hey, Leroy, isn't this where UB40 live?'

'Ya mon. Di house no de far from ya.'

UB40, a Birmingham group who topped the charts during the early 1980s, brought me so much comfort and credibility while I was languishing in TV rooms in American prisons with the gangsters and the gang stars. Even the most die-hard Jamaican reggae fan or Chicago street gang hip hop devotee could never knock UB40, their music, or their incredible integrity and tenacity in ensuring the original Jamaican composers of their songs were financially rewarded. To the average United States penitentiary inmate, nothing else British was worth a fuck, except Lennox Lewis. Shortly after I was released from prison, UB40 – without having any idea how much they had meant to me – sent me copies of all their albums. When I started doing my spoken-word shows, their friends and family would invariably be in the Birmingham audience.

'I don't know them well personally, Leroy, but I'm sure if I knocked on their door, they would let me in.'

'Mi check yesterday an nobody no di de.'

'You checked a hell of a lot yesterday, didn't you?'

'Ya, mon. Because yo af just two night. Mi remember yo say yo wan see some live reggae. Tonight, wi ago a di hot spot. Yo remember yo meet Beano over Morgan Hotel? Lickle more wi go check him.'

We drove west along the coast road to Ocho Rios, a cruise ship pit stop populated by higglers – tourist fleecers – musicians, ganja dealers, cocaine dealers and others who love life and are intimate with death. Rows of detached mansions and renovated plantation houses sat next to luxurious condiminiums. We pulled into a driveway leading to a cross between a stately home and a motel. A friendly guard lying on a deckchair smoking a chalice full of ganja smiled and waved us through. Beano, wearing a metallic blue shirt, Savile Row-style thin black trousers and even more gold jewellery than last time, danced out to greet us.

'Leroy and Niceman. Wi start party now at my place before wi hit de hot spot. Mi hear dat yo like Front-end Loader, Niceman? Mi soon come.'

Prescot appeared with a tray of Front-end Loaders, the guard brought me a chalice, and Beano played a Black Uhuru album. I began to get seriously spannered.

'Would you like to accompany me for a short walk, Niceman? I'll show you the grounds,' invited Prescot, who led the way out through a garden gate.

We walked down a grassy lane past the back of some beautiful but modest houses.

'Several well-known artists and musicians live in this row,' said Prescot.

'Who's the most famous?' I asked.

'That would have to be Mr Ranglin, Niceman.'

'Mr Ranglin? Not Ernest Ranglin, surely?'

'Exactly so. The great man himself.'

'I don't believe it, Prescot.'

'It's easily established, Niceman. We can call in on him. Beano told me he is at home this week.' Dressed in a loose light shirt and green trousers, a kindly-looking elderly man with a radiant face was leaning on one of the gates. Prescot approached him and suddenly switched his speech from precise English to patois. 'Misa Ranglin, meet mi fren. Dem call im Mr Nice.'

I was shaking hands with Jamaica's BB King. Born in Manchester, Jamaica in 1932, Ernest Ranglin taught himself the guitar by studying books and attending events featuring Jamaican dance bands. At sixteen, he was Jamaica's rising star, touring locally and in the Bahamas. Chris Blackwell saw Ranglin play in Montego Bay and contracted him to record Island Records' first release. When the tough urban sounds of American rhythm and blues began to supersede traditional mento, it was Ranglin who first combined the two to produce ska and provide Jamaica with a new sound. In 1964 Chris Blackwell invited Ernest Ranglin to London, where he played at Ronnie Scott's and became its resident jazz guitarist for nine months. At the same time he created the first worldwide ska hit, 'My Boy Lollipop', for Millie Small and was voted the number-one guitarist in the world. I saw him play during this period. He was brilliant and unforgettable, and he is still playing and recording.

'Ah yes. Beano told me about you, Mr Nice. I've borrowed the book you wrote from him. Great story.'

There were all sorts of questions I wanted to ask Ernest, such as did Rod Stewart really play harmonica on 'My Boy Lollipop'? I was too shy to do so and settled for a photograph with the legend.

'Yo will af yo picture tek wid nuff star tonight, Niceman. Mek wi go back dong a Beano now.'

'Why are you suddenly speaking patois, Prescot?'

'I always do when conversing with a Jamaican.'
'But you're talking to me now.'
'You're turning into a Jamaican, Niceman.'

The party had grown quickly. Bottles of overproof rum, cans of Red Stripe and giant glasses of Front-end Loader covered every available surface. In the garden a cameraman was doing a video shoot of over twenty girls aged anywhere between twelve and twenty wearing just dental floss G-strings and fine mesh netting dancing provocatively to the new craze from Spanish Town, Rasta Rocket. Immaculately dressed musicians, with either stunning women or terrifying body-guards, swayed gently as they moved seamlessly from one sound system to another. Crowds of infants, also faultlessly dressed, honed their hip hop moves and hand signals. Every-one was either laughing or singing. Beano sidled up to me.

'So yo meet Mo mi bredren at Tuff Gong place, Niceman?'
'The Rasta. Yes I did.'
'Im ano real Rasta. Im a rent-a-dred or disco Rasta.'
'Disco Rasta! What's that?'
'Rasta is a holy man who nah drink no liquor an nah shave at all because de Bible tell him no. An im no fuck strange women, an im always smoke de high-grade herb. Rent-a-dred do everyting. Im drink liquor, wear dreads because lady dem find dem sexy, im fuck anyting, an smoke anyting. Mo always af good ganja. Yo snort, Niceman?'
'I take most drugs, Beano.'
'Mi af di best cocaine, Niceman. Yo wa some?'
'Sure, Beano. I'd love some.'
Beano pulled out a bag of cocaine the size of a tennis ball. He opened it, dipped the corner of a credit card deep into the flake and stuck a mound of it near one of my nostrils. I sniffed as if it was my first breath. Hot jets of clarity burned through my olfactory membranes and optimism streaked through my brain. This was strong stuff. For the next hour I flirted with all

the women there, thinking I was shagging them rather than just talking about myself, and kept looking for Beano to give me some more cocaine. Instead, I found Leroy looking at me more disapprovingly than ever.

'Alrite, party done. Mi hungry. Mi ready.'

We drove a few miles further west to St Ann's Bay and parked the car at a restaurant surrounded by a tangle of fairy lights and barbecues emitting small explosions. Without asking me, Leroy ordered conch and a cold drink that smelled of turnips.

'Look ya. Ano everybody yo fi tek tings from dong ya. Yo afi watch yourself.'

'I had one line of coke, for Christ's sake.'

'If a from Beano, everybody know dat coke from im a ten time stronger an a line from im a ten time longer.'

'It was excellent coke, I admit. And the duppies have fucked off.'

'Lef de coke alone, mon. Stick to de herb if ya af to take any drug.'

The conch, prepared by chopping it with seasoned rice and putting the mixture in a silver foil envelope on the barbecue, arrived at the table. It was delicious, and I wolfed the lot in seconds – pure cocaine does not destroy one's appetite. I sipped at the drink, which tasted like compost.

'Drink dis. Dem ya roots wi keep yo healty.'

Leroy and I left the restaurant and joined streams of excited people all heading in the same direction. We came across a giant poster that stated in huge multicoloured letters, 'Ruddy Joe Production and Airtight Security Present a Night Call at Jus Cheers, St Ann's'. Then came a line-up of Jamaican music legends: dancehall pioneers Brigadier Jerry and Charlie Chaplin, Ninja, Lloyd Parks & We the People Band, Leroy Sibbles, founder member of the Heptones, Luciano, the outrageous Professor Nuts and the greatest Jamaican singer ever, Ken Boothe.

'All these guys are performing tonight, Leroy? I don't believe it.'

'Dis ago be your best party eva, mon.'

The venue was a large field surrounded by a high fence, outside which were parked shiny red trucks loaded with sugar cane, coconuts and machetes. Succulent chunks of chicken and pork were grilling on jerk barrels – usually fifty-gallon drums cut in half. Piles of cases of Red Stripe served as temporary bars. Ganja dealers shouted, 'High grade. High-grade weed.' Peanut, hot dog, ice cream and candyfloss vendors pushed their contraptions on wheels through the dense crowd at the entrance. Those filing in saluted one another by pointing their forefingers at their temples, as if their hands were guns about to blow their brains out.

Dancehall shootings had begun when security guards at outdoor events fired their pistols into the air to signal support for a particular artist – a bad idea as falling bullets would sometimes injure members of the audience and hit men were able to use the shots as cover for their assassinations. Performers had begged their supporters to leave their guns at home, and the handgun salute replaced the real thing.

I took my place in the queue. 'No, mon. Wi no join line. Ken Boothe no deya yet. Wi go in wid im.'

I noticed a vendor selling magic mushroom tea. Unfortunately, Leroy detected my interest.

'Lef dat shit, mon. Fungus ano herb.'

A car with its headlights full on and a horn like that of an ice cream van was gently ploughing its way through the crowd. Beano was in the driving seat; Prescot sat next to him; Ken Boothe was in the back. He was wearing a safari-style white suit, and his face shone like that of a baby angel.

Ken Boothe is known as Mr Rocksteady for his pioneering of the style, as Mr Evergreen for his forever-young looks, and as Mr Smooth for his stage presence. He has the most powerful and passionate voice, a gritty soulful baritone, reminiscent of Wilson Pickett's. From humble Jamaican origins and a talented dancer, songwriter, musician and arranger, he uses his skills to promote harmony and break down barriers of race and religion. He is Jamaica's perfect ambassador. Ken's international recording career began with his cover version of Sandie Shaw's 1967 Eurovision Song Contest winner, 'Puppet on a String'. He continued to make rocksteady covers of pop and soul hits. In 1974 he recorded and released his greatest hit, 'Everything I Own', which topped the UK charts. It is my favourite Jamaican song.

Beano introduced me and Leroy to Ken, and we followed him through the entrance. The security guards knew Beano, Prescot and Ken Boothe, but not me or Leroy.

'This is my security,' said Ken, pointing to Leroy, 'and this is my producer from London,' pointing to me. The security guards gave us VIP AAA passes.

The VIP area did not resemble the heavily staffed and cordoned-off sections full of minor celebrities one finds in London; it was simply the part of the field nearest the stage where the performers hung out. There were no guards stopping any of the audience from joining them, but no one tried. The punters were there to dance and listen to the music, not hassle those who provided it.

On stage, older guys were positioning microphones, assembling drum kits and connecting 30,000-watt speakers to turntables, mixers and other DJ equipment while kids were carrying up boxes of 45-rpm records.

Beano, Ken and I shared a chalice of high grade, while, somehow, Prescot managed to get me a crude Front-end Loader. Leroy approached me with Leroy Sibbles and a man dressed in flowing shiny white robes wearing a large oriental lampshade on his head.

'Luciano and Mr Sibbles, this Mr Nice.'

Luciano – Jepther McClymont – is a deeply religious man and was responsible for reintroducing spiritual lyricism and humanity to dancehall when many of his contemporaries were stricken with gangsta fever. During the early 1990s, Luciano, so called because of his ability to sound like Pavarotti, alternated periods of extraordinary chart success, including songs like 'Shake It Up', with spiritual sabbaticals and the pursuit of his social agenda. He is a passionate supporter of legalising marijuana. I was honoured to meet him.

Elevated by the ganja, ego-stroked by meeting the reggae legends playing on stage and elated by their music, I determined to dance until everyone else dropped. But this was Jamaica. When dawn broke, not a single person had left or seemed the least bit weary, except Leroy.

'Ya afi to catch de iron bird soon, mon. Time fi lef dis place.'

Groups and families were still arriving as Leroy and I walked back to the restaurant's car park and climbed into the car for an effortless two-hour drive back to Morgan's Harbour Hotel and Beach Club. I quickly grabbed my things and checked out. Leroy took me to the airport.

'Yo see. Mi do wah mi say mi can do. Mi show yo everyting: de four Rs of Jamaica – rum, reggae, reefer and Rasta. An mi show you Henry Morgan's treasure.'

'I know. It's been great. I'm going to miss it, and you. How long before you are back in Britain?'

'Mi no know yet. Mi hav someting fi tek care of. But mi soon come.'

'I've had an idea. Why don't we get a local craftsman to build a statue of Henry Morgan in Port Royal?'

'Money talk an bullshit walk. Anyting yo want an yo have de money, yo can do. Af a safe flight.'

'Bye, Leroy. Make sure the statue's face looks like mine.'

Seven

BRAZIL

I walked downstairs into the dark basement of a West End lap dancing club in Soho. Naked Russians twirled around the poles, lights flashed and music blared. I vaguely recognised the silhouettes of Dave Courtney, Bernie Davies, Tony Lambrianou, Charlie Breaker and other members of the Firm huddled together with the Alabama 3. I moved towards them.

Someone tapped me on the shoulder. 'Thanks for coming along, Howard. Haven't seen you for a while.'

It was Bruce Reynolds, mastermind of the Great Train Robbery and the most gentlemanly of those who live outside the law. I first met Bruce during the mid 1980s. Actor Larry Lamb had played him in the film *Buster* and Larry was friendly with my first wife, Ilze. He had introduced me to Bruce. I met him again ten years later through his son Nick, a talented sculptor and musician who played with the Alabama 3 and with whom I had worked at various spoken-word events. It had been a year or two since Bruce and I had last met, at Farringdon's Tardis Studios, where we had read extracts from our respective autobiographies. He had seemed troubled. I remembered our conversation.

'What's up, Bruce? You seem worried.'

'It's not really a case of worry, I'm just concerned about Ronnie. You know me, my boy Nick, Dave Courtney and Roy Shaw went out to Rio to see him for his seventieth birthday?'

'Yes, Nick told me about it. Wasn't it also the birthday of the robbery?'

'That's right, the thirty-sixth anniversary. We did the robbery on Ronnie's birthday in 1963. We always have a laugh about that. But Ronnie's ill, really seriously ill, and completely skint.'

Ronnie Biggs, fleeing from thirty years in a British prison, had arrived in Brazil in 1970. Four years later, Scotland Yard detective Jack Slipper arrested him in Rio de Janeiro. Biggs beat the extradition attempt as a result of having fathered a Brazilian dependant, Michael, with his girlfriend Raimunda and went on to record 'No One is Innocent' for the Sex Pistols. In 1981 a gang of bounty hunters kidnapped him in Rio and smuggled him to Barbados by boat. A Barbados court decided the rules governing extradition to Britain had not been properly adhered to, and allowed Biggs to return to Rio, where he lived in a dilapidated apartment in petty-crime-ridden Santa Teresa, on the city's outskirts. Biggs made money by selling T-shirts and photographs of himself and entertaining tourists with escape stories. In 1997 the Brazilian Supreme Court rejected a new request by the British government to extradite him. During the next two years he suffered a series of strokes, which left him partly paralysed and unable to speak.

'You know what he told me out there, Howard: "You got me into this, Bruce. Can you get me out of it? I've got one more wish in life, and that's to buy a pint of bitter in a Margate pub."'

'What does he expect you to do?'

'Help him get back to this country.'

'What! He wants to swap a beach in Brazil for a cell in Wandsworth nick? I hope you persuaded him not to.'

'Ronnie thinks he'll get out after a while on compassionate grounds, and that while he's in he can get proper medical treatment.'

'Since when have they been compassionate, Bruce? Those Wandsworth screws would love to see Ronnie Biggs die sewing mailbags, and I don't think the word "proper" accurately describes the medical treatment dished out to Her Majesty's prisoners, unless it's changed since I was there. I'd take my chances with the Brazilian doctors if I were him.'

'Treatment in Brazil would cost a fortune, more than all of us together could raise.'

'Won't some newspaper fork out for an exclusive?'

'I tried that. The media are only interested in covering what goes wrong for him, like all the strokes. The papers will only pay if he gives himself up. And it is his choice, after all. If that's what he wants to do, I've got to help. I did get him into it in the first place. I'll help him get back, I'll get him some money, I'll see him as often as I can, and I'll do what I can to get an early release.'

Several months later Nick Reynolds pushed a wheelchair containing Ronnie Biggs into the departure lounge of Galeão International Airport in Rio de Janeiro. A fourteen-seater jet chartered by the *Sun* was waiting to take him home. Biggs was arrested the moment his feet touched British soil. Friends and relatives arranged a series of fund-raising events to finance his bids to secure early release. This was the first event I had been able to attend.

'How's it all going, Bruce.'

'OK, but Ronnie's health is just getting worse, his family are going through all kinds of hell, and we're finding it hard to raise any loot. Apart from us, no one cares.'

Dave Courtney joined us. 'You're not wrong, Bruce. The fuckers keep harping on about protecting society and all that bollocks. I mean, Ronnie's hardly likely to rob a train again, is he? He can't fucking walk or talk for starters. What kind of poxy society needs to be protected from cripples on their last legs? Sadists, the fucking lot of them. Then there's those geezers who go on about deterrence. It's too fucking late to deter Ronnie. Ronnie's a living commercial for a career of crime. But the creeps that really get up my nose are the ones who whinge about the train driver. Do they know what happens to boxers? What was he doing trying to stop robbers doing their work anyway? Liberty-taking fucker.'

'Well, they did try to stop him doing his work – driving the train,' I said, trying to calm Dave down.

Bruce laughed. Dave tried not to and said, 'You can see which one of us is the stand-up comedian. You all right, Howard? Didn't mean to ignore you. Haven't seen you since that Tenerife nonsense. Anyway, if Ronnie had been a nonce or a terrorist, he'd have been home . . .'

Dave Courtney and Tony Lambrianou were two of the most high-profile senior members of the Firm, the organisation begun by Ronnie Kray in the early 1960s, and they had attended one of my first *Mr Nice Live* shows at the Shepherd's Bush Empire in late 1997. Despite the venue's rigorous security, they had experienced no difficulty gaining access to the backstage after-show party. Dave grabbed me as I walked off the stage, gave me a huge kiss, and told me he too was thinking of embarking on a stand-up comedy career and had come to get some inspiration of the 'If he can do it, anyone can' kind.

We talked for a while, during which time I could do little else but laugh. He is as funny as fuck, one of this country's cleverest raconteurs, and we became and remain very good friends. Shortly afterwards Dave asked if I would join him in a double act at a venue in Tenerife. The almost exclusively British expatriate audience loved the show, but apparently a knife fight had broken out during the second half. After the show Dave, with his considerable entourage, my manager

Giles Cooper and I went to a bar to sign autographs, pat one another on the back and get drunk. All seemed amicable until suddenly a group of about twenty men with Middle Eastern and Spanish features poured in wielding baseball bats. The bar erupted. Giles and I scarpered and sought the sanctuary of our hotel rooms.

'What was all that about, Dave?'

'It happens every time, Howard. There's always a ruck between us and the Lebanese mob when I'm there. Never really understood it. Lucky no one got hurt, as it happens.'

'I thought someone got knifed?'

'That was at the show, not the bar. Nothing to do with us. Some domestic squabble from what I could make out. Anyway, next time we team up you can have my knuckleduster and I'll smoke the joint.'

Bernie Davies joined us. 'All right, butt? You going to Glastonbury next month? It's a first-class line-up they've got – Rod Stewart, Coldplay and of course our lads from the valleys, the Stereophonics and Alabama 3.'

'Not this year, Bernie. Funnily enough, I'm off to Brazil – doing some more research on the Welsh.'

'Old Henry Morgan got out there too, did he?'

'I don't think he did, but I'll check. I'm giving Henry Morgan a break. The reason I'm going to Brazil is I found out the Welsh had a colony there.'

'I never knew Patagonia was in Brazil.'

'You're right, it's not; it's in Argentina. So you know about Patagonia then?'

'Of course, butt. My ancestors on my father's side were the first ones there, apparently. I was thinking of going out myself to try to track down some rich relatives.'

'I'll be going there sometime, too, for sure. We could go together. We must talk about this.'

'Excuse me for interrupting,' said a soft voice, 'but did I

hear you say you were going to Brazil? My name's Jim Shreim, a friend of Nick Reynolds. And this is Michael Biggs, Ronnie's son.' I shook hands with them and offered my sympathy to Michael. Jim had a warm smiling face with a hint of the Middle East. Michael too seemed pleasant but also burdened with concern. 'Because if you are going,' continued Jim, 'you must look me up. I live in Rio, in Santa Teresa, right around the corner from Ronnie's house. I'll give you a great time, I promise.'

The previous week I had filed my article on Panama with the *Observer*. It was well reviewed and some time later won a prize in the Latin America Travel Association's competition for travel writer of the year. The piece had taken me a long time to finish, and I had let socialising and my research into the Welsh slip. London was a bad place to focus on writing; there were far too many distractions. It was just as well I was moving.

The next evening, equipped with a massive hangover, I settled myself into my newly rented apartment in Piccadilly Plaza, York, where essential conveniences such as electricity, telephone and broadband had just been installed. I had chosen York to be near my mother, now in worsening health and living with my sister in Richmond, Yorkshire. My belongings, hastily jammed into a rented van in Shepherd's Bush that morning, arrived safely. I unpacked my books on Wales and the Welsh and the notes I had made, and over the next few days tried to come to grips with what I knew.

My mother had always said that before the Roman invasion all Britain was Welsh from top to bottom and that after the collapse of the Roman empire, the Welsh reigned again through King Arthur. The ages darkened, and hordes of Teutonic Angles, Saxons and Vikings did their best to destroy the Welsh. Merlin said not to worry; a Welsh king riding a red dragon would be back on Britain's throne within the next millennium.

In 1066 England was invaded by the Normans, who under William the Conqueror then slowly pushed the troublesome Welsh into the mountains of the west, trying to contain them with an impressive chain of castles. The Welsh refused to give up and after two centuries of fighting the Plantagenet King Henry III granted Llewelyn ap Gruffudd the title of prince of Wales. Once again the Welsh were able to govern their territories under their own laws and conduct affairs in their own language, but this lasted just a few years. Edward I, determined to unite all the islands of Britain, sought to destroy the prince of Wales. At first Llewelyn did well: castles fell into his hands, and he routinely beat off or destroyed large English forces, who had to devote all their resources to dealing with the malicious, accursed Welsh. Late one lonely night a mugger who had no idea of the prince's identity robbed and killed Llewelyn. The English took control of Wales, attempting to conciliate the Welsh by awarding the title of prince of Wales to the sovereign's first-born son. Challenges to English rule occasionally occurred, most notably the revolt of Owain Glyndwr, but for the next two centuries Wales lived under an alien political system as a subordinate and integral part of the kingdom of England.

White-rosed Yorkist Richard III was the last of the 300-year-old Plantagenet dynasty. He lost his life and the last battle of the Wars of the Roses in 1485 at Bosworth Field, killed by red-rosed Lancastrian Henry Tudor, grandson of Owen Tudor, a Welshman. Henry was duly crowned and Merlin's prophecy had been fulfilled: the red dragon had killed the white and a Welsh king was on Britain's throne. And so the Welsh, represented by Henry VIII and Elizabeth I, presided over a unique century of literary genius, scientific discovery, naval victories, colonisation, exploration and piracy. However, despite Henry VIII's heroic efforts to continue the line, Elizabeth I's virginity resulted in the extinction of the house of Tudor and Wales declined into the status of a region of

England with a funny forgotten past, occasionally visited by culture-vulture nationalists playing dirges on harps in draughty pavilions.

Many Welsh families, convinced that England was intent on destroying their religious, cultural and economic freedom, turned their backs on the country and looked west, beyond Ireland, beyond the Atlantic, to America. During the seventeenth and eighteenth centuries Welsh settlements spread on the west side of the Schuylkill River around Philadelphia, where Welsh became the major tongue in the streets and Welsh names adorned large tracts of land. Today, the still very-active Welsh Society of Philadelphia is the oldest ethnic society of its kind in the United States. Welsh emigration to the Americas continued, and during the nineteenth century extended to Australia and South America.

Optimistically, I surfed the Net. Using the keywords Wales and Brazil, I ploughed through several hundred accounts of football matches and entries about a samba class in Cardiff before finding out that in 1850 a group of 200 Welsh people from Glamorgan gathered by Evan Evans of Nantyglo had settled in the Brazilian province of Rio Grande do Sul intending to establish a Welsh colony. As far as I could discover, this was the first attempt by the Welsh to settle anywhere in South America, but there was no further information. Further surfing provided the following reference: *A volume from the library of H. Tobit Evans, Llanarth, comprising reports by Captain W. R. Kennedy on the Welsh Colony of Chupat, Brazil.* I keyed 'Chupat Brazil' into a score of different search engines but came up with nothing other than this same item. I would have to wait until I got to Brazil; leaving matters to chance continues to be the favoured alternative of risk-takers. It was time I made travel plans.

Several times in Panama and Jamaica I had found myself regretting not having a video camera. There had also been times when a mosquito net, Swiss army knife, and sun-protection lotion would have come in handy. On this trip I would ensure I was well equipped. Unpacking my possessions in York provided the ideal opportunity to ensure I overlooked nothing essential. I opened a large box full of useless travelling accessories and so-called requisites: a receiver capable of eavesdropping on pilots' conversations, radio alarm clocks, currency converters, pocket translators, scientific calculators and various other gadgets which either had never worked, stopped working or been condemned to the graveyard of objects no longer in style. I once bought a professional-looking box of about fifty telephone adaptors and short cables, meant to enable me to download emails from any hotel room in the world, and then stayed for almost two weeks in hotel chains that had their own incomprehensible switchboard systems. First I assembled the adaptors, SIM cards and chargers for my mobile, personal organiser and other electronic crutches. I usually forget or lose at least one accessory and often bring a couple more for gadgets lost on my previous trip. I tested them all but few of them passed, so the next day I familiarised myself with the city of York's retail outlets by buying a top-of-the-range digital video camera, more chargers and adaptors, a mosquito net and a traveller's first aid kit. Then I got a bit carried away and bought a compass, torch, mountain boots, sunhat, sleeping bag and rucksack. Guidebooks, toiletries and clothes filled the rest of my suitcase.

I knew from my schooldays that the Portuguese had colonised Brazil. Although Panama was close, I had never been to South America and never anywhere Portuguese-speaking. I reasoned it might make some perverse sense to go to Brazil via Portugal. To recapture the age of exploration, I would travel the same route – although five miles higher and fifty times faster – as Pedro Álvares Cabral, who had sailed from Lisbon in an attempt to reach India. He gave the deadly calm waters off the coast of west Africa a wide berth and landed at Bahia, a province of today's Brazil.

Some 500 years later, on the hottest day of August 2002, I flew from London to Lisbon and stayed there a couple of days to practise using my video camera and visit the museums of Portuguese navigation. The extraordinary success of fifteenth-century Portuguese exploration and later colonisation is credited to the country's pivotal position on the Atlantic and the work of Prince Henry the Navigator. Adviser to King Alfonso V, Henry persuaded him to invest in shipbuilding, discovery, navigation and cartography. Portugal first colonised the Atlantic islands of Madeira and the Azores then went on, led by Vasco da Gama, to round the Cape of Good Hope and grab a chunk of India. Then Cabral discovered Brazil.

I went to a travel agency in the city centre. As I expected, I had the choice of flying with either the Portuguese or Brazilian national airlines. The flights were the same price. Usually when faced with such a choice, I opt for the airline of the country to which I'm travelling to experience the flavour of my destination as soon as possible. On this occasion, however, I thought it more in keeping with my theme of following fifteenth-century exploration routes to hold on to Portugal as long as possible. I caught a TAP flight to Salvador, the capital of Bahia.

Back in 1500 Cabral had landed in a mountainous paradise whose riverbanks yielded a hardwood of a reddish colour reminiscent of glowing coals or brasa. The land eventually became known as Brazil, but others, who in those times of massive navigational errors were referred to as Indians, had got there first. The Indians had not discovered the wheel and were technologically primitive. When one of them died, the corpse was hung from a tree until dry and then burned. The ashes were mixed with bananas and eaten by friends and family to preserve the spirit. Enemies were eaten without cremation.

But this cannibalism had nothing to do with hunger; there was always plenty of food. The land was ideal for growing sugar cane, and Indians were captured to slave on the plantations established by the Portuguese. Some fled to the vast interior, more died through brutality and disease, but enough took an 'If you can't beat them join them' attitude. The Portuguese settled comfortably at the river mouths, had frequent and varied types of intercourse with the Indians, and supported themselves magnificently by exporting sugar, liquor and tobacco, and importing slaves from Africa and guns and luxury goods from Europe. Gold, diamonds, coffee and rubber were then discovered; these required a larger slave workforce from Africa and the total number of slaves reached four million.

In 1808 the Portuguese prince regent, hearing that Napoleon was on his way to Lisbon, gathered his gang together, fled to Brazil, loved it, and decided to stay, making Brazil the only colony with a resident European monarch. The kingdom became an empire, but despite its prosperity and the eventual abolition of slavery, the monarchy was replaced by a federal republic in 1889. Its citizens inherited a country that produced every mineral, a climate that could grow any crop, and a population drawn from Amerindians, Portuguese and other Europeans and Africans.

At least Cabral had had the advantage of arriving at Salvador, the capital of Bahia and for over 200 years that of Brazil, without suffering the exhausting and disorienting effects of jet lag, nicotine withdrawal and a hangover. I arrived at the Hotel di Roma knackered. Within minutes of checking in, I fell asleep, but an impatient cock's crow woke me long before dawn.

I grabbed my cigarettes. Palm leaves scratched the wall outside in a disturbing rhythm. The moon still shone weakly through the shutter slats and threw its light on a transparent lizard hunting a spider the size of a small saucer. Despite usually championing the underdog, I wanted the lizard to eat that spider. I wondered why I was more disturbed by insects than reptiles. I lit a cigarette. The lizard and spider immediately disappeared. Cats padded across the roof, each step pregnant with anticipated conflict.

Fading moonlight gave way to bright sunshine as a chorus of roosters squawked raucously. A tropical rainstorm wiped out their din and the rhythm of the scratching palm. Ripe fruit thudded on the roof while dogs barked and children laughed as flash floods of sunshine punctuated the torrential downpour. I opened the shutters and blinked at a narrow irregular dusty street of tall colonial houses and villas with red-tiled roofs and walls painted in pink, green, blue and yellow washes. It looked like Lisbon. Joggers criss-crossed the cobbles on their way to the sandy waterfront, where fishermen mended nets and bikinied beauties drank from coconuts. Nearby were ornate places of worship, shopping malls and brick-built shanty towns. Distant high-rises sparkled like sugar cubes above opulent baroque facades, spires and domes. A fifteenth-century whitewashed church stood out like a cardboard silhouette. Salvador, a bit too dangerous and decadent, used to be the place for tourists to avoid, but was now beginning to reap the benefits of travellers' appetites for something different and well away from terrorist targets. Scantily clad holiday-makers were already packing the bars, from which samba blasted and where the booze, particularly *cachaça*, is dirt cheap and always available.

Downstairs, the bounty of Brazilian nature overflowed from the breakfast buffet trays. There were pitchers of freshly squeezed fruit juice, plates of papaya, mangoes and pine-apples, bowls of warm tapioca, sweet milk and cinnamon, cakes, rolls, jam and coffee. I ate until exhausted, then sat in the sun to finish my coffee, smoke a cigarette and possibly drop off.

A man with a gentle manner and a face full of smiles came to my table. 'Excuse me, but I know you are the one who wrote *Mr Nice*, which I very much enjoyed despite my poor

English. My name is Gilberto. I am a photographer and often work for British publications. If you need anyone to help show you around Salvador, it would be my pleasure. In fact, tomorrow I am driving to Cachoeira. You are welcome to join me.'

I had read about Cachoeira, which means waterfall. A river port not far from Salvador where, 200 years ago, gold prospectors and merchants disembarked to load their possessions on to ox carts for exploration further inland. Ships sailing back direct into Lisbon took away their valuable finds.

'Thank you, Gilberto, that's kind of you. I would love to come. Perhaps you could also help me in another way.'

'It would be my pleasure.'

'Do you know anything about the existence here of a Welsh community?'

'I know you are Welsh, of course, but you are probably the only one here in Salvador. There is certainly no Welsh community in this city, and I don't think in the whole Bahia province.'

'What about in Brazil?'

'Well, Brazil is so big, anything is possible, but I have never heard of one. When did the Welsh come here and why? To be missionaries and compete against the Catholics?'

'There might well have been a bit of that, but their main motive was to get away from the English and set up their own colony with their own religion, language and culture. The Welsh seemingly set one up in Brazil a hundred and fifty years ago.'

'How would they have supported themselves?'

'Either by tilling the land or digging holes in it to mine minerals, I suppose.'

'It is true that many miners came from Europe to Bahia looking for work around that time, mainly to Lencóis to the diamond mines.'

'How far away is that?'

'At least a day's drive. I can't take you myself, I'm afraid; I have to be at my office every day. But there is a bus that goes there a few times a week.'

The next afternoon Gilberto picked me up from the hotel and drove off at a pace worthy of Ayrton Senna. We were quickly on the old plantation road to Cachoeira.

'I love this place: the colours, the river, the mountains, the light and the people. Cachoeira is my second home and the only home of Irmandade da Nossa Senhora da Boa Morte – the Sisterhood of Our Lady of the Good Death.'

'Sounds a bit heavy, Gilberto.'

'It is. African religions are best preserved far away from suntan oil, beaches and volleyball games. Supporting them is my greatest passion, my life's work.'

At Cachoeira's bustling market goats anxiously hoped to evade sacrifice; cotton-stuffed voodoo dolls in colourful costumes dangled next to displays of vegetables, fruits, cheeses, spices, oils, juices, bulls' brains and unidentified pigs' organs. In the old days, the slave owners ate the meat and left their slaves with balls, offal and brains, resulting in a national cuisine now served everywhere, including the country's most expensive restaurants. Wearing billowy cotton skirts and a lacy turban and tunic, an imperious mahogany lady with dancing eyes, high rouged cheekbones, an aquiline nose and languid hands covered a makeshift table with a white fringed cloth and set out several shiny tin pans of prawns, batter, dried beans, nutmeg, coconut milk, cashews and peanuts. By her side a cauldron of palm oil, heated by burning coconut shells, bubbled erratically. Beads, crosses and chains swung from her neck, and silver and wooden bracelets weighed down her arms as she fashioned batter and beans into pretty lumps of cholesterol and nectar.

Gilberto and I walked away from the market up a quiet lane and knocked on the door of a humble home bearing a white flag. Dona Filinha de Leman-Ja, the hundred-year-old high priestess of the Sisterhood of the Good Death opened the door, grabbed me and gave me an enormous tight hug. 'We have the same blood in all our veins. You are so welcome.'

We entered Dona Filinha's soothsaying room, a china-shop of miniature bulls. Flagstones of five- and six-pointed stars shone from the floor. Sixteen shells lay on a white towel ready for divination. A massive mural of a beautiful mermaid emerging from the sea hung on one wall. On another hung a painting of a sexy squaw in the most revealing of feathered miniskirts fondling a jaguar while being watched by a monkey peeping Tom. She wore yellow knickers.

'Don't worry, Howard; personal interpretation is highly encouraged. Bond all you can in any way possible. There is no judgement or disapproval. It is all OK. And it will all get better. Now I have to bargain with Dona Filinha. She raises money for the sisterhood by modelling white robes and necklaces and bracelets of shells to satisfy photographers like me.'

We went to the kitchen of the church of the sisterhood. Food cooked here is highly sought after and given freely – sacrificed but not wasted. Outside, popcorn crackled, fireworks exploded and priestesses broke out in song, lighting cigarettes and puffing furiously. One sang a samba, enjoying the everyday naughtiness of the lyrics. No one bowed, signed the cross or genuflected, or showed any sign of humility. Exuding love and fond respect, the priestesses winked, hugged, kissed, held hands and flirted. One asked if I was single.

'I like this religion, Gilberto.'

'Then tonight, I take you to a Candomblé ceremony. Let's go back to the car.'

Brazil has more Roman Catholics than any other country, but large numbers convert from Catholicism to Afro-Brazilian cults. Candomblé is the religion of the Yoruba from Nigeria, the provider of more slaves to the New World than any other

African tribe. According to Candomblé, mankind sprang from a single ancestor, some of whose descendants achieved divinity and were able to control disease, weather, the power of the oceans and other natural forces. Everyone has a spiritual guide, a protective *orixá* and during ceremonial trances, such as the one I was about to witness, the *orixá*s' spiritual energy enters their protégés. Candomblé deities vary from humans with horns and erect penises to mischievous entities who delight in destroying happy marriages and promoting venereal disease. Transvestite and homosexual gods abound: one is the son of two male gods, another is male for half the year and female for the other half.

The Portuguese prohibited Candomblé and force-fed their slaves Catholicism, so its devotees concealed their *orixá*s in the identities of Roman Catholic saints, continuing their African religion by covering it with a veneer of Christian ritual. And in due course Roman Catholic saints and *orixá*s were honoured side by side, each gradually taking on the identity of the other.

Candomblé ceremonies are organised on *terreiros*, terraces or cleared plots of land near houses or small farms. Gilberto stopped his car outside a sprawling complex of huts and buildings decorated with glittering fairy lights named Bate Folha – Hitting Leaves – and walked past a few shrines towards the church. Birds swinging gently in cages suspended from trees nipped enthusiastically at pieces of fresh fruit. Leaves of differing shape, colour and significance, carefully split apples and stiff dark banana peel covered the ground. A paper plate of dried corn kernels, cooked beans and flour lay at the intersection of two dirt paths. A candle sat upright in the plate, and an empty bottle of sugar cane rum lay alongside it. Several unlucky but ecstatic worshippers surrounded the church, which was crammed.

Inside, fringed white crêpe-paper flags covered the ceiling. Vases of flowers, a statue of the Virgin Mary, a brown bottle of water, ceramic dishes and paper bags of bread covered an altar in which were hidden stones containing the spirits of the devotees. Several young brides of the gods glided in like gentle, nervous waves. They wore white lacy blouses and colourful graceful skirts to just above their ankles. Scarves tightly wrapped their heads, stressing the dark bold beauty of their full faces and graceful cheekbones. Confident elderly women, supervising the ceremony, approached the girls, placed their hands on their shoulders, and gave advice and comfort.

Suddenly each of two drummers enthusiastically and ferociously attacked his conga drum. Their fingers frantically hit the leather, and the church exploded into an enveloping rhythm of wild percussion. The church doors were flung open, and an elderly priest, dressed in a white suit, white shirt, white tie, white socks and shoes, shuffled in slowly but still in perfect time to the rhythm. Following him were women dressed in carnival clothes sporting their hair in tight oiled curls, free-flowing waves and straight manes, as well as men dressed as scarecrows, trees and other plants. No one wore ordinary clothes. The brides of the gods began to dance with light steps, lifting their elbows and undulating their ribcages. Slipping into trances as if falling asleep, some nodded while others let the persistent drums take them over. Dreamy-eyed and well out of it, they danced extraordinarily gracefully while thrashing, shuddering, sweating heavily, swaying and sinking to their knees. The older women caught them before they dropped and eased them down.

One beautiful, slim girl collapsed with her head falling forward. Her turban slipped off, letting loose her wavy hair. One of the elderly women gently picked her up, pulled her locks away from her sweaty neck and helped her to the altar. The priest puffed his cigar, took her hand, twirled her in circles and enveloped her in clouds of smoke to identify the spirit. Names of various *orixá*s murmured through the knowing congregation.

The drummers' rhythm became frantic. With eyes rolled up and spit dribbling from their mouths, people whooped, shuddered, whirled around the floor, sang samba songs while making the sign of the cross, ran back and forth, and bounced off the walls. The all-in-white granny first aid team mopped brows, shouted and applauded. The church was metamorphosing into a rave club, and I was beginning to feel as if I had taken ecstasy: loving the beat, loving everyone. I suddenly understood it all: the importance of music, pretty clothes and food; the reverence for extravagance and embellishment.

A man in a straw suit stamped his feet and lunged forward, hooting and whirling around with his dark loose curls flopping over his eyes and the sweat flinging off his skin. With eyes half-closed, he began to waver. An old woman led him to the aisle as he jerked violently and then began spinning, elegantly bending forward and sweeping the air with his curved arm. He stopped, dazed, and the woman gently guided him back to his seat, took his face in her hands and chanted some words. Practitioners sitting on the sidelines sauntered up, cradled his face and blessed him as well. The priest picked up a small boy and lifted him high enough for the crêpe-paper fringe on the ceiling to tickle his face and provoke a cosmic grin. The ceremony ended as everyone returned to a waking state – happy, relieved, sweaty and shiny-faced. They stroked each other's hair, embraced, tucked into the sacrificed food and walked out into the night.

Gilberto and I joined the silent but jubilant exodus into the gentle night air. I confessed to him that the experience had left me emotionally and psychologically drained and asked if he knew of a hotel in Cachoeira at which I could stay. The place had exerted a hold on me, and I felt unable to leave without experiencing the dawn. Gilberto said he understood exactly how I felt and drove me to the Pousada do Convento de Cachoeira, a former convent set around a courtyard with a swimming pool. Although the hotel was fully booked, the manager knew Gilberto well and was eager to please. Gilberto and I exchanged telephone numbers as he and the manager led me to a room with frayed-wire spaghetti hanging from the roof beams. I thanked him warmly and promised to stay in touch.

I lay on the sagging, creaking metal-framed bed as feelings of unease and disturbance seeped into my psyche. I had never given speaking in tongues any credibility, yet now I had witnessed it fully. Was the rest of Candomblé also for real? It made sense that the religion of the first humans in Africa would also be the truest. I thought of my mother's failing health and the inevitability of her death. I felt frightened and alone, then comforted and happy, then terrified. There was no chance of sleep. The magic of dawn helped lift my anxiety, as did the hotel's breakfast, but I was still filled with trepidation and premonitions of impending doom as I boarded the bus back to Salvador.

On arrival, I walked to the Hotel di Roma to freshen up and reassure the staff I had not done a runner. There was a message from Gilberto that he would call at the hotel about 8.00 that evening. I decided to spend the day sightseeing and visited the city's oldest part, the Largo de Pelhourinho, a sloping square along the top of which is a building which has been converted to a museum dedicated to Brazil's best-known author, Jorge Amado. *Pelhourinho* means whipping post. This square once witnessed the daily torture, selling and whipping of slaves but now celebrated their emancipation by frequent processions of African drummers and dancers streaming from the Bar do Reggae. The drumming reminded me of last night's Candomblé and I decided to phone my sister to find out how my mother was faring.

Despite my pre-travel preparations, my mobile rarely registered a signal strong enough to make calls, so I bought a telephone card, strolled down to the seafront, and approached a row of phone boxes. A young beggar caught hold of my arm and asked for money. I refused and picked up the phone. On my third attempt to dial my head was suddenly rammed into the phone box, and I felt consciousness slipping away. A hand grabbed me around the neck and another tore off my gold chain. I struggled to my feet just in time to see my precious gold Buddha glinting in the hands of the young beggar as he sprinted towards the side streets.

My mind flashed back twenty years. I was staying at the Bangkok Peninsula Hotel, and it was my custom to visit the nearby Erawan Hotel, the site of the Erawan Buddha, on a Friday evening. There were many accidents during the hotel's construction and to stop the deaths labourers placed a Buddha in the corner of the construction site. The deaths ceased, and the Buddha become an important shrine for those praying for upward mobility. When there I would usually see my friend Sompop, a flower seller I had befriended and to whom I would sometimes give money.

On one occasion he said, 'Sawabdee, Kuhn Marks, sawabdee, Kuhn Marks. I have Buddha for you. Please wear always.' Sompop had given me what looked like an antique bronze coin, but it clearly wasn't currency. 'Wear always, Kuhn Marks, except when with woman or when in toilet or when in bath, mai dee. Wear in sea or lake is OK, dee mak mak. No harm come to you, Kuhn Marks. You have good luck. Buddha look after you. Now we buy gold chain for Buddha from my friend. Wear always, Kuhn Marks.'

We went to a Bangkok jeweller, got the Buddha gilded, and chose for it a large gold chain.

I put my hand in my pocket for some money. Sompop stopped me and asked me to give it to the poor children.

Since then, the Buddha had been my lucky charm, constantly around my neck except when I was in prison, in bed with a woman or in the bathroom. Now it was gone. I was devastated, angry and convinced that bad luck was on its way. Terrified, I called my sister and learned that my mother although no better was stable. But my worries remained.

That evening I described my unhappy experience and fears to Gilberto.

'Howard, this is common after Candomblé ceremonies, especially when experiencing them for the first time. Don't forget it is the Sisterhood of Good Death. Energies and forces that we usually suppress or deny roam freely in our mind on these occasions. Coincidences do not exist; there is just what is. We call some events coincidences because we know we do not understand them and cannot explain them by what we think is knowledge. Once we think we understand them and think we can explain them, we don't call them coincidences any longer; we give them other names like magnetism, gravity, schizophrenia and God. But they are still simply what they are. Our theories may change over time, but what is remains the same. I know from *Mr Nice* you have studied the philosophy of science. What does gravity explain? Nothing. It is just a name for falling to the floor. The name might change, but things still fall.'

'I know all that, Gilberto; Galileo said the same. And I know that time changes magic first into one science then another. And I know that all scientific theories except some recent ones have been proven to be wrong, so even these recent theories will one day also be proven wrong. But from where do I get this feeling of fear?'

'It is the fear of death.'

'But I am not afraid of death, Gilberto – at least not of my own.'

'What about the death of someone you love?'

'Yes, I am afraid of my mother's death. She is very ill.'

'It's the same. If she is to die, her death must be good. The fear you have is escaping. You must let it go and take no further comfort in your denial.'

'And I am afraid of life without my Buddha; it has been with me for so long. It has saved my life. It is my protection.'

'I am not Buddhist, Howard, but your Buddha, does it

teach you how much control you have over events or how little?'

'How little.'

'Then you have learned your lesson. Your Buddha has moved on to protect someone needing it more than you do.'

'But I let it go through carelessness.'

'Only if you thought you were in control. Forget your Buddha; it was never yours. It found you. It will now find someone else. Are you still interested in finding your Welsh community?'

'Yes, as much as ever. Why do you ask?'

'I have made some enquiries with my academic friends, and they say there has never been a significant Welsh presence in Bahia. However, you should go to Lençóis. It is an interesting place and, who knows, you might find someone of Welsh descent. Don't take the bus the entire way; go by boat and have a couple of days holiday. There is an idyllic island on the way.'

The following day, my fifty-seventh birthday, I caught the early ferry from Salvador to Morro São Paulo on the Ilha de Tinharé. The boat moved gently through the singularly beautiful bay of Bahia, its vast sweep ranging from luscious flora fringing its inlets to glimpses of the distant hills behind. The upper city sits on a steep bluff, eighty feet above the lower town, which occupies the narrow strip between the harbour and the cliff. Soon we entered the turbulent open sea. The trip took about four hours, and I blessed the seasickness pills I had brought from my first aid kit. Landing was nevertheless a welcome relief.

Tinharé has no cars, no industrial noise, no hassle. The beaches are named One, Two and Three. Wheelbarrows carry ferry passengers' luggage through lanes littered with bars, restaurants, Internet cafés and money changers. Delicious crab dishes were on sale everywhere, except at my hotel, which was a crab sanctuary. The hotel's gardens were full of hummingbirds and monkeys, and blue crabs constantly darting in and out of holes in the ground.

As dusk fell, I ventured into a forest of palm trees encircling a Candomblé sanctuary. Between the palm trunks were tree ferns rising to twenty feet and a bewildering profusion of hanging, climbing and parasitic plants, which girdled the boughs with flowers. Then black and white spirits and goblins began to haunt the quiet night. Huge swarms of bats filled the sky. I rushed out to the nearest light, a reggae bar on the beach, and worked my way through several glasses of *cachaça*, eventually achieving a feeling of well-being. I spent the next day in a hammock watching the crabs.

Two days later and well rested, I took the short boat trip from Morro Sao Paolo to the busy port of Valença and climbed aboard a bus to begin the six-hour haul inland to Lencóis. I swallowed some seasickness pills so I could read without feeling dizzy while the bus bounced through the Sertão, north-eastern Brazil's vast and fiercely hot semi-arid interior. Larger than any European country and dominated by rocks, cactus and circling hawks, its soils are poor, and rainfall sparse and irregular. Mere showers cause astonishing transformations: trees immediately bud, cacti burst into flower, shoots appear, and the ground changes colour from brown to green. After a climb, we entered the Chapada Diamantina – the Diamond Highlands. Views of deep valleys, tall isolated peaks, open high plains, shady canyons, cold mountain streams and spectacular waterfalls flanked us all the way to Lencóis, the Queen of the Mines.

Until 1732 India was the world's only known source of diamonds. At first, the diamonds discovered in Brazil were believed to be fake, so the Portuguese took them to Macau and passed them off as Indian. By the mid-nineteenth century, however, Brazilian diamonds had been judged genuine and Lencóis was a boom town infested with criminals, fugitives and adventurers, diamond merchants and the usual service personnel – hookers and the rest. Shops and banks lined the streets. Then the diamonds became scarce and another source was discovered in South Africa. The boom town became a ghost town and stayed that way until seventeen years ago, when an American geologist, Roy Funch, happened to pass through Lencóis and fall in love with it. Almost single-handedly, Roy succeeded in persuading the authorities to turn the Diamond Highlands into a national park. Tonight, he was giving a talk at the Cantos dos Aquas hotel, where I was about to check in.

Roy Funch praised the beauties of the Diamond Highlands, their multicoloured sand caves, riverbeds of millions of tiny white shells, Indian petroglyphs carved into limestone walls, preserved skeletons of giant ground sloths and natural rockslides feeding clear deep natural swimming pools. He spoke of the myths associated with the region's rivers such as the *bicho da agua* – a creature, part animal, part man that walks on the bottom of the river and snores loudly when asleep.

Roy also warned of real dangers should you go trekking. Swamps and rivers – one named the River of the Bats – hosted alligators and pig-sized water rats. Pools provided fertile breeding grounds for rare and deadly bacteria. There were coral snakes that liked to bite fingers, poisonous rattlesnakes that liked to keep quiet, and vipers that just liked being venomous. In addition, there were bombardier beetles, tarantulas and scorpions. The sky was alive with wasps, stinging ants, mosquitoes, vampire bats and aggressive Africanised bees. My mountain boots and mosquito net would be staying in my rucksack.

I shook Roy's hand, introduced myself and thanked him for his talk.

'Howard, you look exactly like the only British resident of Lencóis.'

'Who's that?'

'Jimmy Page. I don't know anything about his music, and he knows nothing about geology, but we're good friends. It's a shame he spends just a few days a year here.'

If I had to blame anyone for my abandoning academia and following the path I had taken it would be Jimmy Page, possibly the best guitarist in the world. I spent an entire postgraduate academic year (1969–70) lying on the floor of a Brighton flat listening to Led Zeppelin, all of whose albums he produced.

Lençóis was small, and there was about a one in hundred chance Jimmy Page would be at home. But turning up like a groupie and ruining his holiday would not be cool. I would have to forget that and decided to walk around the streets that had once teemed with fugitive-filled bars, enticing whore-houses and shops selling Paris fashions. I ought to check the libraries and museums, if there were any, for evidence of the elusive Welsh. I walked up through the hilly town. A car coming the other way stopped. 'You look like a friend of mine. What's your name?' asked the gorgeous female passenger.

'Howard.'

'I thought so. I was lying, actually. You aren't really a friend of mine, but you could be.'

The driver's door opened, and Jimmy Page emerged with an outstretched hand. 'I've read your book, *Mr Nice*.'

I was about to say I'd listened to all his tunes at least a million times but ended up just grinning sheepishly. We arranged to meet for a drink later at the town's central bar.

We drank and talked about ourselves and drank and talked about everything else. At one point drums began to beat furiously outside, and a circle of people surrounded four barefoot young men gripping six-foot bamboo sticks who performed a sequence of martial art movements in a graceful dance form known as Capoeira. Jimmy explained how escaped slaves, realising they would have to defend themselves with their hands and feet, created a style of self-defence to give them a chance against swords and firearms. Recaptured slaves blended these combat moves with long-remembered ritual dances, such as that performed by Angolan males to gain the right to a woman when she reached puberty, and added musical accompaniment. The dance disguise worked for a while but was inevitably discovered, and Capoeira was outlawed in Brazil until 1928, when it became accepted as a sport and art form.

Two Capoeiristas exchange attack and defence movements in a constant flow, observing the rituals and manners of the art. Each tries to control the dance space by confusing his opponent with feints, the speed of the ritualised combat being determined by the many different rhythms of the *berimbau* – a one-stringed musical bow – handclaps and the tambourine. Capoeira is the art of facing danger with a smile on one's face, and a good Capoeirista will face his opponent confidently, but never so guardedly as to inhibit the flow of the game or the expression of the beauty and integrity of his personality. The game serves as a metaphor for life, which requires you to negotiate treachery every day. A careless attitude in life can be disastrous, but an overprotective attitude will stop the flow of vitality, making life static and miserable. The only way to understand the fluid character of Capoeira – or indeed the game of life it mirrors – is to step into the ring with the commitment to push one's limits and see beyond the game itself.

We were well slaughtered when the bouts finished.

'Do you get back to Wales much, Howard?'

'A few visits a year.'

'Have you been to Cardiff Castle?'

'Of course, several times. You?'

'Yes, but so far I haven't been able to get inside it. Mind, I haven't tried since 1973, when the band was on tour there. There just hasn't been time.'

'I saw the gig. It was at the Capitol, which is now a shopping centre and multiscreen cinema.'

'I think you're right; I'm not sure. Remembering tour details is difficult. But I know I stayed immediately opposite the castle at the Angel Hotel.'

'That's still there.'

'But they were renovating bits of it, and visitors weren't allowed.'

'Why the interest; are you keen on castles generally?'

'Not particularly, but the architect who redesigned the interior and exterior of Cardiff Castle, giving it all those towers, pinnacles and stuff, was William Burges. I think he's the best architect ever. He was a friend of William Morris and the Pre-Raphaelite Brotherhood, which I was well into in the old days. In fact, my London house Burges built as his own home. You having another drink?'

'Sure. So you plan to try again?'

More chilled beer arrived.

'Funnily enough, today, just before I met you, I was on the phone to Matthew Williams, the curator of Cardiff Castle. He's writing a book on Burges and wants to have a look at my place. I agreed provided I got a personal tour of the castle. I'll be over there in a couple of months. Let's exchange phone numbers. I'd like to come to one of your shows; I've heard they're hilarious.'

'I'd be thrilled if you did.'

'Don't you get a lot of 1960s has-been rock stars coming along?'

'Yes, but they disappear without coming to say hello. I don't think they like it backstage.'

'Well, the thrill does wear off. It's nice just to be a spectator sometimes, like just now with these Capoeira kids.'

'Why did you choose Lencóis as a home?'

'You can blame my wife for that. She's Brazilian and loves the place. I love it too now, as you can gather.'

During the early 1990s Jimmy and his wife Jimena tirelessly

involved themselves in charitable projects to help and support children and pregnant teenage girls living on the streets of Brazil. Since witnessing an armoured invasion of a shanty town, Jimmy has worked to relieve the plight of Rio's street children. He and his wife associated themselves with Task Brasil, to whom he has made massive donations, including Casa Jimmy, a home for abandoned children in the hilltop district of Rio de Janeiro's Santa Teresa, the same area now lived in by Jim Shreim and at one time by Ronnie Biggs. Fund-raising concerts have provided further money, as have sales of rare rock memorabilia.

We drank another beer as twilight joined us. Ropes of fairy lights twinkled as the sun disappeared behind the hills. Night stallholders displayed their crochet, lacework, trinkets and bottles of coloured sand collected from nearby lake and river beaches. Scores of people of all ages poured into the streets and bars, singing, laughing, dancing and lighting small bonfires.

'Do Brazilians like all music?

'Pretty much. They definitely revere the British sixties stuff. Techno confuses them a bit. They like it if they can dance the samba to it, which they usually can. I'm working with some Brazilian musicians now. In fact, tomorrow I have to go to their recording studio. I never seem to be in Lençóis long enough. Do you need any help in your search for the Welsh? I know most people here. I'll ask around tonight.'

Jimmy disappeared into the dark streets. I didn't hear from him before he left Lençóis, and I doubt if he ever came to any of my shows, but he remains the most talented and genuine 1960s rock idol I have met.

The next morning I went to the Lanchonete Zacão, a photographic gallery that served food, and consumed a breakfast of several different fruit juices, cheese-filled balls of dough and manioc pancakes. I scoured through the old photographs and asked the waiter where I could find information on the names of people who lived in Lencóis years ago. He suggested I visit the town's two churches and the *prefeitura municipal*. I did so but despite examining numerous lists of house owners, mine employees and the usual birth, marriage and death registers did not encounter a single Welsh name. After lunch and a few *cachaças*, I decided to abandon my search. If there ever was a Welsh community here, it had long petered out and left no trace. Maybe they gave up singing hymns, learned the samba and immediately integrated. Who could blame them? In any event, it was time I went to Rio. I had been expected there two days before.

The bus bounced me back to Salvador, where I had no wish to stay; I still couldn't forgive the place for stealing my Buddha. I took a cab to the airport and caught the next flight to Rio de Janeiro.

The city's name (River of January), the photographs of it I had seen over the years and its coastal location led me to believe that I would be landing near a substantial river estuary. Instead, the plane descended from above the Atlantic Ocean through a mile-wide channel between rocky promontories on which forts had been erected and touched down on the shores of a landlocked gulf twenty miles long and five to ten miles wide full of rocky islands of every imaginable shape and size. Only small streams entered this huge salty inlet, and whales were found basking in its brine. Why Portuguese explorer Gaspar de Lemos thought it was a river remains an enigma.

The city of Rio itself exudes confidence and cockiness as if proud of itself for having edged between the hills and the sea, met the jungle and trounced it. Gleaming with the complacence of a successful opportunist, it struts along the southern edge of the gulf shore for several miles, commanding all the space between the water and the mountains behind. These are clothed in luxuriant forest or rise in precipices of grey granite.

I checked into the over-the-top art deco Copacabana Palace, a favourite hotel of royalty and rock stars, and left a message on Jim Shreim's answerphone. I plugged in my laptop and checked for emails. There was one from Gilberto: 'Dear Howard, I hope you enjoyed your holiday and are now tasting the delights of Rio. It's a wonderful city. Today, I visited an old friend working at the Livraria Brandão, the biggest bookshop in Bahia, and found a book that seems to answer all your questions about the Welsh in Brazil. I was very surprised. Can you give me an address to send it to?' I intended to stay for at least a few days, so I gave Gilberto the address of the Copacabana Palace and then went out for a sunset stroll.

Mosaic pavements depicting rolling waves separated the hotel from the palm-fringed Copacabana Beach, which was staging sensual performances by what appeared to be a selection of Miss Universe finalists and male bodybuilding champions modelling the latest swimwear fashions. The musclemen provided daunting competition for any guys hoping to pull, but were heavily outnumbered by the women so you could continue your fantasies without fear of immediate failure and rejection.

I sat down at a beach bar and ordered a coconut full of milk and a *cachaça*. A voluptuous beauty wearing a G-string and two eggcups, whom normally I would ignore as being out of my league as a possible companion for the night, sat down opposite me, introduced herself as Rowena, ordered a drink and said she loved me. She enquired where I was staying and asked if she could escort me back to my hotel so we could have some fun. I was well up for it but felt I was being taken for a ride of the kind well known to anyone other than those who had first arrived in Rio some minutes before. I mumbled something about hotel rules forbidding non-residents from visiting guests' hotel rooms. She suggested using one of the many short-stay hotels just a few yards away. I shook my head. Rowena left, and her place was quickly taken by another top model, Laura, who trotted out the same line coupled with an offer to get me Viagra. I said I had an appointment, stood up, paid for my drinks, including the untouched ones ordered by Rosa and Paula, and returned to the Copacabana Palace, furiously cursing myself for having lost my youthful sense of adventure.

Jim Shreim had called in my absence. He would be busy with his film-making for most of the next day but would be free in the evening.

The next morning I walked swiftly away from Copacabana Beach and took a cab to the Biblioteca Nacional in Avenida Rio Branco, the largest public library in South America, and resolved not to leave there until I had followed through the Internet references to the Welsh in Brazil that I had discovered before coming to the country. I had just two place names to check, Rio Grande do Sul and Chupat. Rio Grande do Sul is Brazil's southernmost province, on the borders of Argentina and Uruguay. Its capital city, Porto Alegre, is the country's sixth-largest city. I turned the pages of every English book and skimmed through some Portuguese ones on Rio Grande do Sul, but there was no reference to anything Welsh. I pored over every large-scale map but couldn't find a single place name remotely linked to any Welsh word. The telephone directories carried every conceivable surname other than Welsh ones. The province appeared to have fewer Welsh connections than any other part of the world. The results for Chupat were even worse: the place simply did not feature in any map or publication. The library shut at 8.00 p.m. I left empty-handed. It seemed that as far as Brazil was concerned, Wales ceased to exist when Pelé knocked them out of the 1954 World Cup.

Jim Shreim was waiting for me in the hotel bar. We hugged each other and laughed.

'So you're here at last, Howard. Welcome to Rio. This is Johnny Pickston, a close friend of Ronnie and Michael Biggs.'

Johnny, a few years older than me but fitter despite having to use a walking stick, gripped my hand.

'Good to see you, Howard. Jimmy said he'd met you in London at the benefit gig for poor Ronnie. Blinding book, by the way. Got a copy for you to sign if you don't mind. So what brings you to Brazil? Not that anyone needs a reason. Look at these birds coming in. Beats Bognor, don't it?'

'Certainly does, Johnny. I'm impressed with what I've seen so far. The women are friendly.'

'And cheap.'

'I was going to ask you about that, but I mustn't get too distracted; I'm on a bit of a mission trying to track down Welsh people in Brazil.'

'I think Tom Jones came here a few times. Seriously, though, what do you mean?'

'Well I read months ago there used to be a Welsh colony in Brazil. I've spent all day today in the library, and it seems as if I'll have to go to Porto Alegre—'

'Don't mention that fucking place.'

'Is it that bad? It didn't look too great from the books I saw, I must admit.'

'I don't know about that, but Porto Alegre is where those dirty bastards who tried to kidnap Ronnie were pretending to make a film. They made out they were taking him there for a shoot, then stuck poor Ronnie in a bag and took him to Barbados. Me and me missus, Lia, were with Ronnie just before. We did all we could to get him back, and we did. Those dirty bastards, they ought to be shot. That's all I know about Porto Alegre. I won't go near the place.'

Jim Shreim tactfully changed the subject: 'You know the Super Furry Animals, don't you, Howard?'

'Sure I do. They're fellow Welshmen and amazing musicians. Why do you ask?'

'They're coming here soon. Maybe you could hook me up with them?'

Johnny chipped in: 'There you go, Howard. Wait here in Rio with us until the Welsh come to see you. You'll have a lot more fun than in Porto Alegre, I promise you. Is that a video camera you've got?'

'Yes it is, but I've hardly used it.'

'Can you video me with a message to Ronnie and get it to him?'

'Of course. You want to do it now?'

'I've got a better idea. Tomorrow I'll take you up Corcovado and we'll do it there. You should see it, anyway. Ronnie used to love the place. Tonight, we should go to Help – it's the biggest disco in South America. It's rammed wall-to-wall with hookers and will blow your mind, I guarantee. It's on the same street as your hotel here, the Avenida Atlantica.'

Whatever happened next took all night, and Johnny and I were as hungover and tired as we had ever been when our cab dropped us at Rua Cosme Velho, where a funicular train took us almost vertically up Corcovado to the 100-foot-high, 1,000-ton statue of Christ stretching out his arms in cosmopolitan welcome. I recorded Johnny's tearful and heartfelt video message to Ronnie Biggs. Then we threw coins into a shrine and silently made our private wishes – I prayed for the health and long life of my mother.

Gilberto's parcel was waiting for me at the reception desk of the Copacabana Palace. I opened it as soon as I was in my room. The book inside was *City of Frozen Fire* by Vaughan Wilkins. It concerned the nineteenth-century discovery in the forests of Brazil of a Welsh civilisation that, without the rest of the world's knowledge, had existed there since the twelfth century. At last I was on to something; my trip to Brazil was proving worthwhile.

Then came a voice message from my sister: my mother's health had taken a serious turn for the worse; she urged me to come home immediately.

Eight

BUSTED

Several months later I realised I would never escape from the trauma of my mother's death. I might become familiar with the loss, but I would not recover from it. For a while life became frighteningly empty and pointless. My capacity to concentrate evaporated, childhood memories filled my mind, and I looked forward to nothing. It seemed silly to carry on with the search for my ancestry when I had just lost the most precious part of it. Great-aunt Afon Wen had also passed away, with her cloudy memories of my Native American, smuggling and Welsh Druidic heritage. Great-aunt Katie was still alive, but her health was failing. My track record uncovering ancestors was poor; I had only found a new descendant.

I discovered the references to Chupat, Brazil I had found on the Net should have been to Chubut, Argentina. They related to Patagonia. I eventually read *City of Frozen Fire*, the book Gilberto had sent me in Rio de Janeiro, and it was indeed about the discovery of an ancient Welsh civilisation in the forests of Brazil; Paulo Coelho's recollection had been correct. But it was a poorly written fictional boys' adventure story providing nothing of interest and plenty of disappointment. I continued living in York, waking up early every morning, walking around the city walls, breakfasting at British Home Stores and returning to my flat with a firm resolve to resume writing. But the blank screen just got blanker. I stopped doing my column for *Loaded*; I couldn't even write 1,000 words a month.

I could, however, still manage to do shows, and I plagued my tireless manager Giles Cooper to get me as many gigs as possible, as this was now my only source of income. I performed in Amsterdam, Oslo, Moscow, the Channel Islands and Tenerife. I did spoken-word tours of Germany, Italy, Spain, the Republic of Ireland and the United Kingdom, doing shows in several London venues, every provincial city and most towns. I never changed the script: I just changed the audience.

Although I would start each tour with the best of intentions by reading a guidebook to wherever I happened to be, taking a sightseeing tour if one was available and visiting the local museums, these plans never lasted more than a day or two. It became impossible to do more than get up, check out, travel to the next place, check in, prepare myself and the stage for the show, do the show, unwind, sometimes by DJing at a bar or club, and get to bed. I was living like a minor rock star, smoking ounces of skunk, drinking gallons of booze, snorting grams of cocaine and filling my dressing room with the rich and sexy. Every night was the same routine, but everywhere was different. If you don't change inside, you have to keep moving. It was the exact opposite of prison, where you can only change inside and never change your surroundings.

It would have been a cliché if I had lost myself in powder, become an alcoholic, developed cannabis psychosis and checked into the Priory, but the rock-and-roll lifestyle pulled me out of my gloom. I began to travel and write again. Visiting Georgia, Estonia, Cuba and Vietnam, I wrote travel pieces for the *Observer* and the *Daily Telegraph* and reviewed books for other publications.

At some point between trips in spring 2003 Scott Blakey telephoned me. It was his daughter Sara's second birthday. Scott said he was intending, for reasons he would explain to me when we next met, to transfer seed production from Switzerland to Spain. Seeds have always been legal in Spain. Mr Nice Seedbank had done well there with seed sales, mainly through Cañamo, who produce an excellent monthly marijuana magazine and had also published the Spanish version of *Mr Nice*. We agreed to meet in Barcelona.

I flew from Leeds/Bradford airport to Barcelona and took a taxi to a café just off the Ramblas. As is usual in Spanish cafés, the television was blaring. I was early, and Scott had not arrived. I ordered a beer. The waiter gathered I was British and asked if I would be watching the football on television: Barcelona were playing Manchester United, kicking off in about ten minutes. I said I would, and he provided me with some free tapas.

I hadn't seen a football match, live or televised, since I was a football correspondent for the *Evening Standard* five years earlier. One day during early 1998 the sports editor Simon Greenberg had telephoned me and asked if I would be prepared to travel to France and cover the World Cup. I told Simon I was a rugby fan but did admit to getting fed up of standing in drizzles watching various Welsh teams getting comprehensively hammered. I explained I had never been to a football match and wasn't too sure about the rules. As far as Simon was concerned, this was perfect. The *Evening Standard* weren't after someone to write a blow-by-blow account of each match – there were sports writers to do that – they needed to cover other aspects such as getting tickets and overnight accommodation near the venues. In other words, they wanted me to mix with the touts and the hooligans. I agreed. In order to understand the sport's rudiments, Simon took me to Wembley to watch a pre-World Cup warm-up match between

England and Saudi Arabia. I learned that Alan Shearer was the captain of England and that Gazza and Paul Gascoigne were the same person.

Eurostar took me to Paris, and I hit the bars in the always lively rue de Lappe looking for a ticket for the Jamaica v. Argentina match and a cheap hotel. The area had changed since I was last there in the 1980s, when the doormen had been pretty girls enticing impoverished drunks to spend their last few coins on cheap drinks and other desirables. Now they were bouncers enforcing dress codes and determining the acceptable state of inebriation of high-rolling punters. I found a hotel but couldn't get a ticket so decided to try my luck outside the Parc des Princes.

Several tens of thousands had had the same idea but had abandoned their search to enjoy the party put on by the Jamaica supporters. The Argentina fans, no strangers to carnival madness themselves, joined in with some frenzied techno tango. Opposing supporters danced with each other. Twenty minutes after the kick-off, I eventually got a ticket for 1,000 French francs. Argentina won 5–0. The Jamaica fans carried on partying. The next day I took the TGV from Paris to Toulouse, where Romania were playing England.

There was no accommodation anywhere in or near Toulouse. I went to the station café, which was full of fellow ticketless nomads, and joined a group of England supporters marching to the Stade Municipale. Touts were charging fortunes for the few tickets still left, so along with several others I chanted, 'You can stick your tickets up your arse' to the tune of 'She'll Be Coming Round the Mountain'. I was carried by the crowd into a bar near the ground with eight TV sets.

Within minutes England had conceded a goal and a fight broke out in the pub. It was nothing to do with football; an old personal score was about to be settled. The first blood spilled was mine – caused by flying wine bottle shrapnel. One of the combatants grabbed a steak knife; it was getting messy and vicious. The ambience changed from misery over England being 1–0 down to fear of mutilation. Peace was persuasively restored by those not fighting. The blood and glass were wiped up and vocal encouragement for Glen Hoddle's men began, again, to build up momentum. England equalised. The bar erupted. Lager-bearing arms, red legs and tattooed bodies gesticulated madly. They'd settle for a draw. Romania scored again. Misery returned, but peacefully. That had been my last experience of watching football.

Scott did not arrive for two hours, by which time Barcelona had won.

'Sorry, I'm late, mate. Got caught in this shit,' said Scott, pointing at the television. 'The city is solid with cars full of people yelling and screaming. I guess Barcelona must have won.'

'They played brilliantly, Scott; they deserved to win. It was a good match.'

'I thought you Welsh were like us Aussies, only interested in rugby.'

'Don't you mean only good at rugby?' I asked.

'Same, isn't it?'

'I suppose. But Wales are getting to be good at football these days. They've got some excellent players. Ryan Giggs was man of the match.'

'Doesn't seem like he got too many goals, looking at the score,' taunted Scott.

I changed the subject: 'How are things in Switzerland these days?'

'Not good, mate, not good.'

Scott explained how, in the last couple of weeks, the Ticinese authorities had busted and closed down dozens of cannabis shops, including some of the ones I had called in to during my last visit. This change had come about because of recent communal elections, where the winning party had declared in their electoral campaign their intention of closing all cannabis shops within Ticino.

'I thought the Swiss Supreme Court had ruled that growing cannabis was legal. How can they bust people making the equipment for that?' I asked

'They did rule that way, but Swiss law is weird, mate, weird. Each Supreme Court verdict is just that, a verdict on one single case. A Swiss Supreme Court verdict does not change or create a law: it's just an interpretation to fit the circumstances.'

'What does that mean?'

'Fuck knows altogether, but it obviously means that grow shops can be busted.'

'Come to think of it, Scott, it's not that surprising if the grow shop I went to in Chiasso was anything to go by. Dope was being sold there openly. Anyway why does it matter? I didn't think Mr Nice Seedbank or Gene Bank Technology owned any grow shops.'

'They don't. But it's the thin end of the wedge. The Ticino authorities aren't going to stop with busting grow shops. Businesses producing seeds and other cannabis products will be next, I bet. I want to get out before that happens. Every bone in my body feels it coming. Spain is the place to set it up now. It's not illegal to have seeds or grow them here.'

'But Spanish law is also a bit weird. I know – I was wrongly extradited to America in 1989. It's legal to do just about anything with growing dope, but if public order is affected or threatened, the authorities can bust you for that alone.'

'What does "public order" mean?' asked Scott.

'Whatever the Spanish cops want it to mean, from what I can make out. But I suppose if seed production is done without too many people knowing about it, public order can hardly be affected.'

'That's how I was going to do it anyway, and I've already

found a place to rent. I just thought I would run it by you first. I'll give the guys in Lugano a call now and arrange to get the parent plants I need brought down here. No drama.'

Scott stepped outside to make his call. He returned after about ten minutes, his face white.

'Well, mate, the shit has hit the fanny. The Swiss have just busted Gene Bank Technology, with all its equipment and any dope there. They've destroyed hundreds of thousands of plants. The cops have detained hundreds of people, including carpenters, lawyers, gardeners, florists. It happened this morning. I told you I could feel it coming.'

'Jesus Christ! What the fuck is going on? How could it have been legal yesterday and not today without any change in the law? I thought I read the other day the Swiss are debating decriminalising cannabis. What's made them do a U-turn?'

'Outside pressure – it's obvious,' answered Scott.

'From the fucking Yanks?'

'No, not this time, mate. Somewhere much closer to Switzerland – next door, in fact.'

'You mean Berlusconi and his gang of fascists?'

'For sure. You could probably have bought as much as fifty kilos in that grow shop in Chiasso. Those places weren't just selling five to ten grams for personal use. Loads of Italians come to Lugano, Chiasso and other parts of Ticino, to work among other things. Lots of them smoke dope, which is cheaper in Switzerland than in Italy. It didn't take them long to figure out they could make some money smuggling it back to Italy. They use every method you can think of, from sneaking over the border on foot to the old smugglers' routes used during the Second World War. The Italian cops know all the dope they are busting in Milan and just about everywhere else has been grown in Switzerland. The grow shops were even sticking up their flyers in Italian clubs. Berlusconi has got wind of it and cracked down.'

Marijuana. Leaves of Grass

Shantibaba. The world's
best marijuana botanist

Goldie Lookin Chain
at Glastonbury 2004

Gruff Rhys and his
lady, Catryn Ramasut

Kelly Jones

Rob, Alabama 3

Bernie Davies, Tel Currie

Bernie Davies, Rhys Ifans at Glastonbury 2004

Dona Filinha De Leman-Ja, High Priestess of the Sisterhood of the Good Death

Rio de
Janeiro

Oxford Union

Tango. It took two

Mr Nice on Ice

It made sense. Switzerland isn't independent and neutral because it scares other countries: it keeps its privileged position by caving in to them all equally.

'What gets me is that Swiss law says cultivating marijuana is legal unless you intend to "extract narcotics" from it. I didn't "extract narcotics" from it,' said Scott.

'But how can you prove you didn't intend to?'

'Don't they have to prove I did?'

'You mean you're innocent until proven guilty? I wouldn't rely on that one, especially not in Europe. The Napoleonic Code governs most law here, which means the defendant carries the burden of proof. Although I suppose if you can prove beyond reasonable doubt you cultivated cannabis intended for legal activities, like producing a contract for hemp beer production, you shouldn't have any problems.'

'I've got stacks of contracts like that – I really didn't extract narcotics.'

'I know. You did the exact opposite: you got hold of all the non-narcotic bits and sold them to the Yanks to make perfume. But maybe that did break Swiss law.'

'How?'

'Because the only way you could get the non-narcotic bits was to extract the narcotic bits, which, technically, is against Swiss law, as you just said.'

Scott looked at me as if I was mad. I looked back at him as if I was.

'Anyway, Scott, taking all that THC out of six tons of dope just to satisfy the Yanks was against some higher ethic, if not the law. I knew it had to be bad karma the moment you told me you were doing it. Shiva wouldn't have been pleased.'

'Let's have a smoke,' said Scott.

Night fell as we left the café. Scott rolled a strong joint, which we smoked as we walked through the labyrinthine tributaries of the Ramblas.

'I've just been thinking, mate. They've busted everyone

connected with Mr Nice Seedbank other than me – the breeder – and you – Mr Nice himself. Why do you think that is?'

'Probably because we weren't in Switzerland this morning. I don't think either of us will be going back there in a hurry.'

'But I haven't broken any fucking law.'

'If they think you have or think they can get you anyway, they'll still bust you. Trust me.'

Scott looked sadly at the ground.

We walked back to our hotel and agreed to meet next day for breakfast at 9.30. I woke up at 9.00 a.m. A note had been pushed under the door.

> Dear Howard
>
> I'm going back to Campione d'Italia. I have nothing to fear as I know I have not broken any law. And I promised Sara I would take her swimming. It's 7.00 a.m., and I don't want to wake you. Also, you would probably persuade me not to go back. But I know I must. I'll be back in Barcelona within a week. Hope to see you here then.
>
> Love,
> Scott

Worried sick, I flew back to London. The next day I received an email from Martin, Scott's dad. Scott had been busted by the Italian police. I had often teased him about his failure to serve time in prison despite having worked with cannabis all his life and had accused him of shirking his apprenticeship. Inwardly, of course, I had been happy he had reached thirty-nine without enduring such an experience and was convinced he would never have to. Anger and sorrow played havoc with my mind.

In March 2003, a few weeks before our meeting in Barcelona, the Swiss authorities, as part of Operation Indoors

– seizing plants grown indoors before they could be moved outside for the warmer weather – had issued an international arrest warrant for Scott which charged him with heading an organisation that exported tons of cannabis from Switzerland and laundering the earnings. They claimed they had evidence of his transporting truck loads of drugs to destinations throughout Europe and depositing millions of euros in Swiss bank accounts. Acting on the warrant, Italian police arrested Scott at the usually unstaffed border between Campione d'Italia and Switzerland. After an exhaustive investigation, the authorities were unable to find any evidence of Scott – an Italian resident – breaking Italian law. The Swiss asked for his extradition, and Scott, as keen as ever to clear his name, agreed immediately. It took sixty days, during which time he was kept in an overcrowded high-security prison in Como in the most disgusting conditions.

In August Scott was extradited to a Swiss subterranean holding unit in Mendrisio, Ticino, still waiting to find out the specific charges against him. Confined in a windowless cell and interrogated daily for sessions lasting as long as seven hours, Scott truthfully answered all the questions put to him to encourage the Swiss authorities to charge him with a specific offence and get the matter resolved. If he had refused to answer, the Swiss could have kept him for two years while they conducted their investigations. Lawyers were not allowed to attend these deeply unpleasant, threatening interrogations. The prosecutors in Ticino will use virtually any means to get what they want – usually an admission of guilt – but there was no criminal conduct for Scott to admit to.

Cannabis growers throughout the world were outraged. During October 2003 the following petition was posted on the Internet.

The Australian geneticist, Scott Blakey, founder of Mr Nice Seed Bank, has been in prison for the last two

months in Mendrisio (Switzerland) accused by the
authorities of the canton of Ticino of marijuana
trafficking. Scott Blakey is not a drug trafficker; he is a
dedicated cultivator and breeder and has discovered
several new cannabis seed varieties. He has taught many
cultivators some of his knowledge of hybridising distinct
varieties of marijuana. We ask for solidarity throughout
the world's cannabis community to help petition for his
immediate release.

Next to the petition was a photograph of Scott, smiling and
reading a copy of the Italian translation of *Mr Nice*. Thousands
signed the petition, which, of course, had no effect on the
authorities. They never do.

I have fought and campaigned to legalise cannabis since I
smoked my first joint in 1964. I wasn't alone; I merely
followed the lead given by rock singers, artists, poets, writers
and politicians of the day. A few years later, in 1969, the
Wootton Committee, set up by Harold Wilson's Labour
government, concluded cannabis should be decriminalised. It
stopped short of legalisation, mainly because the members of
the United Nations appeared obligated by international treaty
to keep it illegal; the penalties for transgression, however, were
left up to each nation's discretion and varied from no punishment at all to the death penalty. The Wooton Committee
suggested no penalties. At the time you couldn't have asked
for more.

However, without providing any justification, Home
Secretary James Callaghan refused to carry out the committee's recommendations. The penalties for cannabis use and
dealing were not removed; they were increased. British
cannabis users were furious. Some became dedicated dope
dealers and spent years in prison. On my release, I took my
activism to the limit: I smoked joints on stage, in pubs,

restaurants and outside police stations, inviting arrest. Although I was forcibly ejected from a few bars and clubs I was never arrested by the police, who invariably had more important problems. I also took part in hundreds of debates and discussions at university unions and on television and radio, and wrote scores of articles for newspapers and magazines. I was a member of the European Commission-financed British Drug Policy Review Group, a behind-the-scenes group of police, judges, members of the House of Lords, clergymen and academics who wished to see drugs legalised.

In 1997 some stalwart from the Norwich-based Legalise Cannabis Alliance asked if I would stand for Parliament in their constituency. After determining that ex-convicts were allowed to stand and that the only requirements were to be alive and to have £500, I agreed. It was thought at first that I should stand as an independent, but as this would oblige me to be familiar with things like education and hospital services, about which I knew nothing, we formed the single-issue Legalise Cannabis Party. I could therefore only be expected to know questions about cannabis, and the local knowledge I would require would be confined to that concerning the dope-smoking community. I went through all the procedures, paid up, and was accepted as a bona fide Parliamentary candidate for Norwich South. Charles Clarke (Lab.), who went on to become, briefly, home secretary, was standing against me.

'Howard Marks of the Legalise Cannabis Party. Mr Marks, have you ever actually smoked cannabis?'

'Yes. I have smoked cannabis every day for—'

'Thank you, Mr Marks. Moving on to Charles Clarke of the Labour party. Mr Clarke, have you ever smoked cannabis?'

'Yes, I have, but it was many years ago,' answered Charles Clarke.

The audience murmured in disbelief. This was the first time an MP had publicly admitted smoking cannabis. I saw my chance and to loud protests shouted, 'Mr Clarke, as there are no statutes of limitation in this country, would you report your crime to the police and be prepared to face the same punishment as has been handed out to several of our party members for similar conduct?'

'I only smoked it once and didn't like it. It's a very bad drug,' said Charles Clarke, squirming slightly.

The hustings chairman changed the subject.

Next to Norwich South lies Norwich North. I've never been keen on borders so decided to stand for Parliament there as well – you can stand in two or more constituencies but sit for only one. Campaigning in two constituencies was excellent fun. Cameramen and journalists followed me all day. Instead of standing on a soapbox announcing boring policy objectives and imploring people to vote for me, we bought a battered van, decorated it with fairy lights and giant marijuana leaves, and banged out non-stop techno from speakers on the roof. We drove through every street in Norwich delivering the following through letterboxes and distributing it on flyers to restaurants, pubs, and clubs:

Dear Voter

I am standing in your constituency as Parliamentary candidate for the single-issue policy of the full legalisation of cannabis. I am doing so because:

- I, as an independent, am able to say things which party politicians cannot.
- I regard the laws banning cannabis use and cultivation to be unsound, unjust and unrealistic.

The effects of this prohibition are to:

- Turn community members into criminals, despite the absence of victims.

- Leave supply in the hands of profiteers who might also sell harmful drugs or accept stolen property as payment.
- Burden police, courts and prisons at excessive cost to the taxpayer.
- Stop the sick and infirm from using a natural medicine.
- Render impossible the quality control of the available cannabis.
- Stop research into the uses of the cannabis hemp plant as fibre and fuel.
- Ban the cultivation of cannabis for its seed, which can be used as a food.
- Deny people the relaxation and recreational pleasure obtained by consumption of cannabis.
- Repress the human and civil right to choose one's own lifestyle, beliefs and religion.

All major government reports on cannabis have suggested some form of legalisation, yet politicians refuse to openly debate or discuss the matter. I am standing to give you the opportunity of expressing just how important you know this issue to be.

Take care

Howard Marks

Word got around, and I was asked to stand in two other constituencies, Neath and Southampton Test. Simultaneously campaigning in the public halls, squats, techno clubs, shebeens, brothels, illegal raves, recording studios and opium dens of four constituencies proved exhausting. I managed to get an average of 500 votes, losing my deposit in each constituency. I was disappointed of course, but there was never any chance of my being elected, and we had certainly succeeded in bringing our cause to the attention of the public.

Wondering in which direction I should next proceed to advance the cause of re-legalising cannabis, I soon after happened to be reading the employment section of *The Times*. In it was advertised a newly created post in the Cabinet Office – the UK Anti-Drugs Co-ordinator – whose brief was to eradicate illegal drug trafficking in the UK. Realising that by legalising all drugs I could fulfil the brief easily and quickly, I wrote to the Cabinet Office. They sent me an application form, on which the following words appeared in large bold type: 'UK ANTI-DRUGS CO-ORDINATOR, ALSO KNOWN AS "DRUG CZAR".' I had never dreamed I would have the opportunity of being promoted from a mere baron to a czar. The salary was £75,000 a year, much less than the average drug baron's but not bad for a job with a built-in alias, and I have always been fond of pseudonyms. There was also a £5,000 removal allowance. I could make good use of this to transport a container of my personal effects which had been sitting around in Kathmandu since the 1980s. I presumed there would be diplomatic immunity. Another page outlined the core personal requirements for the post. These included proven leadership qualities, negotiating and influencing skills, and the capacity for strategic planning linked firmly to the delivery of results. I found this encouraging as the authorities already had proof that I had been the head of the largest marijuana-smuggling organisation in the world; were aware of my successful negotiations with the *Mafia* and other inter-national organisations, and knew that I had delivered well over a hundred tons of hashish. The page finished by stating that the successful applicant would require credibility in the drugs field. I felt I was in with a chance and wrote the following:

My own experiences in the study of illegal drug transactions began at the University of Oxford in the early 1960s and were continued at the Universities of London and Sussex. Shortly after obtaining a master's degree in nuclear physics and postgraduate qualifications in philosophy, I was recruited as an agent by MI6, the British secret service. I'm hesitant to detail here my drug-related work during this period, but presumably the Parliamentary Secretary for the Foreign Office is empowered to show you any relevant files. Suffice it now to state that for twenty years I was intimately connected with illegal drug trafficking in the following countries: Wales, England, Scotland, Ireland, Germany, France, Italy, Spain, Holland, Portugal, Morocco, Kenya, Lebanon, Pakistan, India, Nepal, Thailand, Philippines, Hong Kong, Canada, United States of America, Colombia, Jamaica and Mexico. In many of these countries I worked closely with senior law enforcement, forging long-lasting professional and social relationships. I have been granted unique access to many clandestine illegal drug processing plants.

I have held directorships of Panamanian media companies, Liberian record labels, British travel agencies, Dutch boutiques, Chinese publishing companies, Thai massage parlours and Swiss investment consultancies. I owned and managed a language school in Pakistan, not far from the Khyber Pass.

For the first half of the 1990s I was employed by the United States Department of Justice, permitted to enter the Federal Bureau of Prisons' convict section, and allowed to teach incarcerated drug traffickers. I did that for seven years. I can keep down a job. At the same time, I posed as a marijuana addict and entered a drug abuse programme to familiarise myself with the problems of denial and recovery.

I have written a book on illegal drug trafficking. It has sold over 750,000 copies in Britain, been translated into six languages, is still a best-seller, and is available from all good bookshops.

I have written articles on drugs and crime for almost every national newspaper. I have appeared dozens of times on major TV and radio channels as an expert on illegal drug trafficking, false passport acquisition and money laundering. I regularly give talks and lectures at rave clubs, music festivals and business conferences. I would gladly risk and even sacrifice my life right now to achieve the eradication of all illegal drug trafficking in this country. I am 100 per cent committed.

I posted the completed application form to the Cabinet Office. Eventually I received a reply.

Dear Mr Marks
Thank you for your application for this post. The selection team have carefully considered it along with all the other applications, and I am sorry to inform you that we were unable to include you among the candidates for interview.
May I, nevertheless, thank you for your interest in this post and for taking the trouble to apply. I hope that your disappointment will not prevent you from applying for other positions which the Cabinet Office will advertise in the future.
Yours sincerely,
Colin Welch,
Recruitment Manager

Again I was disappointed, but at least the door had not been closed.

None of my tireless work appeared to have the remotest effect. But now, while Scott was languishing in a Swiss prison for legally growing cannabis, a wind of change was puffing its way through the British cannabis community. More people were smoking more joints than ever before. Those on the dole could grow stronger marijuana than gangsters could import. The police were fed up with busting honest, otherwise law-abiding kids, and police chiefs were advocating turning a blind eye. Rumours of impending legalisation swept through the streets. At last, the government, after refusing for decades to even debate the issue, was going to sort it.

There was some cause for optimism. At the end of 2001, Home Secretary David Blunkett had asked the Advisory Council on the Misuse of Drugs to review the classification of cannabis in the light of available scientific evidence. Drug offence penalties are graded into one of three classes according to the personal or social harm attributable to the particular drug. Class A, carrying a maximum penalty of life imprisonment, included heroin, cocaine, ecstasy and LSD; Class B, with a maximum of fourteen years imprisonment, included cannabis, amphetamines and barbiturates; while Class C, with a maximum of five years imprisonment, included steroids and tranquillisers. Although the Advisory Council found cannabis could produce dilatation of the conjunctival blood vessels (red eyes), disrupt blood pressure (a whitey) and increase heart rate, it stated that such cardiovascular symptoms are similar to the effects of exercise, and most unlikely to constitute a health risk. It further found that cannabis did not increase risk-taking behaviour, did not contribute to violence – either to others or to oneself – did not cause mental illness or brain damage, and did not lead on to other drugs. The Council concluded that cannabis was much less harmful than the other substances within Class B and should therefore be reclassified as Class C. Polls showed that most of the voting population agreed. The reclassification was implemented in law during early 2004, and many cannabis smokers felt they could smoke with impunity.

In fact, the change in law was slight. Although penalties for individuals consuming cannabis were less, those for other cannabis offences remained the same. The government had not downgraded cannabis from Class B to Class C; it had formed a new and different class. Subject to police officers' discretion to arrest or not, cannabis possession, sharing a joint, allowing someone to smoke a joint in your home, consuming cannabis in certain areas and cannabis cultivation were all still arrestable offences and punishable by up to fourteen years imprisonment. Nevertheless, there had been progress of a kind. Other European countries debated following the British initiative. The tide was changing.

But this swell of shifting attitudes could not help Scott. After months of interrogation and several unsuccessful bail applications, the Swiss, under pressure from the Australian embassy, moved Scott from the Mendrisio bunker to a more civilised prison near Lugano. The spartan conditions of the underground prison had taken their toll on Scott's health, but now he had access to a gymnasium and quickly regained his fitness. He was also earning 400 Swiss francs a month ironing clothes in the prison laundry.

Eventually Scott was formally charged with contraventions of the Swiss federal law on narcotics ranging from smoking marijuana – which he wasn't about to deny – to smuggling tons of the stuff – which simply wasn't true. The trial took place in March 2004.

The judge found there was nothing to suggest that Scott had sold marijuana or had made any economic gain from its sale, as the prosecution had repeatedly claimed. The judge also ruled that Mr Nice Seedbank's commercial activities were perfectly legal. Scott's only offence was to bring into Switzerland his plant genetics (seeds) and his expertise – which happened to lead to great improvements in the quality of the marijuana grown generally in Switzerland. For that Scott received a sentence of four years imprisonment followed by ten years expulsion from Switzerland and an undisclosed fine. This reasoning is typical of both the Swiss and the American legal codes. If you should have foreseen or accept the possibility that the outcomes of your actions might incidentally cause or aid criminal activity, then you have broken the law, even if your actions themselves were legal. In other words, if they want you, they will get you whatever you didn't do.

Everyone who knew about Scott's case was appalled at the obvious injustice of his punishment, including the Swiss Court of Appeals judges, who a few months later reduced the sentence by half. To the relief of all, especially his three-year-old daughter, Scott was released in October 2004. Mr Nice Seedbank continues its legitimate business.

Other than fleeting visits of a couple of hours each to attend to matters relating to my mother's death and ensure the house stayed clean, burglar and weather proof, and in one piece, I had not visited Kenfig Hill for over two years. It was time to break my self-imposed exile. I took a train from York to Bridgend, where I rented a car and drove the familiar five miles to Waunbant Road. I parked outside the house expecting to be drowned by waves of sadness, pierced by pains of nostalgia and disoriented by déjà vu. Instead, the house twinkled in the twilight and glowed with welcoming winter warmth. The door opened easily without a creak, revealing spotlessly clean rooms. My parents looked at me from their portraits on the walls, as they always did when I entered the living room, but this time their faces did not arouse in me intense feelings of everlasting loss; they smiled with relief, robbing death of its dominion.

The attic was in the same state as when I had visited when performing at the Porthcawl Royal Pavilion. Bric-a-brac and pamphlets still littered the bookshelves and overflowed from cardboard boxes and suitcases. Would it ever be sorted and classified or would it just wait until irrelevant to anyone left alive and end up in a skip? Poking around aimlessly, I found a stash box I must have left behind years ago. Inside was a matchbox containing enough hashish for a strong joint. It was reddish brown. Could it be Red Lebanese, the favourite smoke of the 1970s? Had it lain here for over a quarter of a century? I started rolling a joint, and the hash crumbled into tight little buds. Perhaps it had decomposed beyond use; I had no idea how many years hashish remained fit to smoke. Despite repeatedly resolving to keep a sample from every consignment I imported, I hadn't managed to hold on to any for longer than a few months. If it was good, it had to be smoked. As the tiny buds disintegrated, I smelt a familiar odour, and my heartbeat quickened.

Memory is seemingly unable to conjure up a smell from the past in the same way it can recall sights and sounds from long ago, and whenever I recognise an old smell, I am shocked and surprised. This dope reminded me of the Panama Red given to me by Living Stone in Panama three years before. I had smoked some in Bocas del Toro and Portobelo but had forgotten I still had it with me in Jamaica. I must have unknowingly brought it to Kenfig Hill on one of my brief visits. Or had my father or some other cool ancestor acquired it in Panama decades earlier? I smoked it and still couldn't determine which.

Beautifully stoned, I rummaged around for hours, picking up bits and pieces and reliving the times I had last seen them. I found a boxful of Elvis Presley 78 rpm acetates, sheet music of his early hits, some Elvis badges and a collection of Elvis cards given away with bubblegum from slot machines. I came across a tin cabin trunk stuffed full of *National Geographic* magazines, maps, charts and guidebooks to countries all over the world, and began sorting into one box anything relating to South America.

There were ashtrays inset with moth wings from Brazil, ceramic figurines from Peru, a marble statuette of Christ of the Andes, a Uruguayan basket made from the carapace of an armadillo, guide booklets to Inca, Aztec and Mayan monuments, and cheap souvenirs from most of the continent's capitals. My obsession with Welsh–South American connections went into overdrive and butterflies started dancing in my guts. I felt excited and adrenalised, but safe and secure as if surrounded by guardian angels. I saw a small battered brown leather wallet, opened it and found a spread-out caul affixed to a small white envelope. A caul is the shimmery transparent membrane that on rare occasions covers the face and head of a child at birth.

In cultures throughout the world, the presence of a caul means the child has supernatural abilities, such as sight into the future or a third eye. The child is intended for greatness. Jesus Christ was born with one. Cauls are considered protection against drowning at sea and are therefore prized and sought-after by sailors, who pay large sums of money to own these talismans. Gathering the caul onto paper was an important tradition. The midwife would rub a sheet of paper across the baby's head and face, pressing the caul onto the paper. This would then be presented to the mother to keep as an heirloom. I knew my father had always carried a caul with him when at sea as he had often referred to it, but I had no idea whose it was.

On the back of the envelope was written 'Patrick McCarty'. Both my great-grandfather and great-great-grandfather were named Patrick McCarty. Had one of them been born with a caul? The wallet also contained a small, faded black and white photograph of a narrow channel of rough sea bordered with sharp-pointed mountains. On the back was written 'Patagonia', the seeming home at various times of ancestors on both sides of my family. A feeling of comforting tiredness enveloped me.

I awoke about nine o'clock, my mind full of thoughts of Patagonia, and switched on the radio. It was St David's Day, 1 March, the only Welsh holiday. I had completely forgotten, partly because February is always catching me out with its meagre ration of twenty-eight days, but mainly because I hadn't spent a St David's Day in Wales since I was a teenager. In other countries the patron saint of Wales is paid scant notice.

Both Merlin and St Patrick, another Welshman, foretold the sixth-century birth of St David, whose mother Non was a niece of King Arthur. St David was baptised by his cousin St Elvis, an effeminate bishop who had been suckled by a she-wolf, assisted by a blind monk named Movi, who held the young David underwater. Some of the water went in Movi's eye and miraculously healed him of his blindness. St David went on to become a pupil of St Paulinus, whose blindness he also cured. Paulinus' first sight was of a field of daffodils. David was tall, strong and gentle, and led a frugal life, eating only bread and watercress and bathing regularly in a lake of cold water, the only liquid he would drink. During a battle against the Saxons the saint advised the Welsh to wear the same clothes as the enemy but to put leeks in their hats so they could identify one another. The Welsh won the battle. He became Archbishop of Wales, restored Glastonbury, where his remains now lie, and raised a widow's son from the dead on his way back from a pilgrimage to Jerusalem. David lived for over 100 years. His last words were, 'Do the little things.'

The Welsh remember him by wearing a leek or a daffodil on 1 March, the anniversary of his death. I resolved to do so today, for the first time in forty-five years. I thought I might drive to St David's. It would take no more than two hours. I could even check whether there was a parish of St Elvis, as Eddie Evans had told me three years ago. I telephoned Marty Langford and asked if he wanted to come with me. He couldn't; he had promised to take his mother for a drive to the seaside.

The radio played a few Welsh hymns and then broadcast a ten-minute programme on Patagonia, stressing that there too St David's Day would be celebrated. I telephoned Gruff Rhys to wish him a happy St David's day. He told me he was doing a solo tour of North Wales, but that he and his girlfriend Cat had just come back from Patagonia. They'd had a fantastic time; the place was wild. I told Gruff I was about to drive to St David's, and he asked me to pay his respects to Haverfordwest, a small market town on the way, where he was born.

I drove west, stopping in Carmarthen to buy a daffodil for my lapel, sang a hello to Haverfordwest and reached St David's by noon. Despite being the world's smallest city and despite today being its very own day, St David's had ample room to park. I joined the crowds, many in traditional Welsh costume, visiting the cathedral, and found a café serving my favourite Welsh dish of lava bread, bacon and cockles. Then I drove to a tourist information centre just outside the city and enquired about St Elvis. The woman in charge said there was a farm called St Elvis four miles away on the road to Haverfordwest near a place named Solva. So Eddie Evans was right after all. I asked if she had any books or pamphlets on St Elvis; she didn't think so, but there were some on Solva – maybe they would help. I looked through the racks but none mentioned Elvis. By way of compensation, I found *Solva Blues*, the autobiography of Meic Stevens. A quote from Gruff Rhys, 'A world-class guy – he's my hero', was on the front cover. Meic is one of my heroes too.

Known as the godfather of Welsh folk, he has been in the forefront of Welsh music since the 1960s. A Valium addict married to a chronic schizophrenic, Meic grew up in Solva and jammed with Pink Floyd founder Syd Barrett before crossing the Atlantic to look after the Grateful Dead's touring stash of half a million acid tabs. He became a close friend of Bob Dylan, who described him as Britain's greatest songwriter. I bought the book.

Solva lies around a natural harbour at the mouth of a winding river valley of small fields which have obviously been farmed for centuries. Its position made it ideal as a base for trading ships in the eighteenth century, and a strong seafaring and smuggling tradition developed. Now it is populated by painters, writers and gourmets. The chapel has been converted into an art gallery, and the old chemist's and printing shops are restaurants, but the streets still stink of that ancient and fishy smell common to seaside villages. There are several pubs, including the Cambrian Arms, where I popped in for a pint hoping to run into Meic Stevens. The place was rammed, but he wasn't there. I gathered from one of the customers that he was now living in Cardiff. A picture of Elvis – the pelvis rather than the saint – hung above the bar mantelpiece, and the radio, accompanied by thirty drunken Welsh people in full song, was playing Elvis's 'Crying in the Chapel'. We were reminded the song had first been released exactly forty years ago.

I asked the landlord for directions to St Elvis Farm, drove off and found a small sign on the roadside about a mile away stating I was entering the parish of St Elvis. Comprising two farms and fewer than 200 acres, it is the smallest parish in Great Britain. I turned right, came across a farm, stopped the car and rolled a joint. A young farm worker in denim jacket and jeans approached.

'Lost, are you?'

'No, not all. I was trying to find St Elvis Farm. They told me at the Cambrian Arms it was down here.'

'Fair enough. You've found it all right. But the boss is away today, gone to St David's for a bit of a booze-up, like, for the holiday. He'll be too pissed to drive back tonight, that's for sure. Can I give him a message or will you come back tomorrow? Are you from the university? What's your name?'

'No, it's all right, thanks,' I answered. 'I haven't come to see your boss. I was just looking around for anything to do with St Elvis.'

'Well that pile of stones over by there is St Elvis Cromlech, and that pool is St Elvis's Holy Well, and that's about it. My dad, God bless him, a bit of a nutter, like, used to talk about it lying on the intersection of ley lines or something and being magical, but I think he just wanted to believe that because he was a fanatic Elvis fan. Are you an Elvis fan?'

'Yes, I am.'

'Thought so. You didn't strike me as an academic researching Welsh saints. We get a lot of those wankers here. We get a few Elvis fans too, but nothing like as many as you would expect, given he's a descendant.'

'What! Elvis Presley is descended from St Elvis?' I felt sure the kid was having a laugh but was enjoying the story too much to stop him.

'Yes, on his mother Gladys's side, according to my dad. And he was right about that. All sorts of people checked it out. Gladys's great-great-grandfather, William Mansell, was a Welshman descended from St Elvis.'

I couldn't let him get away with this. 'Hold on. Like I said, I'm an Elvis fan and know a bit about him. All right, his mother was called Gladys, and Gladys is a Welsh name. But his father's name was Vernon Elvis Presley, so Elvis's name came from his father, not his mother. And anyway saints don't usually have children.'

'Some did, though they kept it quiet, like. St Elvis definitely did. He was a bit of a lad by all accounts. According to my dad, one reason Vernon attracted Gladys was because his middle name was the same as her ancestor's. William Mansell married a Red Indian squaw called Morning Dove White. Dad said lots of Welsh and Red Indians married one another in those days.'

This at least made some sense. I made a mental note.

'Is there nothing else here connected with St Elvis?' I asked.

'Only St Elvis's Rock.'

'What a fantastic name!' I said. 'Where's that?'

'On the beach. About an hour's walk from here. I usually take the dog for a walk there every night, but he's gone with the boss today. Today is the first day I haven't been there for ages. Tell you what, if you give me a lift to the Harbour Inn in Solva, we could walk there in about ten minutes now the tide's out.'

We got into the car. It stank of dope.

'Nice smell. You are Howard Marks, aren't you? My dad used to mention you a lot. Said he always wanted to meet you.'

'Yes, I am. What's your name?'

'Can't you guess?'

'When did your dad die, Elvis?'

'Five years ago. Went out in a sailing boat and disappeared. They found the boat but not him. I suppose he could be still alive, but I know he's not.'

'Where did he sail from?'

I knew the answer.

'St Elvis's Rock.'

Elvis and I drove to the Harbour Inn and walked past rows of disused limekilns towards the sea. Crossing over the brow of the low headland, Elvis pointed to a rocky outcrop close to the shore. On top was a wooden cross. We stared in silence. The wind picked up as heavy rain clouds frowned and wept and then billowed and bullied their way to land.

'Let's get going. It's pissing down,' said Elvis.

We walked back to the Harbour Inn. Gusty howls and sighs and hissing rain prevented conversation. We dripped into the bar, and I bought Elvis a pint.

'You know where those winds came from?' asked Elvis.

'Tell me.'

'They're the south-westerlies. They come from Patagonia. If you went direct south-west from St Elvis's Rock, the first thing you would come to after thousands of miles of empty ocean would be a Welsh fishing village, just like Solva. Dad would always tell me that. Strange, isn't it? Well I'd better get back home. I live just around the corner. Thanks for the drink, Mr Marks. It was good to meet you.'

I didn't need any more messages, signs or coincidences. I drove back to Kenfig Hill and made my plans to visit Patagonia.

Nine

PATAGONIA

The distant and alluring land of Patagonia occupies most of the southern parts of Argentina and Chile. Flying to anywhere in Argentinian Patagonia from outside the country usually means changing planes at Buenos Aires. I had decided I would spend a few days in the capital, rather than just a few hours at the airport. I could sample some city life before venturing forth into the deserted plains of Patagonia while at the same time work out why I was going there, what I was hoping to discover and how to go about it.

We were coming in to land. Buenos Aires is an enormous regular grid hovering just above sea level. Grand North American metropolis-type avenues, accommodating as many as fourteen lanes of traffic and lined with sixteenth-century buildings, cross one another at perfect right angles. High-rise office and apartment blocks dwarf the insignificant hills. London Docklands-type regeneration developments blend into active ports, colonial plazas, booming light industry plants, and malls of cafés and bars. Ezeiza, the international airport, is efficient, and I soon took my place in the orderly queue at the accommodation desk. Friends had told me there was only one hotel to stay at when in Buenos Aires, the Alvear

Palace. It was full, of course, but the staff's suggestion of the centrally placed Amerian Buenos Aires Park Hotel in Reconquista seemed acceptable.

Ninety-seven per cent of the thirteen million inhabitants of Buenos Aires, the *porteños*, are of European descent, two per cent of African, and a mere one per cent of Native American Indian. Accordingly, Buenos Aires seems more European than all the European capitals, which, for better or worse, now have immeasurably larger non-Caucasian populations. Despite the Spanish being the colonial masters of Argentina, inhabitants of Italian blood now easily outnumber them so Spanish, the official language, is spoken with an attractive Italian accent. Italian coffee bars and open-air restaurants sprawled along the pavements, French bakers churned out croissants and cakes, Spanish tapas bars provided their usual titbits, Irish pubs allowed smoking, while German delicatessens made every sausage imaginable. Culture vultures nested at café tables outside news-stands displaying copies of *OK* and *Le Monde*, as well as English translations of Machiavelli. Multispace venues offered courses on everything from tango to basic Portuguese. Multiscreens showed rare English indie films and forgotten 1960s French classics. Eclectism was the ideology. Both prostitution and public drunkenness had just been decriminalised. The streets were tumultuous, diverse and unpredictable, but appeared easy and attractive to explore.

I unpacked my belongings at the unpretentious and comfortable Amerian, switched on my laptop, took out my file of notes on Patagonia, and began to draw up a proper plan for my visit. I had to see for myself whether there still was a Welsh community in Patagonia's Chubut Valley, not just a museum, theme park or other relic preserved for the tourist and travel industries. My failure to find any evidence of a Welsh colony in Brazil had made me sceptical about travel writers and the Internet. In addition, I had to find evidence, if there was any, of the existence of my great-great-grandfather, Patrick McCarty.

Bruce Chatwin wrote in his *In Patagonia*, 'The history of Buenos Aires is written in its telephone directory.' This was probably true of the whole of Argentina, so a search through the Patagonia telephone directories might help. I could have done this any time on the Net from anywhere, but I felt that coming to the communities themselves would increase the possibility of coincidence, give me a better chance to stumble fortuitously across a distant cousin. I also had lists of the hangouts in Patagonia of Butch Cassidy, the Sundance Kid and other fugitives from the Wild West. Many were in the Chubut Valley where, according to my Auntie Katie, Patrick had studied Welsh, so I would start my McCarty search there. Finally, I had to check if any of Bernie Davies's ancestors were in the first group of Welsh colonists to arrive in Patagonia and whether any of his relatives were still there. I was about to linger on the possibly spiritual and probably mad reasons for Patagonia providing the solution to the problems of Wales and wondering whether I would see any penguins when the telephone rang.

'Hi, Howard. Welcome to Argentina. It's Martin, owner of Pacha's in Buenos Aires. Dave Beer from Leeds told me you were coming here for a few days, and one of my associates happened to be at the hotel when you checked in. How are you?'

'Very well thanks, Martin. It's nice of you to call.'

'Not at all. I was hoping we could meet but unfortunately I'm in Uruguay for another week.'

'That's a pity. Perhaps I could see you on my way back from Patagonia.'

'For sure. And if you want someone to take you out tonight and show you the secrets of this wonderful city, I'll give you the number of my good friend Eduarda, who will sort you out with Pacha's VIP facilities. Enjoy Patagonia.'

I took down the number but immediately resolved not to go to Pacha's. I knew what would happen if I did: I would get spannered for three days, fall in love with an Argentinian stranger, rent a flat in Buenos Aires, miss the deadline for this book and run out of money. I had to be disciplined. On the other hand, it would be good to spend just a few hours with someone who knew the place.

A few hours later I was at La Boca, a café and former brothel, drinking maté, Argentinian speed, with Eduarda, a sexy, fiercely academic woman of about thirty-five. She was staring with disgust at my torn jeans, but her duty was to entertain.

'Martin told me you were here for just a short time. Do you like the *maté*? Argentinians drink five times more maté than coffee, usually in the form of a sharing ritual with friends, family, and co-workers. Every Argentinian is addicted to maté, plastic surgery and psychotherapy. We can commit suicide by jumping off our egos. As well as drinking maté, you must also eat our meat, watch professionals dance the tango, visit gauchos in the pampas, go to the Delta, and see our city's many historical sites, cemeteries and museums. Try to see a football match too. Tonight we will do just two of these before Pacha's: walk down Caminito, the tango street, and eat some beautiful beef. By the way, have you noticed who else has visited this café? Look on the wall.'

Prominently displayed was a photograph of Bill Clinton, who had dropped in for coffee on a presidential tour. Even more prominent was a photograph of Maradona and some of his mates.

Along Caminito dozens of couples danced furiously to the tango while hundreds applauded, shouted and danced – less furiously – with one another. Sexual and musical excitement sent heartrates soaring. The tango, sometimes described as vertical lovemaking, was originally danced by men with men. European immigrants in Buenos Aires to seek their fortune visited bordellos to ease their loneliness and, while waiting their turn for prostitutes, invented a dance. Not surprisingly, it was symbolic of the struggle to possess a woman. When the men started dancing with the prostitutes rather than with each other, the dance became less melancholic and more sexual, resulting in the disapproval of the *porteño* elite and the enthusiastic support of their rebel offspring. The dance became a craze in Paris and then a religion in Buenos Aires.

Dusk fell. Eduarda had a Mercedes waiting for her. We drove to La Cabana, more of a museum than a steakhouse, to sample the world's best beef. Argentinians eats kilos of the tastiest and most tender beef every day and almost nothing else. Vegetables are hard to come by; there is no demand. While some British believe cow consumers are playing Russian roulette with insane steaks, Argentinians consider vegetarians to be seriously mentally defective because of their aversion to eating the world's best and most succulent beef. Their revered ancestors brought over herds of cows to graze in the country's massive green pastures; it would be sacrilege to refuse the reward. A fossil of the world's largest carnivore was found in Argentina. There is something about the place that makes one want to eat meat. The beef at La Cabana was first class, as was the wine, another Argentinian success story. Eduarda told me she held postgraduate qualifications in geography and anthropology, gained while living in New York.

'You must have found North and South America very different,' I said rather lamely.

'Yes, but there are many likenesses, too.'

'Are there? Like what?'

'Each is crossed from north to south by a great volcanic mountain chain nearer to the western than to the eastern coast. In each there is an independent mountain range on the eastern side. Each has two gigantic rivers. Each has on its western side a desert that contains an inland river basin with lakes. The shores of each are washed by the mightiest ocean currents.'

'I hadn't thought of all that, but these are just geographical likenesses, you must admit.'

'The similarities are not merely physical, Howard. Both continents were inhabited by races unlike those of Europe. Both were easily conquered by Europeans because of the superiority of the invaders in arms and discipline, and the immunity they possessed to the diseases they brought with them. The countries of both revolted against European control.'

'Are there any differences?' I asked with mild sarcasm.

'Of course. And these, I think, are far more interesting than the likenesses. In South America there was a large sedentary population of aborigines cultivating the soil and others who had worked in some sort of industry for many generations. The Spanish and Portuguese conquerors immediately turned them into serfs, and intermarriage occasionally occurred. In North America, however, the English and French met aborigines scattered over a vast region, who lived mainly by hunting animals and had formed no habits of regular industry. They were mostly fierce fighters and it was found impossible to make slaves of them or use them for any regular labour.'

'So was there never any question of Native American slavery in the United States?' I asked, feeling increasingly inhibited by Eduarda's textbook torrent.

'Absolutely not.'

'What about intermarriage?'

'Very rare. The settlers usually brought their women with them. Apparently the only example of a mixed race – half-white, half-Native American – was when the Welsh came to America in the twelfth century.'

'Whom?'

'The Welsh.'

'I'm Welsh, Eduarda.'

'I know from your features and accent. But I'm not Native American, I'm afraid. I am one hundred per cent Spanish. My family is from Ibiza, where the first Pacha's opened. It's a coincidence, no?'

I thought probably not but said nothing.

'So, shall we go to Pacha's, Howard?'

Buenos Aires clubs use film, theatre, acrobatics, song and dance to take the punter on an erotic journey through pain and pleasure – a heaving carnival for the senses. Pacha's, especially, attracts outrageous fashionistas, debauched hedonists and switched-on celebrities. Eduarda and I were escorted to join some of them in the heavily cordoned-off VIP area. The waiter brought two house specials. They tasted sweet and herbal.

'These are fantastic drinks,' said Eduarda. 'A bit like ecstasy but completely legal.'

We each drank two more.

The DJs mixed garage, disco, drum 'n' bass, punk, hardcore house, new wave and heavy metal. Erotic, exotic, chaotic and narcotic circus characters wove through the dancers. French maids with feather dusters and rubber-clad slaves with confetti cannons patrolled the edges of the crowd.

'Let's dance, Howard,' Eduarda commanded.

We walked to the dance floor. Discordant cacophonies of something like sound suddenly made me stumble as I unsuccessfully tried to tune in to a head-fuck mix of bass lines, wolf whistles and catcalls. Eduarda held out her hand to help me up and fell on top of me. Her eyes were ecstatic, her nostrils were smoking. Familiar but wonderful feelings tingled through my guts and skin. We swayed back to the VIP area.

Several hours later, I was sitting in the back of Eduarda's Mercedes with her head on my lap. She had fallen asleep, still clutching a half-full bottle of Pacha's champagne. Our clothes were drenched with sweat and booze, and the car reeked of alcohol and cigars. The chauffeur, fed up of driving us up and down avenues gleaming with early-morning sunshine, woke her up.

'Howard, it is almost nine a.m. I must get home. I have had a most wonderful time and will miss you and your wonderful accent. I have a friend, Raoul, who lives in Trelew. He works for a tourist company there. I'll fax his number to your hotel. My driver will drop you off and then take me home.'

'You don't fancy coming in for a coffee?'

'I actually fancy coming in for something far more exciting than coffee, but I won't. I have a busy day. See you again, I hope. You will enjoy Patagonia, I know.'

I staggered into the hotel, legless and disoriented, and lurched through the lobby. The hotel had been invaded by about thirty Brits on tour with Saga, a company specialising in group holidays for the over-50s. They were at the bar having a welcome drink and getting to know one another. I could hear at least one Welsh accent.

'I wish they would hurry up and check our bags in. I can't wait to take off these bloody long stockings and have a shower. Eleven hours is too long for me. I told you before we left it would be.'

'Gareth, will you stop complaining just for a minute,' a woman, clearly Gareth's wife, protested. 'You haven't stopped. They're giving us a drink while we wait, fair play.'

'It's not a drink I need, it's some bloody breakfast. I thought that was included.'

'Not on the first day, Gareth. Saga made that very clear before we left home.'

I couldn't resist interrupting. 'Where's home, then?'

'South Wales.'

'I thought so. Same as me.'

'Well? Sit down and join us. I'm Gareth Powell. This is my wife, Bethan. Have a drink with us by here. It's free.'

'Thanks. I'm Howard Marks. You're on holiday, I suppose?'

'Doesn't bloody feel like it. Eleven hours on a plane!'

'Stop it, Gareth, for God's sake. Yes, we are on holiday, Howard. Where are you from in South Wales?'

'Kenfig Hill. Do you know it?'

'Know it! I should say. Gareth and I often used to go and pick dewberries on Kenfig dunes, didn't we, love?'

'That's not all we did there, mind,' added Gareth. 'Well! Well! Kenfig Hill. Haven't been there for donkey's years. From Blackwood, we are.'

'Gareth's mother used to love making dewberry tart. It was her favourite after gooseberry.' Bethan was clearly on one.

'That's a coincidence. I was in Blackwood not so long ago.'

'Were you indeed? What the hell were you doing there?'

'Just a bit of research – I'm a writer.'

'Really! What's there to research in Blackwood, other than why anyone would go there in the first place? Kenfig Hill's better.'

'Apparently Henry Morgan owned some property and lived in Blackwood. Some people even think he was born there.'

'Oh no! Don't you bloody start, please, about Henry bloody Morgan, for Christ's sake. That's all I hear about from Idwal from morning to night. He doesn't stop. And he's meant to be my best friend. He keeps going on about Captain Morgan having lived in one of our locals. So bloody what? I'd have thought someone with his loot would have had better taste than to move to Blackwood.'

'Gareth, some people are interested in history. And Blackwood's lovely, Howard. Don't listen to him. My mother's family came from near Kenfig Hill – I think it was Pyle. We called in on them when we went to the eisteddfod in Bridgend. It didn't stop raining all day.'

'Gareth, you must mean the Monkey Tree, yeah? People kept telling me it was haunted by Henry Morgan's relatives,' I said, sidestepping Bethan's wittering.

'I bet you didn't see any ghosts; it's hard enough to get a drink. The only spirits there are well behind the bar. History writer, are you?'

Gareth and Bethan were just that little bit too old to have

spent their formative years taking substantial quantities of drugs or to have taken much interest in the trials of a major marijuana smuggler. I dodged the opportunity to tell them my life story: 'Sort of. I write about social issues, music, and sport as well. Where are you off to next?'

'They're taking us all over Patagonia for ten days.'

'To the Welsh community?'

'I bloody well hope not, Howard; I'm trying to have a holiday. Although that's probably the only place we'll be able to watch the Wales v. France match. We've done well this year, haven't we? Did you see the games against England and Italy?'

'Of course I did. Fantastic, weren't we? Do you think we'll win the Grand Slam?'

'No doubt in my mind. We've got that old seventies magic back at last.'

'So if you aren't interested in the Welsh community, Gareth, why are you going to Patagonia?'

'Well, I am a bit interested, but I'm not fanatical. I've lived all my life in Wales without bothering to learn Welsh, so it's no use me pretending I'm that keen. What I'm looking forward to is seeing the glaciers in the south of Patagonia. It's the best part of the world for that.'

'I want to see the penguin colony,' said Bethan. 'I love penguins. I'm not a bird lover generally, but the way penguins walk is fantastic, I think. I'm not fussy about seeing the sea lions, though. Mind, I would have liked to see the whales, but they're out of season, according to the guidebook.'

The tour manager announced the group's bags had been checked into their rooms. Gareth and Bethan got up to go.

'I'll give you Idwal's number in Blackwood tomorrow at breakfast down by here. He will tell you all you want to know about Henry Morgan, and a lot more, I'm sure. It's a job to stop him talking, I'll warn you now.'

The next morning Gareth and Bethan were waiting at a

table; they had finished their breakfast some time ago. Gareth
was dutifully clutching a piece of paper.

'Here's Idwal's number. We're off in a few hours. I wouldn't
have minded staying here for a few more days, but that's what
it's like on these tours: you never get enough time.'

'I'm also going to Patagonia, funnily enough, probably the
day after tomorrow. Shall we exchange mobile numbers?'

'Mine doesn't work over here, Howard, but I'll take yours.
All the best. We'll meet again, I'm sure.'

I spent the rest of the day reading my guidebooks on
Argentina, moving from one culture café to another. In the
evening I made notes and ate another mountain of beef. The
following morning I took a city tour to bring the right measure
of reality to my guidebooks. The bus stopped at Teatro Colón,
the world's largest opera house, drove past Aristotle Onassis's
first business (a river ferry) and drove through the old artists'
quarter of La Boca, where I had drunk maté with Eduarda and
where Maradona's football club, Boca Juniors, had turned
itself into a shrine. A little later I gazed at the balcony where
Madonna had sung 'Don't Cry for Me, Argentina' and paid
my respects at Eva Perón's grave. I watched professional dog-
walkers exercising up to thirty leashed dogs at a time through
the city's lush parks and some old men pissing at street
corners.

The next morning I checked out of the Amerian, took a cab
to Newberry, Buenos Aires's domestic airport, and caught the
first flight to Trelew in the Chubut Valley. At least Trelew was
a Welsh name. I hadn't found any Welsh place names in
Brazil. Trelew means home of the lion, which failed to make
much sense. Perhaps the Welsh words for puma and lion were
the same.

After a few hours over a barren wilderness, the plane landed
at a small airport. A great statue of a penguin with a black head
dominated the arrivals hall. Murals of dolphins, sea lions and
whales covered the walls. Signs warned against the dangers of

bringing in animals, foodstuffs or other carriers of viruses or bacteria into Patagonia, the world's biggest complex of nature reserves and wildlife sanctuaries. I could find no hotel accommodation desk so just walked outside to where passengers were boarding a public bus destined for Puerto Madryn. I couldn't believe my luck. Puerto Madryn was named after Madryn Castle, the former North Welsh home of Sir Love Jones-Parry, one of the founders of the Welsh colony in Argentina. Punta Cuevas, where the Welsh first landed over 150 years ago, was part of Puerto Madryn.

I got on the bus, which for fifty-body shaking miles bounced along a straight and empty grit road spearing through thousands of square miles of flat military-green thorn scrub. The sea magically sprang into view, and I could see the tops of buildings nestling in a cove on the coast. A long pier with a massive cruise ship on each side stretched out into the ocean. Shops by the harbour sold motorboats, kayaks, canoes, jet skis, windsurfing boards and deep-sea fishing and diving gear. Puerto Madryn was not a typical Welsh village; it was a thriving North American-style water-sports resort and marina.

Somewhat disappointed, I got off the bus and located suitable accommodation, the Hotel Peninsula Valdes, checked in, and went for a walk into town looking for anything Welsh. Eventually I came across streets named Matthews, Roberts, Humphreys and Love Jones-Parry. Relieved, I walked down Love Jones-Parry until I came back to the promenade. A large monument, designed in 1965 by the famous Argentinian sculptor Luis Perlotti, commemorated the centenary of the Welsh landing in Punta Cuevas. Now excited at making some headway at last, I took a cab to Punta Cuevas and asked the driver to wait for me. Strolling along the shore, I was confronted by a statue of a Native American Indian perched on top of a pile of stones. He was holding a bow in one hand and shielding his eyes from the sun with another. A notice stated that this was *El Indio*, another Luis Perlotti statue. It commemorated the gratitude of the Welsh to the Tehuelche people, whose shared expertise had ensured their survival. Some caves with boarded-up openings were nearby. I read another notice, which stated the Welsh had landed here and lived in these caves. There was no other acknowledgement of their presence. Disappointed again, I got back into my cab and returned to the hotel.

Why had the Welsh chosen to come to this desert steppe – ravaged by icy gales in the winter and sucked dry by suffocating hot winds in the summer – in order to live in prehistoric living conditions? Had things really been that bad back home in the valleys? Where were their families now? Confused and unsettled, I ate some magnificent shellfish, drank a bottle of Malbec, and resolved to call Eduarda's friend in the morning.

My Spanish hadn't entirely deserted me: *'Buenos dias. Puedo hablar con Raoul, por favor?'*

'Quien llama?'

'Soy Howard Marks, un amigo de Eduarda en Buenos Aires.'

'Ah! Bien! Bien! Soy Raoul, Raoul Roberts. Como está, hombre?'

We met in the lobby of my hotel. Raoul Roberts was stocky and dark with twinkling blue eyes and a mouth permanently itching to smile. Although of Welsh male ancestry, he did not speak Welsh, but he had learned English as part of his tour-guide training, and that together with my street and prison Spanish enabled us to communicate effectively.

I gathered from Raoul that the Welsh had chosen Punta Cuevas as their landing point because of reports sent to Wales by two of the potential colonisers, Lewis Jones and Edwin Roberts (no relation to Raoul), who had made a preliminary investigation of the area. Puenta Cuevas lay in a sheltered natural harbour comprising a semicircle of rocks some eight miles wide and twenty-two miles long, where building materials in the form of soft clayey cliffs and timber from a nearby wreck were available. Jones and Roberts were obviously not experienced colonisers as they had neglected to find out whether there was fresh water immediately inland. There wasn't. Five members of the 153-strong group died within a month.

With cold, hunger and thirst as their permanent companions, search parties crossed the desert on foot, nourishing themselves by sucking blood from vultures and praying that no Indians would attack them. How could they possibly succeed where the Spanish, French and English had failed? The Welsh adventurers eventually found fresh water near the estuary of the Chubut River and set up smallholdings and a fishing community at a place they named Trerawson.

Argentina was not simply being generous in offering the Welsh a large chunk of its land; such a colony in the area also suited Argentinian interests. The government needed to strengthen its presence against threats from Chile and from England because of the Falklands/Malvinas dispute. England was the common enemy of Argentina and Wales. The Argentinian minister of the interior, Dr Rawson, keenly supported the establishment of a Welsh colony and gave his name to the country's first Welsh settlement, where they were officially granted rights of abode. Used to working in mines, the Welsh found farming difficult. At first ignorant of the different seasons in the southern hemisphere, they sowed crops in autumn instead of spring and had to face one failure after another.

They were saved from starvation by athe Tehuelche tribe, who set up camp close by, thereby beginning an astonishing relationship with the Welsh settlers, teaching them how to handle cattle, ride horses and hunt. The two communities bartered meat and pelts for bread and butter and even staged their own sports fixtures. The Welsh won the shooting; the Tehuelche won the equestrian events. The bond established between them has held until the present day. Nevertheless, the first few years were tough for the settlers, and the population fell. Over the years, the Welsh learnt to irrigate their fields and were eventually able to export wheat. The population recovered and then increased. Remembering their debt, the Welsh took abandoned Indian children and orphans into their care and taught them Welsh. Intermarriage with local Spanish-speakers was encouraged, provided they learnt Welsh.

Raoul said there were few if any people of Welsh descent now living in Rawson, but he would gladly take me there to show me their first chapel – Capel Berwyn – and the only Welsh cemetery. Then, by way of contrast, he would take me to where the Welsh were now living.

The grit road from Puerto Madryn to Rawson was in the same condition and went through similar landscape to the one from Trelew to Puerto Madryn. But Raoul drove faster than the bus. We were overtaken just once by a dust storm on wheels. As we entered Rawson, another water-sports resort, a large building in the distance swamped me with an uncomfortable and familiar feeling. A battered sign showed that it was the Servicio Penitenciario Federal Instituto de Seguridad y Resocializacion, a maximum-security prison. I pondered the irony of land symbolising the triumph of Welsh freedom ending up as a high-security nick. On the other hand, Patagonia's first chapel provided me with a comfortable familiar feeling; it was like so many I had seen as a child. Next to the chapel and partially obscured by it was a large painting of a sailboat, the *Mimosa*.

Named after one of the arms of the Southern Cross, this shabby tea clipper, well past its sail-by date, had spent May 1865 lying in Liverpool's Clarence Graving Dock waiting to transport 153 emigrants to their promised land 7,000 miles to the south-west. Carpenters constructed partitions in the hold to separate the men's sleeping quarters from the women's and built tables, benches, storage boxes and a makeshift gangway. The female figurehead was removed and replaced by a simple scroll. The fare was £12 and £5 for children, but those unable to pay were still accepted: the Reverend Michael D. Jones, who had first envisaged a Welsh colony in Argentina, would pick up the bill. No one knew how long the voyage would last. They took provisions for six months.

Mimosa's captain, George Pepperell, recruited a crew of eighteen, mostly the dregs of Liverpool. Discovering that his passengers were almost all Welsh-speaking, Captain Pepperell signed on a young Welshman, Richard Berwyn as purser. At 10 o'clock on the morning of Thursday 25 May, *Mimosa* was towed out into the vast basin of the Victoria Dock, and on Sunday 28 May, a pilot guided her down the Mersey toward the open sea. The voyage took 65 days. Despite the daily issue of lime or lemon juice, many of the passengers began to suffer from boils and bleeding gums. Five children died on the voyage; two babies were born. They stopped at a Brazilian port to restock with provisions. Captain Pepperell, weary of the voyage, tried unsuccessfully to persuade the passengers to join a colony already settled in Brazil, presumably the one I failed to find.

Finally, just before dawn on Thursday 27 July, *Mimosa*, flying its unique flag of a Welsh dragon superimposed on the Argentinian colours, reached its destination and dropped anchor. By late afternoon Lewis Jones and Edwyn Roberts had rowed out to where *Mimosa* was anchored and were on board. Disembarkation took just over a day, after which the colonisers gathered on the beach and held a short service of thanks. Captain Pepperell lost no time leaving with his ship. The original painting of the *Mimosa*, completed in her sailing prime when she lay outside Sydney Harbour, used to be exhibited in the Parker Gallery in Pimlico, London, until a collector from the Isle of Wight bought it. On his death, the painting changed hands then disappeared. Bernie Davies might be interested. On the other hand, perhaps the painting already graces the walls of a Valley Commandos clubhouse.

Raoul then took me to Moriah, the Welsh cemetery. Any lingering doubts I had ever had about there having been a strong Welsh presence in Patagonia quickly evaporated. Apart from a few in Spanish and English, all the several hundred gravestones were inscribed in Welsh. I failed to find any bearing the name McCarty, but there were some Davieses. According to Raoul, Trelew, just a few miles away, was home to some Welsh people, but now other groups easily out-numbered them; the heart of the existing Welsh community was a bit further away at Gaiman. He suggested we went there and call at Trelew on the way back.

At first Gaiman seemed like a ghost town, and I expected to be taken to another cemetery. One a day is more than enough. But Gaiman wasn't dead; it was merely a bit drowsy. There was a monopoly of Welsh street names, dusty rows of flinty Welsh cottages, hacienda-style houses, stern-looking chapels and more tea houses than there are in all Wales. We parked the car in Avenida Jones, where Welsh teachers opened Patagonia's first and still-active secondary school. The motto chiselled above the entrance – *Nid Byd Byd Heb Wybodaeth* (There is no world without knowledge) – was precisely the same as that of Garw Grammar School, which I attended.

We walked a few yards to the nearest tea house, Casa de Te Gales, which, despite it still being morning, was serving afternoon tea. Raoul signalled me to go in alone while he looked for Manolo, a friend of his who although not of Welsh ancestry was learning the language to please his fiancée and could also speak fluent English. He had just returned from a visit to Wales. Familiar Welsh paintings and tea towels covered the walls. Welsh arias and the aromas of my childhood saturated the atmosphere. Fine old ladies loaded blue and white gingham-covered tables with munchies and cosy covered teapots full of proper miners' brew ready for the dozens of Argentinian aristocrats who had driven hours to sample the delights of a traditional Welsh high tea. Croeso

Cymru, the Welsh tourist board, could learn a few lessons by visiting here.

For several minutes I lost myself in a surreal nostalgic reverie, smiled at everyone and chatted to anyone who returned the smile. A young woman wearing a white blouse sporting both her name, Bronwen Lopez, and a prominent Welsh dragon brought plates of Welsh fruit cakes, tarts, spiced breads, jams and scones to my table.

'*Siarad Cymraeg?*' she asked.

'*Odw,*' I replied, feeling more unreal.

Bronwen was delighted to meet someone from Wales and introduced me to her companion waitresses Dolores Jones and Claudia Williams, great-great-granddaughters of two of the passengers on the *Mimosa*. We talked at length about Wales and I explained my rather confused quest to find out whether any Davieses here came from Mountain Ash and whether any McCarty had ever lived in the Chubut Valley. They suggested I visit the keeper of the town's museum, Tegai Roberts. Her great-aunt was born during the *Mimosa*'s voyage and her great-grandfather, Lewis Jones, was reputedly the first Welsh person to set foot in South America. Trelew was named after him, not after a lion or puma after all. She would be able to help.

Leaving a message for Raoul should he return before I did, I followed the waitresses' directions to the yellow-bricked museum, which was once a railway station. I spotted a familiar figure frantically darting in and out of every bar, café and shop. It was Gareth, AWOL from Saga.

He saw me and rushed up. 'Do you know anywhere with a television round by here? I get so confused with the bloody time difference. They must have already started the second half.'

I had forgotten. It was Saturday, the day of the Wales v. France match.

'I don't, Gareth. And I doubt very much if the match would be broadcast here. Where's Bethan?'

'Buggered if I know. Watching Patagonian hares and ostriches, I expect, with the rest of the crowd. They're supposed to be bloody Welsh here, though, aren't they? And they've got to be able to get Sky Sports, surely? I'll keep trying. Let me know if you find one.'

It was the briefest meeting I had ever had with a fellow Welshman.

Tegai Roberts is the elder stateswoman of Welsh Patagonia, and no Welsh person would ever be forgiven for visiting Gaiman and not paying her homage. With enormous grace, she welcomed me to the museum in Spanish. I answered in Welsh, and her eyes sparkled. I asked if she had a list of the names of the *Mimosa* passengers and from where in Wales they had come. She nodded and pointed to a display cabinet. I looked to see if there were any Davieses. There were dozens, mostly from Mountain Ash, adding much credence to Bernie Davies's claim that his grandfather was one of the first colonists. Tegai had no idea why so many had come from Mountain Ash, but she said there were hundreds of Davieses in the Chubut Valley, many of them direct descendants of the *Mimosa* colonists. Some of them might know. She knew of no McCartys or old stories of any Irishmen having come to learn Welsh here but thought it well within the bounds of possibility.

I left the museum with some sense of achievement and walked around Gaiman, fascinated still by the predominance of Welsh names on houses, hotels, post offices and other official buildings.

'Howard! Howard!' Gareth, his arms open wide, was tearing down the hill, skipping as best he could. 'I called home from the post office. France eighteen, Wales twenty-four. Only Ireland to beat now for the Grand Slam. And that's at Cardiff.'

We walked arm in arm through Gaiman's small municipal park, looking for a café that sold something stronger than tea and ran across a graffiti-defaced statue in its centre.

'Christopher Columbus? What the hell is he doing here? I know he has a tendency to end up in the wrong place, but this is ridiculous. They'll be saying Henry Morgan came here next. What's the inscription say, Howard? I can't read Spanish.'

'It commemorates Columbus's discovery of America.'

'Never! Would you bloody believe it? Prince Madoc discovered America, not bloody Columbus. Here of all places, where they're meant to be proud to be Welsh, they stick a monument to Columbus. And there's nowhere to watch rugby. It's a bloody disgrace.'

Gareth spent the next ten minutes adding '300 years after Madoc' to the statue's graffiti.

'Right, I'd better get back to the group. They're at the chapel around the corner. They've opened it especially for us. I'll be in trouble with Bethan if I don't go. Do me a favour, will you, and come with me? I get embarrassed being the only Welshman in the group and not being able to speak Welsh.'

Decades had elapsed since my last visit to a Welsh chapel. That had been when I married my first wife, Ilze, in 1967. I had forgotten the smell of the spartan wooden pews, the stained-glass light exposing the dust and the polish, the echoing whispers, the harsh silence, and the thoughts of the presence of God. The Saga group huddled near the pulpit trying in vain to comprehend the stilted English of their local guide, Prygethwr (Preacher) James. None of them spoke Welsh or Spanish.

'He speaks Welsh,' shouted Gareth.

'*Dewch yma*,' boomed Prygethwr James, his eyes beaming.

Timidly, I approached the pulpit. Prygethwr James gave me a bear hug.

'*Croeso. Beth yw enw?*'

'*R'wyn* Howard Marks.'

'*Croeso*, Howard Marks.'

Prygethwr James then asked me to translate any questions

asked him by the group. I said I would do the best I could. The group reacted with total silence. So Prygethwr James explained to his impromptu congregation how the Welsh were able to keep their traditions and language and organise their community life under a municipal democracy, while peacefully coexisting and trading with semi-nomadic Native American Indians and exporting the produce of both cultures to the outside world.

Out of the desert the Welsh settlers had created fields, meadows, orchards and gardens. They built roads, irrigation systems and a number of chapels of which sixteen remain. These also served as primary schools and meeting halls, and published their own newspapers. The Welsh saga was a paradigm for peaceful colonisation. Welsh, the first non-native language, still dominates in most spheres of communication, social relations, culture, religion and education. Eisteddfods and choral singing have helped keep Welsh alive as the language of the community for almost 150 years. Chubut is the only place in the world where Welsh has greater currency than English. Most other immigrant communities in Argentina lost their original language within three generations.

This had been difficult to translate, given that my Welsh fluency and vocabulary are that of a seven-year-old child, but Prygethwr James helped me, occasionally substituting the Spanish words when he noticed my blank looks on hearing his Welsh.

'How big is the Welsh settlement in Patagonia?' asked one of the group.

Prygethwr James admitted he had little idea as to how many of the population would call themselves Welsh, but large Welsh settlements in Patagonia were established as far north as Luis Beltran on the Río Negro, as far south as Sarmiento on the border with the province of Santa Cruz, as far west as Chile, and as far east as the Atlantic. The area the Welsh occupied was about twice the size of Wales.

'Ask if I could look at the hymnal on the pulpit,' asked Bethan.

Permission granted, Bethan stepped up to the pulpit, picked up the hymnal, turned over some pages and started trembling. 'I can't believe it. It's exactly the same as the one in the chapel back home, exactly the same. Even *"Calon Lan"* is on the same page.'

She burst into song. Gareth, Prygethwr James and I joined her in full voice.

The tour group looked bemused as they boarded their bus. 'Thanks for that, Howard,' said Gareth. 'We're off to Trelew now, staying the night. If you're going through there this evening, we could have a drink. All the best, anyway.'

Feeling disoriented, as if I had just been on a brief visit to heaven, I walked back to the Casa de Te Gales. Raoul had returned and brought along his friend Manolo – short hair, tinted glasses and face permanently fixed in an expression of concentration. His English was excellent, tinged with thick Cardiff and South American Spanish accents, and his T-shirt advised you to 'Smoke Bush Not Iraq.'

'Ah! Mr Nice himself. Encantado, hombre. I thought from what Raoul said it had to be you. I've met some friends of yours in South Wales. I've read all your books, went to your show in Porthcawl, and I saw you in *Human Traffic*. Wicked, man.'

Directed by the young, brilliant, award-winning Justin Kerrigan, *Human Traffic* is a film about Cardiff nightlife at the end of the second millennium, focusing on how five best friends deal with their relationships and personal demons over a weekend. Starting on Friday afternoon with their preparations for clubbing, the film follows their progress from ecstasy-induced fun through a booze-laden comedown early on Saturday morning followed by the weekend's aftermath. I played myself in a cameo role commenting on the way spliffs were smoked and passed around at parties. It was my first acting role.

'I had great fun doing that. When were you in Cardiff?'

'Eight years ago as a student, which I remembered nothing about until *Human Traffic* reminded me. But I go back there at least once a year. That place rocks, man.'

'What did you study?'

'I got a scholarship from here to do Welsh studies at the University of Cardiff but ended up learning English and becoming a resident DJ at the Emporium.'

'Really! I DJ'd there when Tim Corrigan was in charge. He runs the Soda Bar now, doesn't he?'

'That's right. Tim used to be my boss. He's a dude. I also used to play at the Club Ifor Bach. I heard you DJ'd there once with Gruff of the Super Furry Animals. I missed that. I've got his new solo album, by the way, the one that's all Welsh. Anyway, Mr Nice, what brings you to Patagonia?'

'Just having a look around to see the place for myself, really. It's incredible, isn't it? I'm also vaguely doing research for my new book.'

'New book? Great! What's it about?'

'Good question, Manolo. I guess where I come from, what's happening to me now and where I'm going.'

'What's that mean, then? Are you here to look for long-lost relations? DJing at a Welsh tea house? Or do you have plans to grow marijuana here? That would be great.'

'All the above. Is it possible to get any dope here?'

'There's no dope scene here really, but I did bring a ready-rolled one with me when I knew I was meeting you. I brought some skunk back with me from Cardiff. I can't miss the chance of smoking a joint with Mr Nice, can I? We'd better not smoke it inside here though, just in case.'

The three of us went out and walked to the municipal park. Manolo sparked up a joint, took a few drags and passed it to me. Raoul seemed oblivious to what was happening. I sucked at the joint. It's amazing how well it works after a few days' abstinence. Manolo and I talked about the usual – skunk, pills, cocaine, music, films and football. He lived in Dolavon, just west of Gaiman, and offered his services as a guide to the Chubut Valley. He had things to do today, but he and his car would be at my disposal tomorrow for a few days' exploration, if I liked the idea.

Manolo then sped off, while Raoul and I got into his car and drove back to Trelew to have a drink at the Touring Club hotel, where anyone who matters today hangs out and where all the bad guys hung out a hundred years ago.

Butch Cassidy, born Robert Leroy Parker in Utah, was the most prolific bank and train robber of his day. After numerous run-ins with the law and a couple of years in prison, Cassidy organised a group of outlaws, including Harry Longabaugh aka the Sundance Kid, which became known as the Wild Bunch. During 1896–1901 the Wild Bunch robbed over a dozen banks and trains throughout the West until the Pinkerton National Detective Agency began to make such robberies highly risky. In 1901 Cassidy and Sundance, with the latter's girlfriend Etta Place, fled to Argentina to pursue a career in ranching. All they wanted was to lead a life hidden from the world. Their home in Cholilo, at the western end of the Chubut Valley, was often the scene of music, well-attended dances and other revelry, much loved by the dignitaries of the area. To buy supplies and sell their produce, they would travel 400 miles to Trelew and stay for long periods in rooms that now form part of the Touring Club hotel.

The public area of the hotel was a huge cowboy saloon with fans suspended from a high ceiling, newspapers on sticks, old peeling mirrors, polished light-wood tables and chairs, antiquated but functioning cappuccino machines and a bar longer than a cricket pitch. Shelves carried hundreds of spirit and wine bottles, beer and cider cans; and black and white group photographs lined the walls. I looked at each faded photograph intently. Many bore the names of the people pictured. I looked for McCarty. And there it was. Rubbing my eyes and dusting off the frame, I treble-checked. There was no doubt; I had read the name correctly – Patrick McCarty. He and a few of his mates were leaning against a white stone wall making hand gestures similar to those made by today's hip hop artists. I could not detect any family likeness, and there was no hint where the photograph had been taken. However, this was no coincidence: I had found my great-great-grandfather.

I joined Raoul back at the table and told him the reasons for my obvious excitement. I asked if he would mind enquiring from whoever was in charge if there was any chance of buying the photograph. I would happily pay a good price. Raoul ambled off behind the bar. He returned shaking his head. No photographs were for sale, but if I had a camera I was welcome to take a close-up shot, as long as I didn't remove the photograph from the frame. I had no camera other than the one in my mobile, which I still hadn't figured out how to use. I'd have to buy one and come back.

My problem was solved by another surprise appearance from Gareth, who seemed as if he had expected to meet me here.

'The rest are at the Palaeontological Museum round the corner looking at models of dinosaurs. I don't mind a bit of history, but that's taking it back too far, in my opinion. Mind, I liked *Jurassic Park*.'

'Do you have a camera, Gareth?'

'I certainly do, and it's a digital one at that. I've got it with me. It takes excellent pictures, excellent. Shall we ask your mate to take one of us two together? We could sit down by there, next to that poker table. I'm sure those Indians wouldn't mind moving over for a minute.'

After quickly introducing Gareth to Raoul, I explained to Gareth my discovery and need for a camera. Within a few minutes Gareth had taken several exposures of the priceless photograph.

'I can download the photos and email them to you. Marvellous what they can do with computers these days, mind, isn't it? Who would have thought it? So your great-great-grandfather was from round by here. What was his name?'

'Patrick McCarty.'

'Was he one of those original Welsh colonists that the preacher kept going on about today? Bethan was fascinated.'

'No, he was Irish.'

'I guessed that with a name like McCarty. But there were plenty who came from over the water to work in the Welsh pits. I used to court an Irish girl myself before I met Bethan. She lived in Merthyr Tydfil. Two years it lasted. Bethan still goes on about it. Was he one of those?'

'No, my great-great-grandfather went over the water the other way, to America. Then he came here, learned Welsh, disappeared for several years and finally turned up in Kenfig Hill under the name Marks and led a quiet religous life. He changed his name because he was related to Billy the Kid.'

'You're kidding. I never knew that was Billy the Kid's surname. I suppose he must have had one. Billy Marks. Well I never.'

'No, Gareth. Billy McCarty.'

'Right! Of course. Now I've got you. Well I suppose we're all belonging to one another in some way or other. My father always used to say he was Bob Hope's cousin, something I would have kept a bit quieter about if I was him. Well I'd better be off. See you again, I'm sure.'

'OK, Gareth. Let me give you my email address.'

'Oh dear. Almost forgot already. Thanks, Howard.'

Meanwhile Raoul had been thumbing through the local phone directory searching for McCartys. He had found three MacKarthys, rang them, but none answered. He would try again tonight after he had driven me back to my Puerto Madryn hotel.

*

As arranged, Manolo, wearing the same T-shirt, turned up at the Hotel Peninsula Valdes just after breakfast.

'All right, Mr Nice? Raoul called me before I left. He checked on those MacKarthy numbers in the phone directory, but the people insist they're neither Welsh nor Irish and have no connection with either. So that's not your family. They seemed a bit upset to be bothered. They're probably Yanks. We don't like Yanks much down here.'

'I'm not that keen on them myself.'

'I'm not surprised. What was it like in that maximum-security prison?'

'Brutal and barbaric, but survivable. You just do your time until they let you out.'

'I suppose so. Wouldn't fancy it myself, though. Anyway, enough of that. Those days are over, I hope. Let's get going.'

I checked out of the hotel and asked to leave my bags with the concierge for a few days. Manolo got into his car, a red Mercedes much like the one I owned before I was busted, and arranged the soft drinks, snacks and ashtrays. I climbed into the passenger seat.

'Nice car, Manolo. I used to have one of these.'

'Not bad, is it? We like European cars in Patagonia. You'll hardly ever see an American one. We'll go to my place and pick up some CDs and blankets. It's on the way. You can meet my missus, Olwen. She knows all about you and has even read your book in Spanish. Don't mention dope in front of her, though. She's nervous about all that stuff. Best to keep it quiet.'

We traversed the now-familiar sixty miles of wilderness to the Chubut River, passed through Gaiman, and thirteen miles further west came to the seemingly unconscious tiny hamlet of Dolavon. Unlike Gaiman, Dolavon had preserved the character of an early pioneering settlement – whitened brick buildings and not a tea shop in sight. Manolo's home was at the edge of the village, a quaint grey cottage with railway sash windows next to a municipal campsite. Boots and gardening tools lay next to the doorway, which exquisitely framed Olwen, a beautiful mix of Welsh, Spanish and Indian features.

'*Swt mai, Mr Nice? R'wyn falch iawn i cwrdda chi. Croeso i Dolavon. Dewch mewn.*'

We walked in and sat down on some antique chairs. The usual trilingual Welsh/Spanish/English conversation then took place, substantially aided by a nearby pile of dictionaries and some maté to focus concentration. After about half an hour Manolo picked up his CDs and a pile of blankets, and we said our goodbyes to Olwen, who insisted I see the garden before leaving. The simultaneous yellow blooming of the native thorny *calafate* and the imported daffodil, a common symbol of the Welsh nation, heralds spring in Patagonia. A Tehuelche legend relates how an old woman too feeble to travel was left behind by her tribe one winter and turned into a *calafate* bush to feed the small birds with her berries and provide them with shelter from the icy wind. In Olwen's garden each *calafate* bush was surrounded by a carefully planted circle of daffodils in gratitude for its winter-long protection.

Manolo and I drove into the centre of Dolavon and parked the Mercedes near a disused railway station, next to a stream. Weeping willows, curious irrigation waterwheels and other hydro-devices lined the stream banks.

'Weird, aren't they? These saved the original Welsh settlers and enabled them to be self-supporting after years of their harvests failing. They used the Chubut River to feed irrigation canals, pumping the water through with machinery like this. Soon, the valley was a blanket of yellow wheat. No one makes bread like the Welsh, do they? Lovely stuff. The Indians here learned that quickly enough and used to swap loads of ostrich feathers for a few loaves. The Welsh would flog the feathers to other European colonists and use the money to buy what they needed.'

'Why didn't the other Europeans buy feathers direct from the Indians?'

'They'd be scalped if they tried that, wouldn't they? Only the Welsh insisted on treating the Indians as equals. All the other Europeans, except for a handful of individuals, used to really fuck them over. Anyway, while all this bread-bartering was going on, a guy from Dolavon called Benjamin won first prize in the wheat contest at the Universal Show of Paris. I think it was in 1899, the one the Eiffel Tower was built for. Four years later Benjamin won the same prize at the Chicago National Show. Chubut wheat really took off then and was exported to Europe and North America. To stop the middle-men ripping off the profits, the wheat boys formed the Chubut Mercantile Company, which everyone called the Welsh Co-op. There's one of the old mills still working just around the corner. It's a restaurant, too. Fancy lunch before we go? They do fantastic Patagonian lamb there.'

After eighty years of use, Harinero Mill is still in working order with the original machinery. Manolo and I had to walk through the mill, where the noise was deafening, to get to the farmhouse-style restaurant. Bilingual Spanish/Welsh recipe books, jams, and bread were available to buy.

'How's the lamb?'

'As good as any back home. I suppose they brought the sheep from Wales.'

'No. The first sheep here actually came from the Malvinas.'

'Really! From the Falklands?'

'Don't use that word here, for fuck's sake. What a stupid war that was – two bald men fighting over a comb. But yes. An Englishman, Henry Reynard, brought the first sheep over. The English do have their uses, sometimes.'

Leek soup had preceded the stuffed shoulder of lamb. A selection of Welsh black cakes followed. The waiter topped up our carafe of red wine throughout the two-hour meal.

'All right, Mr Nice. Let's be off and do what the Welsh did over a hundred years ago – head west.'

Manolo stuck a CD into the car's sound system. 'Your Mother's Got a Penis' by Goldie Lookin' Chain, Wales's answer to two decades of American hip hop, boomed out of the back speakers.

'I love these guys,' said Manolo. 'I've got the whole album. The track about the soap bar really cracks me up.'

The terrain gradually became more mountainous and punctuated with alien-shaped sandstone outcrops which looked as if they had transplanted themselves from Arizona's Monument Valley. Coming into a small town named Las Chapas, Manolo turned up a lane towards a ranch house. He pointed to a gable.

'Recognise that?'

A white cement eagle proudly surveyed its domain.

'Of course. It's the insignia of the Free Wales Army. Are they out here too? Inside that ranch?'

'It's rumoured they are. Locals have heard rifle shots and sounds like people training, but I don't know. One of my friends knocked on the door once. The people who live there are Welsh, sure enough, but they said the eagle was in honour of the Welsh name for Snowdon, Yr Eryri – Eagle's Nest. Take your pick.'

Next stop west was the small community of Las Plumas – Valley of the Martyrs – where we bought petrol. There had to be a tale attached to such a name.

During the last years of the nineteenth century the Argentinian government had embarked on its appalling so-called *Conquista del Desierto*, the ethnic cleansing of the Patagonian wilderness. Indians were massacred, imprisoned in barbaric conditions or banished from their homelands, provoking an unsurprising upsurge of hostility and distrust towards white men. The twenty-year-long friendly coexistence which had prevailed between the Welsh and the Tehuelche Indians, whom the Welsh called their 'brothers of the desert', was threatened. On a day never forgotten in these parts a few Welsh settlers were mistaken by Indians for Argentinian government soldiers, brutally murdered and dismembered. One of the Welsh party, ex-*Mimosa* passenger John Daniel Evans, 'Evans the Miller', miraculously escaped and went on to found Trevelín – Mill Town – the westernmost outpost of Welsh Patagonia over 300 miles away. Although saddened to the core, the Welsh sought no vengeance and continued to refuse to join the government's persecution and extermination of Patagonia's indigenous population.

Motoring further westward another fifty miles, this time accompanied by 2 many DJs' remix of 'Where's Your Head At', I noticed the sandstone outcrops were steadily increasing in size to massive mountains of rock, Grand Canyon-style. Plateaus capped cylindrical mountains as if expecting the onset of the next close encounter with a flying saucer. The red sun overtook us and headed for bed. Manolo noticed the scenery had grabbed me.

'Something else, isn't it? Straight out of *Star Wars*. We call this place the Altars. Forget California; this is the real Death Valley. Shall we stop here for a rest? We're about halfway.'

We smoked a joint Manolo produced from his pocket.

'Do you recognise it?'

'Recognise what?'

'The dope you're smoking.'

'I can't say I do, other than it's extremely strong skunk. What is it?'

'It's Mr Nice Super Silver Haze.'

'You're having a laugh, aren't you? How did you get hold of that?'

'Do you know a girl called Polly from Kenfig Hill?'

'Of course.'

'Well I got this skunk from her a couple of weeks ago. I telephoned her last night and told her I had met you here. She was gobsmacked. Small world, isn't it?'

'I suppose so. But you wouldn't think so, looking at this bit of it, would you?'

The horizon seemed infinitely further away than I had ever experienced. Monstrous rock altars filled my field of vision in every direction. Birds of prey, graceful and menacing, hang-glided among them. Visions of dragons and dinosaurs tickled my subconscious as I came to terms with my own insignificance. Bertrand Russell's words jumped into my mind: 'If the history of the universe were ever documented, it's doubtful if the human race would be even mentioned.' Night fell, switching on the lights of the Southern Cross. Its right arm, Mimosa, winked at me as I sought the solace of dream. Winds howled around the petrified pyramids. Beady eyes of curious foxes and guanacos – wild Andean llamas – glinted creepily in the starlight.

'You take a blanket and lie on the back seat. I'll wrap myself up on the ground – I prefer it that way.'

I took up Manolo's offer and immediately fell asleep. We both woke up after just a couple of hours.

'OK, Mr Nice, let's make a move and try to get to Tecka before daylight.'

Manolo produced a plastic bottle of red wine and a Tupperware munch box, and we had a lively breakfast of home-made bread, hard sausage, pears, sharp cheese and walnuts before getting back on the road.

Dawn broke as the monumental rock formations gradually gave way to fertile plains, lakes, hills and streams. The snow-capped peaks of the Andes shed their clouds of morning mist and announced their dominating presence. We stopped for petrol just outside the small town of Tecka. A roadside mausoleum lay nearby.

'You've probably not heard of Incayal, but he was the greatest chief of the Tehuelche. Tecka was his favourite place to camp. When the Argentinian government started killing all the Indians, Perito Moreno, the guy who discovered the glaciers down south, persuaded the authorities to allow him to live in peace as keeper of a museum in Buenos Aires. After Incayal died, Moreno moved his body back here. It's become a shrine now. There's nothing else to see in Tecka, so we'll keep going on this road. In a few hours we'll get to Arroyo Pescado, and we don't want to stop there either. It's where a Yank murdered a Welshman, another event we don't forget. It's still full of Yanks. They come here for fishing holidays. I hate the place.'

Manolo related how the Welsh colonists, having been deprived of the Tehuelche as commercial partners, badly needed to export their products. They planned to extend the railway, and a brilliant engineer, Dafydd ap Iwan, came to work on the project. Dafydd ap Iwan established rail terminals at Puerto Madryn and Trelew and then conducted feasibility studies and surveys from Trelew to the Andes. He also became manager of the Arroyo Pescado branch of the Chubut Mercantile Company. In December 1909, Dafydd ap Iwan was held up and murdered in cold blood by a North American bandit named Wilson. Plans to complete the Welsh Pacific–Atlantic railway died shortly afterwards.

We drove for a few hours through gentle mountain passes past chuckling creeks until we reached the westernmost Welsh colony, Cwm Hyfryd, now split into the Andean foothill towns of Esquel and Trevelín. The colony boasted a police station and telegraph office. A hundred years ago its chief of police, Eduardo Humphreys, had made friends with his good neighbours Butch Cassidy and the Sundance Kid. Cholilo was only a few miles from Esquel.

Plateaus and plains came into view. A short distance away small troops of gauchos in their full regalia of flat-topped black hats, colourful bandannas and handlebar moustaches were rounding up a herd of Herefords.

'It's a cowboy movie, isn't it?' said Manolo. 'See those black rocks over there? That's where Butch Cassidy and the

Sundance Kid murdered a Welshman for no reason. We'll pass by their place in a little while.' A lonely abandoned shack lay rotting in a corner of a field. There were no notices and no visitors. 'Good enough for them,' said Manolo. 'They did the place no good at all.'

We entered the dusty town of Esquel. Posters and signs referred to the Old Patagonian Express, the Welsh Co-op's downfall. Local wheat couldn't compete in price with the grain the train bought down from up north. At the Cassis Restaurant we had a delicious lunch of trout carpaccio followed by roast lamb. Manolo went to the bar to make a phone call. He turned round, put his thumb up and put down the phone.

'Got some news for you about your great-great-grandfather, Mr Nice. That was Raoul. He's had a word with Tommy Davies, a good man who knows just about everything that's ever happened here. My dad thought a lot of him. Tommy is pretty old. He'll be a hundred in a year or two. Anyway, he said his father had often talked about an Irishman called Patrick who had come to live in Gaiman and who did learn Welsh at the school there. But for some reason he left to go to live in Ushuaia.'

'Where's that?'

'It's the end of the world.'

'Which country?'

'This country, Argentina. It's right at the bottom of Tierra del Fuego. Next stop is the South Pole. I expect you'll be off there now, won't you? Why don't you stay here and help me grow some weed?'

'I've got to go there, Manolo, especially if it's the end of the world.'

Ten

THE END OF THE WORLD

I arrived back at the Hotel Peninsula Valdes in Puerto Madryn in the early hours two days later. Reclaiming my bags from the concierge, I found the Saga tour group had just left. I had been looking forward to recounting my recent adventures and discoveries to Gareth. No matter. I was sure we would meet again one day in the Welsh valleys. My room was the same one I had had before. Feeling sore and stiff, I showered off the dirt and dust of the desert. It was a relief to have a proper bed again, and it did not take me more than a few minutes to fall asleep. I dreamt of deserts and prehistoric monsters.

I was still sleeping ten hours later when the telephone rang. Manolo was downstairs. I joined him.

'All right, Mr Nice. Raoul and I have your flights sorted to Ushuaia. You can pick up and pay for the tickets when you leave. The direct flights were all fully booked; you'll have to change and stay overnight at Calafate.'

'No worries, Manolo. Calafate? Isn't that the name of those flowers that Olwen likes so much?'

'That's right. The place is full of them, but people usually go there to visit the glaciers. You'll have plenty of time to do that. You arrive late tomorrow morning and leave the next evening. A good mate of mine, Carlos, lives near Calafate. I've spoken to him this morning, and he is going to meet you at the airport, take you to a hotel and make sure you are all right. His last name is Guevara, so as you can imagine everyone calls him Che. Not only that, he's a doctor specialising in allergies and weird stuff like that, just like the real Che Guevara, and he even looks like him.'

'Che Guevara was Argentinian, wasn't he?'

'Right again. Most people thought he was Cuban until *Evita* came out. You'll like Che. He doesn't say much, hardly anything, and he is a bit eccentric, but a great guy. I told him all about you. He'll take good care of you. Don't worry.'

'Thanks, Manolo. You've done a lot for me this last week.'

'My pleasure, Mr Nice. Raoul found out a bit more about your ancestor Patrick. While he was here learning Welsh he became close friends with another guy also learning Welsh, a Chilean called Juan Williams. The name probably doesn't mean anything to you, but he was an admiral in the Chilean navy and fought in the war against Spain in 1865. For some reason he later resigned from the Chilean navy and came to live here. He and Patrick were inseparable, apparently, the best of mates. They left here together at the same time, probably for the same place, Ushuaia. That's all Raoul was able to find out. Not much, but it's something.'

'That's great, Manolo. I'm sure it will be a great help. Thanks, again.'

'Raoul can't take you to the airport tomorrow but someone from his company will pick you up here at eight o'clock in the morning. Raoul said to say goodbye and good luck. He would like to stay in touch. Me, too. I'll see you either in Cardiff or back here.'

I took a long stroll around Puerto Madryn, reliving the excitement I had felt on first seeing Welsh street names. Although just a week had passed, I felt nostalgic. I went shopping and armed myself with books, CDs and souvenirs in case I never had the good fortune to return. At the hotel I surfed the Net for any information on Chilean admirals called Williams, and to my surprise found some. During the middle of the nineteenth century Juan Williams Rebolledo, a captain in the Chilean navy, took possession of the Straits of Magellan, claiming them for Chile during a war against Spain. He fought again during the war between Chile, Peru and Bolivia but in 1880 fell out with the Chilean government. There was no mention of any connection with Welsh Patagonia or Ushuaia. Partly comforted and partly disappointed, I went to bed.

Raoul's friend turned up with his taxi the next morning and we headed off along the now-friendly road through the wilderness. About halfway to Trelew airport I asked him to stop the car and got out. I wanted to stand alone once more in those magnificent silent plains and deserts that aroused such strange feelings in me. Was Patagonia really the ancient habitation of giants, whose footprints on the seashore had amazed early European explorers? At the airport I collected my tickets and boarded the flight to Calafate. The landscape changed from desert to fertile mountains as we flew south-west.

At Calafate airport I picked up my bags, walked into the arrivals hall and saw Che Guevara. Despite having been warned of the physical likeness Manolo's friend bore to his namesake, I was not expecting such an impressive carbon copy. He wore shades, combats, army shoes with the laces open and a green Chinese Red Army cap. He was smoking a cigar, inhaling deeply.

'You must be Che. I'm Howard, Manolo's friend.'

Without saying a word, Che shook my hand, quickly turned and walked towards the exit. I followed him to a black van with the engine running and climbed into the passenger seat. The inside of the van was a combination of pharmacy and pet shop. There were cages of birds, frogs and reptiles; bottles of preserved animal parts; jars of herbs, spices and crushed insects; boxes of bandages, antiseptic and antibiotics; and some new scientific equipment.

After ten minutes of driving in complete silence through colourful woods and fields we crossed a small river, and just before entering Calafate town parked outside the Hotel La Loma. Che spoke, for the first time, in precise impassive English: 'It's two star but comfortable. Please check in. You are expected. I have to go to a small village near here to attend to a patient. You are welcome to go with me. You will find it interesting, I am sure. I will wait here until you return.'

I checked in, put my bags into a homely old-fashioned little room, and rejoined Che in his van.

We drove for a few miles down a well-used country road and stopped at a ranch named Estancia Alicia. Trees stripped of their bark stood like great white skeletons. Flocks of birds flitted around searching for food and nest-building materials. Some were quietly feeding in the shadows of scarecrows; others were pulling the scarecrows to bits and carrying off the straw. Che grabbed a couple of cages and other bits and pieces, put them into a yellow holdall and got out of the van. We walked down a path to a wooden hut and in through its open doorway. Lying on a blanket, a naked young girl racked with fever sobbed continuously. A belt of fierce red blisters ran round her waist with a circular gap of unblemished skin at her navel. The girl's father, his head in his hands and an open Bible on his lap, sat motionless on an upright chair next to a table. He looked up at us with pleading tear-soaked eyes.

'If that gap closes,' whispered Che in my ear, 'she will die.'

Che took off his shades, revealing one brown and one blue eye. He knelt on the floor beside the girl, grabbed his pen, drew a strange design on the clean patch of skin between the inflamed areas, opened his yellow holdall and pulled out a dome-shaped cage containing a brownish-yellow warty toad with heavy eyelids. Che held the toad and gently rubbed it against the blisters. The enraged toad swelled up to bursting point and exuded a viscous milky-white substance from its warts. Che held the toad away from the little girl and dabbed its warts with cotton wool. Closing his eyes and saying a prayer, he rubbed the cotton wool into the girl's navel. Within twenty minutes the secretion had dried and acquired the colour and texture of cement. The lethal red belt began to recede, and the girl's fever subsided. Che smiled for the first time since I had met him. The father was praying furiously, but now in thanks not desperation. He got out of his chair and lay next to his daughter. Che placed the toad on the table and put the cage next to it.

I took the place of the young girl's father and sat in the upright chair. I realised the toad might be one of the rare kind whose warts contained DMT. DMT stands for dimethyltriptamine, a powerful hallucinogen found also in some tropical plants and naturally produced in the brain by all animals, including us. Take DMT out of migrating birds, they lose the ability to orbit the world. Take it out of hibernating animals, they can't sleep. DMT production increases when we dream. Every zoological death is accompanied by an overdose of DMT. It sends us on our way when we die, flooding the mind with a tunnel of afterlife light, a mixture of euphoria, fear, insanity, disorientation and insomnia.

Throughout history the toad has been a bridge to the other-world. They have always fascinated me. Able to spend their lives in water and on the land, toads are born in the spring-time, a rainy season in most parts of the world, and frequent associations have been made between toads and sexuality, fertility and rain. Primitive charms relating to sexuality and fertility mention toads. Ancient cultures viewed the toad not only as a trickster and a master of escapes and spells, but also as a symbol of re-creation and a keeper of the secrets of transformation and immortality. Toads are born in mud, cannot breathe with their mouths open, have no teeth and swallow their own skin as they shed it. Toads thus consume themselves, in a constant cycle of death and rebirth. In many shamanistic traditions of Central and South America hallucinogenic compounds gathered from toads are used for rituals of communion with the spirit world. The Christian Devil's coat-of-arms was believed to feature three toads. A true witch will have an image of a toad in her left eye.

'Che, is this one of those DMT toads?'

'Yes.'

'I would love to try some DMT.'

'No problem,' said Che, who was now lying on the floor next to the girl and her father. Soon all three were asleep and snoring.

The toad, still outside its cage, also seemed to be knackered. It was six inches long and heavily built with bony ridges over its eyes meeting above the nose. Its hind feet had leathery webbing between the toes, but its front feet were unwebbed. It had large swollen glands on its shoulder behind each eardrum. Suddenly, the toad sat upright, opened an eyelid and fixed on a large fly walking on the tabletop. The fly disappeared as the toad swallowed, its tongue too quick to follow with the human eye.

It made a few short rapid hops towards me. I grabbed it and pressed my tongue against its warty lower back. The toad struggled to get free, its powerful back legs trying to prise open my grip. I could already feel the moisture sinking into my tongue – a sticky, viscous mixture, warm at first, then as it penetrated cold as metal. I ran my tongue across the toad's back. It tasted of pear drops, chemically enhanced fruit-flavoured confectionery. How much should I take? How strong was this toad? I licked again, then one for luck, then another for more luck. The toad hopped away back into its cage and shot back an angry and frightened look, as if accusing me of rape.

Che woke up with a start. 'Stop at once. That is not the way to do it.'

'Sorry, I thought you said there was no problem in my having some.'

'Not like that.'

'But I've read you have to lick the toad to get the DMT.'

'Californian hippy nonsense, dangerous and disrespectful to the toad. Smoke the DMT, don't swallow it.'

Che got up, went to his yellow holdall, pulled out a flat sheet of spotless glass about twelve inches square attached to a stand that held it vertical, and a small glass pipe. He lovingly picked up the toad with his left hand and held it in front of the sheet of glass. Holding it firmly, with the thumb and forefinger of his right hand he squeezed near the base of one of the swollen glands until a viscous liquid squirted out onto the glass. He did the same with the other gland. Che scraped the substance from the glass and put it into the glass pipe, which he gave to me. I lit it and inhaled.

As with any hallucinogen, once taken there is no turning back. No regrets or you are doomed from the start. Within seconds something was building in my toes – warm flushing sensations, a tingling of sparking nerve ends exploding underneath my flesh. My face felt as if it was being stung by nettles. I saw fluorescent red, green and yellow dots weaving in and out of white lines, moving like blood cells through capillaries. Diamond patterns undulated across my visual field. I heard a sound like chirping crickets running across my mind. Although I was indoors, I sensed the feel of the earth, the dry desert soil passing through my fingers, the scent of cactus. I experienced a feeling of wonder and well-being and relaxed into a deep, peaceful interior awareness.

But my mind felt crowded. When I started on a thought, another one came along and clashed with it. I tried to speak to Che, but the words wouldn't come. I felt cold, as if I was being slowly submerged in icy water. The water started rising, faster with every inch. My waist, hands, arms, chest and neck took it in turns to freeze. My vision slipped. I saw sparks, exploding pockets of thick ozone. I could no longer feel my legs. It felt like my bowels were about to give way, then they simply disappeared altogether – bowels, intestines and stomach – all gone. Panic overtook me.

My eyes poured water like taps. No, it wasn't my eyes; I was seeing water. Everything was made of water and was now returning gracefully to its original liquid form. The wide open plains that had dominated my perceptions and thoughts for the last few days slipped away, running off across the barren land. Small bushes bubbled and vaporised into hanging projections of twisting pale blue and rose-coloured masses that swapped places with the sky. Satellites passed overhead, hooting like owls. Dark mountains moved, grew and shrank, swelled and breathed.

Feelings intensified and had a race, made a final mad dash for my brain, trying to get me. My skull shook as if in the centre of a violent thunderstorm. Thick plates of prominently carved bone rattled underneath my skin and blood vessels. I saw the hideous owl from Jamaica picking away at a duppy's eyes. A giant crab wearing a pirate's hat showed me its pointed teeth. Then the panic receded. My lungs took a breather; they stopped. Why not? There was no need to breathe. A wave of membrane washed up and towered above me. It had me. I was engulfed. This is my last breath of air, I thought. From now on, I'll breathe water. I can't drown. I've got a baby's caul.

Cold tentacles stabbed in with frightening speed and penetrated my brain to its core. A bright blue caterpillar flashed inside that central point in my brain, primeval jelly inherited from my caveman ancestors. Another burst of blue light, and the cold tentacles turned instantly hot. A white dot swelled, pulsed and turned into little wet tentacles with segments, then into silver microchips. They morphed into larger and more intricate machines, coming alive with lightning and bursts of electricity. From the edges came helices, spiralling and changing as they rolled towards the centre, turning from sphere to cube to pyramid. Flickering-static TV screens bleated out semi-seconds of news, squawks of sitcom laughter and jolts of programmes on war, ice cream, corruption, drugs, drug wars, tobacco, industry, mobile phone ringtones, pornography, hair dye, gossip magazines, murder and holidays to tropical destinations.

I could hear a bass drum banging, deep and low. The movement of everything around melded into the drumbeat, jumping as one. The ground and air were shuddering. The bass drum became a snare, then a cymbal, then a crunching clatter overhead. I felt myself ducking, taking cover. Something big and heavy was coming down on top of me. I collapsed inwards. Arms moulded with chests legs and arses into an armour-plated bubble. Something hit hard, vibrating every nerve ending in my body, rattling them like the inside of a church bell. Black mountains shuddered, crumbled and retreated in fear, while the ground turned into a thick green brittle rock with razor-sharp edges that glinted in the stark white light. The ground grew, filling gaps with thick purple-grey cracked earth and rocky outcrops. Mountains glowed in the distance. Above them was an atmosphere in which night, day, stars and clouds coexisted. A purple mist gathered overhead like a thick simmering soup. It sank, headed towards me, booms of crackling thunder bursting my eardrums. The mist engulfed me. I lit up with a purple aura, white and violet sparks bursting from the pores in my skin. I could feel no weight, only existence. The purple force field was holding me there. I existed, held there in my purple bubble. The mist held everything together, powering all of us, expanding and threatening. Purple was the colour of eternity. Without it we were surely doomed.

Suddenly, Che was standing in front of me. He walked towards me holding the toad. 'You see,' he said, 'you have found the answer. What colour is it?'

Che's eyes were the eyes of two men, two souls, two natures.

'Purple,' I replied. My head emptied. Nothing functioned; there was just an empty hole where scientists believed intelligence once existed.

'You are right,' said Che. 'It's purple.' Che flickered and blurred and changed into a giant in animal skins and a thick cowboy hat, holding a pistol. 'Damn right,' he said in a Welsh accent, grinning with a face that had been around a long time. He vanished in a blink.

I held my hand up in front of my face. It aged and died in less than a minute. When I blinked it was back – reborn, solid and swelling, purple and blue, pulsing with life. It was everywhere – in the ground, in the mountains, in the sky. We were all connected in one way or another. No amount of television could destroy that. The purple rope of life held us all together.

The TV sets switched off. The synchronised power-down echoed around the universe, sending shock waves far beyond my understanding. Twisting fornicating snakes of DNA built up a picture in seconds – fractal mosaics, leaded windows, and Mayan and Egyptian carvings.

The TV sets collapsed into microchips that turned into toads, all clambering over one another, half immersed in thick blue muddy toad juice. On the ground ten yards in front of me toads hopped and crawled from a large round pool. Giant neon-blue skulls with eye patches hovered in the distance. Deep-sea angler fish with bulbous eyes, long bony bodies, evil fins and large vicious self-illuminating teeth flashed vivid sunshine-yellow smiles. The toads were everywhere now. I was surrounded. Their croaks, bleats and squirts occasionally joined in unison. There were billions of them. They all turned and looked straight at me. A deadly silence fell.

Then the croaks started again, a random mass pulling back to unison, a pulse that increased in pitch. I could feel it hitting my body in jolts. The toads jumped, danced, frolicked with no control and flipped in the air like broken-boned kids frantic on sugar drinks.

'That's him,' said a voice, high-pitched and rough like an old record.

'That's the one who licked a toad, who licked one of us. We'll charge him now. How shall we find him?'

'Guilty,' croaked another. 'We find him guilty.'

I had disappeared off the radar screen. Mobile phones, computers and global positioning systems could no longer see me. I was alone in the middle of nowhere beneath exploding volcanoes, battling ancient cavemen and giant lizards with fake horns glued to their heads. I called on those forces within my being to realign and submit, to let go of all my compelling fears and just exist. I realised I had been cleaned and purified in the savage lands with which the future has not connected and which refuse to accept the outside world. These plains of Patagonia had not been left behind; they had just wanted no part of whatever else was around. I was now part of them.

Familiar feelings began to pour into my stomach. Pangs of hunger and waves of tiredness fought with flashes of memories. I was coming down. The DMT trip was ending. I was no longer in the house; I was in a line of people of all nationalities queuing for tickets. I looked for Che. He was nowhere to be seen. Someone asked me for 200 pesos. I pulled the money out of my pocket and was given a ticket. I got on a boat, sat in a row of seats and gazed out of the window. I had never been so far away from home.

The icebergs were getting larger and more menacing. Some looked like ancient Greek ruins, tossed haphazardly into the depths by some third-millennium Atlantis catastrophe. Others resembled the giant disembodied faces of Mount Rushmore, their enormous eyes gazing sternly at us as we floated under their noses. The boat's engines coughed harshly and died. In ghostly silence we drifted helplessly towards an unending chaotic mountain range of pure ice. One of the giant heads gave a cruel look and crumbled into the water, creating huge waves with the sound of a hundred simultaneous thunderstorms. Some of the passengers started shouting in various incomprehensible languages and rushed in panic to the side of the boat. Confused and scared, I joined the panicking throng and pushed my way to where I presumed the lifeboats were being lowered. An ugly craggy black rock jutted over the boat's deck. Perched on the rock was the biggest bird I had ever seen or imagined, a giant vulture with a massive pink head and a bloodthirsty smile. I assumed it was God. This had to be the end. I prayed to the bird of prey and let the crowd carry me to my fate. We all have to die sometime, some way.

> Bird of prey
> Bird of prey
> Flying high
> Flying high
> Am I going to die
>
> Bird of prey
> Bird of prey
> Flying high
> Flying high
> Take me on your flight

'Just my bloody luck. Would you believe it? The batteries of the bloody camera have packed up. Now of all times. I told Bethan to buy new ones yesterday. She forgot, of course. Typical.'

'Gareth! Where did you come from? Where am I?'

'Oh you recognise me now, do you? Thank God for that. The doctor said you might be delirious for a bit longer. He wasn't kidding. You've been talking complete nonsense. Nasty thing, mind, snakebite. I got bitten by one in Italy once.'

'What doctor, Gareth?'

'Your buddy, the one who's the image of Che Guevara. Nice bloke, I thought. Didn't say much.'

'Do you know him, then?'

'Well no. You both came into the bar together. I'd never seen him before.'

'Which bar?'

'I can't remember what it's called. I only went in for a piss while the others were visiting the ranch next door. As I was leaving, I saw the two of you at the bar. You looked terrible.' This made some sense.

'Shouldn't we be getting off this boat, Gareth?'

'Off the boat? I think we would be wise to wait until it docks, another half an hour, I think.'

'But didn't they just call abandon ship?'

'You're still a bit delirious, I think, Howard. Let's go and sit outside on the deck.'

'Sure. But why was everyone rushing to the side?'

'Doing the same as I was – taking pictures of that bloody condor. And then the bloody camera batteries gave out.'

The giant otherworld vulture which I had thought was a Fatboy Slim remix of God was the rare Andean condor, the world's heaviest flying bird with a wingspan of ten feet and a lifespan of up to seventy-five years. It spends most of its time riding thermals in the company of jets and fighting with vultures and eagles over the carcasses of sea lions. A condor was perched at the mouth of a small cave in the face of a rocky bank, which explained the stampede.

'Where are we, Gareth?'

'Didn't you hear a word of what the guide was saying before my camera went kaput? We're cruising on Lago Argentino, Howard, going through the National Glacier Park. Next question.'

'Are we anywhere near Calafate?'

'Of course. That's very close to where we got on the boat, and it's where we'll get off.'

'Where's my doctor friend?'

'No idea; he didn't get on the boat. But he gave me his card to give you. Here it is. Bloody hell! He really is Che Guevara. Well, well, well. I thought he'd been killed in Bolivia or somewhere ages ago. I must be mixing him up with someone else. I suppose it could be his son.'

'He's not Che Guevara, Gareth; he's just got the same name. He idolises him, and tries to look like him.'

'I've got you. It's a bit like one of our neighbours in Blackwood. He changed his name to Elvis Presley. He didn't look like Elvis, though, no matter how much he tried.'

We went up on deck and sat down. I watched the luminous blue glacier slip back up the valley from where it had come. The DMT was flashing back. The glacier sparkled, twitched, glowed and squirmed like a segmented blue worm with a black centipede's head. Thick mandibles chomped on swollen blood vessels. It looked dangerous but seemed otherwise occupied.

'Are you all right, Howard?' asked Gareth. 'You were looking a bit better; now you seem a bit odd again.'

'I'm fine. I've just had a funny old day.'

'What have you been up to? I was wondering.'

'I've been with that doctor on his rounds. He doesn't half use some strange medicines – stuff from all different types of animals and plants. I tried some just for a laugh, and I've been feeling weird since. I wasn't really bitten by a snake.'

'What did you take?'

'Something from a toad.'

'Well, that's odd. My Auntie Ceridwen used to keep toads,' said Gareth.

'Was she a doctor too?'

'Hell, no. She was a bloody witch, a real one. She used to feed her cats from spare nipples that she had in her armpits. There aren't many witches left these days.'

'Is she still alive?'

'I doubt it very much. She disappeared without trace over ten years ago, and she was pretty old then. She might be still alive, but everyone assumes she's dead. Ilfant, her son, my cousin, has inherited her house and all her stuff. In fact, as you'll know being a Welsh speaker, *ilfant* is the Welsh for toad. Shows how much she thought of toads. Not that she treated them very well, mind. She mangled them to bits, took lumps out of their heads and cut off their tongues. She would even clean the handle of her broomstick by rubbing the poor buggers up and down it. Ilfant told me that he once found her using it like a vibrator. She wasn't married, of course.'

'I've read about witches doing that,' I said. 'The pus from the toad's skin used to get them high, and they would think they were flying.'

'Well, I never knew that, Howard. You learn something new every day. It makes sense, though. I always thought the idea of them actually hurtling through the sky on brushes was a bit far-fetched. She used to feed the toads with flies' wings and special tiny mushrooms she called *bwyd yr ilfant*.'

'That's Welsh for toad food,' I said. 'Maybe they were toadstools.'

'That's a point, a very good point. I hadn't thought of that.'

We were silent for a few minutes, then Gareth said, 'Let's have a drink at the bar here on the boat. They've got local brandy with glacier ice. I've not tried it, but it might clear that toad shit out of your system.'

I hadn't seen Gareth since the meeting at the bar in Trelew. 'So, how's your holiday going? Are you still with the Saga group?'

'Yes, quite a few of them are on the boat. Bethan isn't here; she's gone to see those bloody penguins she's been on about since before we left home. I thought I would rather go on a boat trip round the glaciers and take some pictures. I had enough of wildlife yesterday. We went to a sea lion colony. Bloody huge they are – sixteen foot and four tons, according to the guide. They go out to sea and gorge as much as they can and then come back to lie on the beach and fart all day. It smelt worse than that sewage place near Kenfig Hill where me and Bethan used to pick dewberries. I got some good photos, mind. And I took some great ones today until the bloody camera gave up the ghost.'

'Is it the camera or the batteries?' I asked anxiously.

'Well I can't be sure, I suppose. I think it's the batteries. I bloody hope so; otherwise, I've lost all my photos. You're thinking of the one I took in Trelew, aren't you? I'm sure it's the batteries. Don't worry. I'll get some as soon as we're off this boat.'

Just as the sun was setting over the pale blue lake, the boat docked at somewhere named Puerto Bandera. It looked familiar.

'Is this where I got on, Gareth?'

'Of course. And that's the bar where we ran into each other,' answered Gareth, pointing out a wooden building in the distance. A sign, 'Estancia Alicia', pointed in the same direction. I began to feel normal.

'Shall we meet later?'

'I would love to, believe me, but I have to have dinner, all-inclusive, with the rest of the old codgers at the hotel, and I promised Bethan we'd have a quiet night in tonight. She feels cheated if we stop at a posh hotel and don't feel the benefit of it. We could meet tomorrow morning, if you like. I'll come over to yours. Hotel La Loma, wasn't it?'

'That's it. See you tomorrow, Gareth. Not too early.'

'Don't worry about that. I can see the toad has taken the bollocks out of you. You have a lie-in. I'll probably have a bit of one myself.'

Gareth caught the Saga bus. I took a taxi to the hotel and lay on my bed to dream about witches, babies' cauls and naval heroes.

*

There was a note waiting for me at reception when I went down in the morning for breakfast:

> Dear Howard.
>
> I came over, but you were obviously fast asleep. That toad shit seems a lot more effective than Horlicks. I couldn't have stayed anyway: Bethan is poorly. It's nothing serious, just a bit of tummy trouble. She didn't stop eating last night. Either that or she caught bird flu from the bloody penguins. But I ought to stay with her and get the doctor. (I hope he's not called Che Guevara.) I bought some batteries, and the camera is as right as rain. Good luck with your mission, and get in touch when you are back home.
>
> All the best.
>
> Gareth.
>
> PS You won't believe this but there's even a Welsh tea café right here in the main street of Calafate. So they're expanding well beyond Gaiman. They might get to Wales soon.

Later that day, I caught the two-hour flight from Calafate to Ushuaia, Tierra del Fuego. It was snowing. I took the courtesy bus to the Las Hayas Resort Hotel, checked in, left my bags at reception for the staff to take to my room, and took a seat in the restaurant. I was starving, and my hunger had been severely inflamed by my in-flight reading. Ushuaia's culinary delights included the Antarctic king crab – also called the centolla or spider crab. One of those and a bottle of Malbec from Bodega Escorihuela would be a sensible way to begin a visit to the end of the world.

Tierra del Fuego was discovered in 1520 by Fernão de Magalhães – known in English as Ferdinand Magellan – a Portuguese navigator engaged by the Spanish crown to find a route to the East Indies by sailing west from Spain. After crossing the Atlantic and heading south, Magellan found a narrow seaway cutting through the southern tip of the South American land mass and the Pacific Ocean at its western end. Smoke and fire, presumably made by the indigenous Indians, rose from the island south of the strait as Magellan sailed through. He named it Tierra del Fuego – Land of Fire. At the bottom of Tierra del Fuego, on the shore of the Beagle Channel, lies Ushuaia, repeatedly referred to in all the tourist leaflets, thereby reducing the isolation they are trying to promote, as the southernmost town in the world. South of the Beagle Channel, which also joins the Pacific and Atlantic Oceans, lie hundreds of largely uninhabited and variously sized and shaped islands petering out at Cape Horn. Sea and ice alone form the physical landscape between there and the South Pole.

I went to my room. Innumerable large snowflakes blotted out most of the view in the dark night, but I could see from the slow-moving ships' lights that I was close to the sea. I overlooked the Beagle Channel, named after the ship that had carried the father of evolution, Charles Darwin, to his discoveries during the 1830s. Ushuaia makes the most of its connection with Charles Darwin, and a copy of his book *The Voyage of the Beagle* lay on my desk next to the Gideons' Bible and hotel services folder. I had read it years ago while studying the history of science as an Oxford postgraduate but forgotten most of it. Skimming through the conclusion, I read the following:

> In calling up the images of the past, the plains of Patagonia frequently cross before my eyes: yet these plains are pronounced by all most wretched and useless. They are characterised only by negative possessions; without habitations, without water, without trees, without mountains, they support merely a few dwarf plants. Why then, and the case is not peculiar to myself, have

these arid wastes taken so firm possession of the memory? Why have not the still more level, the greener and the more fertile Pampas, which are serviceable to mankind, produced an equal impression. I can scarcely analyse these feelings: but it must be partly due to the free scope given to the imagination. The plains of Patagonia are boundless, for they are scarcely practicable, and hence unknown: they bear the stamp of having thus lasted for ages, and there appears no limit to their duration through future time.

A blinding dawn suddenly blazed through the windows. I got up to shut the curtains and saw a backdrop from Dungeons and Dragons. The morning sun blazed from the clear blue sky behind the Martial Mountains as they surveyed what was clearly their domain, like white-capped, chocolate-faced giant wizards poring over a magical potion. They were huge and magnificent, and a bit too close for comfort.

Lounging around the hotel reading local newspapers and magazines, I read that George Bush had been here fishing at a $1,000-a-night lodge, and CNN's Ted Turner had just bought a ranch. I also found out that Ushuaia had been built by those incarcerated nearby at what was once Argentina's biggest penal colony. The prisoners, mainly anarchists sent down from the north, built the steep criss-crossed streets of houses and bridges, and a fifteen-mile railway track. I consulted the telephone directories. There was no one called McCarty or even Williams.

I had woken up wanting to eat more Antarctic king crab. The hotel's Martial Restaurant did not open until the evening, but the staff recommended Volver, reputedly the best crab restaurant in the world and open from eleven o'clock. The snow had stopped, and I took a taxi to the main street, San Martín, a non-stop parade of shops stuffed with world's end souvenirs, penguin paraphernalia, duty-free whisky and cigarettes. Volver was an old-fashioned restaurant at the water's edge. Inside, shelves carrying hundreds of old photographs and piles of bric-a-brac jutted out from walls covered with yellowed newspapers. The menu offered crab pâté, crab salad, crab soup, crab pasta, crab goulash and crab. I ordered crab. Soon afterwards, Ernesto, who told me he had served his apprenticeship as a waiter in Bournemouth, brought to the table a plate on which a crab, its spindly legs spanning over a yard from tip to tip, was lying on its back. The meat was delicious.

I gazed at the photographs. There were no obvious portraits of a Patrick McCarty. While browsing though some bits and pieces I noticed some empty boxes labelled 'Fabrica Centolla, Puerto Williams'. I was on to something.

'Ernesto, where is Puerto Williams?'

'About twenty kilometres away, sir, on the island of Navarino just south of Ushuaia.'

'But I thought Ushuaia was the southernmost place in the world.'

'It is if you ignore Chile, sir, which Argentinians always do.'

Stupidly, I hadn't realised that Tierra del Fuego, like much of what was originally known as Patagonia, is divided between Chile and Argentina. The Beagle Channel forms a large part of the border. Puerto Williams, just across the channel, was in Chile.

I walked to the harbour, where tour operators were offering trips down the Beagle Channel. Two featured Puerto Williams as a stop. One, on a luxury liner, was leaving tomorrow for a week-long cruise through the Chilean fjords and then calling at Puerto Williams on the way back. Another, on a catamaran, went there via a sea lion colony and came back the same day through rocky outcrops housing colonies of cormorants. It was leaving in just over an hour. There were ten other passengers, half of whom were American yachties, returning from a duty-free shopping trip in Ushuaia to boats moored in Puerto

Williams and chattering animatedly about prices in voices louder than the catamaran engines.

We rocked and rolled for an hour through choppy sea, passed some thick-necked sea lions shooting out clouds of hot breath at delighted sea lionesses basking on a wreck-strewn beach, and pulled into Puerto Williams. Chilean police boarded and examined our passports.

In misty rain, I walked past huge steel freight containers functioning as offices and stores, and rows of old-style wooden bungalows topped with brightly painted corrugated iron roofs with smoking chimney pipes. A pile of firewood, a flagpole and a dog kennel stood outside each one. Four youths, each holding a lead, were taking their king crabs for a walk. Apart from a small but closed anthropological museum dedicated to the long-extinct Yamana Indians, there was nothing to suggest that Puerto Williams had existed for longer than a few decades. Maybe the Chileans had recently built it just to boast they had the southernmost town in the world. It couldn't possibly have had anything to do with either my great-great-grandfather or a nineteenth-century Chilean naval hero.

Drenched, disappointed and a bit depressed, I ambled back to the waterfront. Through a clearing in the drizzle I could see a sunken tugboat lying in a sheltered inlet connected to the shore by a bridge. Walking towards the bridge, I could see the tug's top decks were now the Club de Yates Micalvi. A few multimillion-dollar cruising yachts were tied up alongside, refuelling and provisioning, with gruesome sheep carcasses hanging from their rigging. I walked into a cosy lounge bar, its crackling wood fire warming and drying groups of yachties, hell-bent on sailing to Cape Horn and Antarctica, tourists cruising through the Chilean fjords, and Chilean naval personnel. One of the yachties, a large, pleasant, red-faced woman wearing a navy-blue baseball cap, hailed me as I went up to the bar. 'How you doing? I saw you on the boat coming over.'

'That's right. I remember seeing you.'

'You're British, right? You remind me of someone. I'm Erin, by the way.'

'I'm Howard. I'm just getting a drink. You want one?'

'Here, let me get you one. I have an account here. I'm trying to think who you look like. What are you having, Howard?

The bar was stocked with hundreds of whiskies, including my firm favourite, an Irish brand named Redbreast.

'Redbreast, please. No water, no ice.'

'That's a new one on me. I guess I'll try the same.'

We took our drinks to a small unoccupied table overlooking the misty channel. The menu described Puerto Williams as a natural door to the white continent; it was not founded until 1953, and then just as a radio station. Puerto Williams later developed as a naval base, and service personnel had built the wooden homes I had just seen. It was baptised Puerto Williams in honour of Chilean naval hero Admiral Juan Williams. So there was a connection.

'Weren't those sea lions awesome?

'Sorry?'

'I said weren't those sea lions we saw on the boat today awesome?'

'Yes, they were. Sorry, I was just reading something interesting here.'

'On the menu? It's fairly regular chow. I could ask them if there was anything else you wanted. I know them real well. Hey! Look at the weather.'

The whiskey pounded through my temples as I watched the rainstorm turn into a snowstorm and back into a rainstorm. Mists swirled around like ghostly dervishes. The fog lifted. I saw what I had never seen or heard of before, a straight horizontal rainbow. Shrouded in mist, the multicoloured and spectral carpet played havoc with my understanding of optics. Then I saw something I had seen before, rows of towering granite needles pointing at the sky.

'The Teeth of Navarino. Aren't they just the neatest little hills you've ever seen?'

I was unable to speak. There was no doubt. They were the spiky hills in the photograph I had found alongside the baby's caul in Kenfig Hill.

'I didn't realise the time. I must go. I've got to catch the boat,' I whispered to Erin, halting over each word.

'Time flies when you're having fun. Bye, Howard. Nice to meet you. Have a good trip back to Ushuaia.'

Back in my room I checked my mobile. There were five missed calls from withheld or unknown numbers but no messages. Suddenly it rang.

'Thank God, I've got through, I've been trying for ages. How's it going, Howard? It's Gareth it is.'

'Gareth! You're home already. Is everything all right?'

'Not so bad, thanks. We had a good flight. It landed on time, fair play. Idwal met us at the airport and drove us to Blackwood. Very good of him, really, considering he's eighty-five next year. I've got some news for you, Howard, very interesting news. Will this call cost me a fortune? It's a bloody long way. Not a bad line, mind.'

'No, Gareth; it's on divert, so I have to pay the charges. It will cost *me* a fortune.'

'All right, I'll carry on then. You remember Idwal?'

'I don't think so.'

'Yes, you do. Idwal Jones. I told you about him when we first met in Buenos Aires. Bethan mentioned him to you first. He's the one obsessed with Captain Morgan – goes on about him non-stop.'

'Oh yes, I remember – the one who thinks Henry lived in your local pub.'

'That's him. Well, I was telling him about you and what you were up to, more to stop him from talking than anything else. It's hard to get a word in edgeways. Tell me, Howard, was one

of your relatives in Kenfig Hill called Morgan Marks?
Everyone used to call him Mock Marks.'

'Yes, for sure. He was my grandfather Tudor's brother.'

'There you are then.'

'Morgan Marks died not long before I was born. In fact, it's
his grandfather in the photograph in the Touring Club in
Trelew. Did that come out, by the way?'

'Don't know yet. I have to wait for my son to come back
from holidays. He's going to download it on a memory stick,
whatever that is. Anyway, according to Idwal, Morgan Marks
moved from Kenfig Hill to Pontypridd and became a friend
of Edgar Jones, Idwal's father. We're going back a bit now,
mind. I told you Idwal's eighty-five next year, didn't I?
Morgan Marks used to say he was belonging to the Henry
Morgan family and that's why he was called Morgan. I don't
think too many believed him, but Edgar had a lot of time for
Morgan, and they used to spend all day researching into
Captain Morgan. As a boy, Idwal would help out sometimes,
and that's how he became so fanatical. So we've got your
family to blame for Idwal driving me and everyone in
Blackwood round the bend with his Captain Morgan stories.
Small world, isn't it?'

'Yes it is, Gareth. I'm at the end of it. It's snowing.'

'Funny enough, we had a few flakes here this morning. I
thought April showers were meant to be rain. Bethan says it's
something to do with global warming. I can't see how, myself
– it's bloody freezing. Idwal has got Henry Morgan's family
tree if it's any use to you.'

'Does it show Morgan Marks?'

'No, no. It's just of his ancestors, not his descendants.
Seems he was a descendant of Hywel Dda, the Welsh king who
gave us all those laws.'

'That's really fascinating if it's true, Gareth, because Hywel
Dda was a direct descendant of King Arthur.'

'Did King Arthur really exist, though, Howard? Idwal's got his doubts. Thinks it's a bit far-fetched.'

'I'm sure he did. There's even evidence that King Arthur is descended from Jesus.'

'I never knew Jesus had children. With that Mary Magdalene woman was it?'

'It's complicated, Gareth, and apparently involves the Holy Grail.'

'I'll ask Idwal about it. Funny to think you might be descended from Henry Morgan and King Arthur, though, isn't it, Howard?

'And Jesus,' I added.

'Come off it, Howard. You'll be saying you're descended from Adam next. There was something else I had to say too. What was it? Oh yes. Bloody hell! I almost forgot the most important bit of all. Are you still there?

'Yes, go on, Gareth. I'm listening.'

'Morgan Marks used to go on to Idwal about his grand-father, Patrick McCarthy, who had made his fortune in South America, then changed his name to Marks when he moved to Kenfig Hill.'

'That's definitely him.'

'Couldn't be anyone else, Howard. Couldn't be. I asked Idwal if the name might have been McCarty, not McCarthy, and he said yes, easily. I also asked him about Billy the Kid, but Idwal's got no interest in cowboys whatsoever, even if they are Welsh, so it wouldn't have meant an awful lot to him even if Morgan Marks had told him about it. It's the sort of thing he'd forget.'

'Does Idwal know how Patrick made his fortune?'

'Yes, and this will make you bloody laugh. Patrick was doing all right for himself trading this and that and had some important friends including some big Indian chief and top brass in the Chilean navy. You mentioned something about that, didn't you? That day you were poorly with the toad, when you had that funny turn.'

'That's right, Juan Williams was in the Chilean navy. Go on, Gareth.'

'This is the bit that will make you laugh: the chief gave Patrick the Straits of Magellan.'

'What do you mean?'

'Just what I said. The Indian chief gave Patrick the Straits of Magellan for nothing. Didn't charge him a penny. Then Patrick went up and down the straits collecting the bird shit and not letting anyone else have any. He collected tons and tons of it, made millions, but then had to scarper because he got caught up in the fighting between Argentina and Chile over the border.'

'Gareth, there's no way that can possibly be true. You don't believe it, do you?

'Idwal is never wrong. He might go on a bit, but he's always right, always.'

'I'm not saying Idwal's wrong, Gareth, but Patrick might have made up the whole story. Or Morgan Marks might have made it up or got it wrong.'

'Idwal has seen the proof with his own eyes. Says it's a matter of record. He made all sorts of notes about it. When Idwal's not talking, he's writing. And he's meticulous about references and that sort of thing.'

'Has he still got the notes?'

'He's looking for them now. It will take him a while, mind. His house is nothing but papers – Bethan thinks it's a fire risk.'

'Did Idwal tell you the chief's name?

'Something like Quasimodo. Not Quasimodo, of course; he was the hunchback of Notre-Dame, wasn't he? But it was a name like that.'

'Casimiro? He was a famous Indian chief from Patagonia.'

'Casimiro, that's right. You see, Idwal is never wrong.

Funny to think you've been traipsing all round the bloody world looking for your ancestors, and the answers are all here in Blackwood, next door to Kenfig Hill. What are your plans now?'

'I really don't know, Gareth, especially after what you just said. There doesn't seem much point hanging round here anymore, I'll probably just come back to Britain.'

'Well come down to Blackwood. Me, you and Idwal can have a drink at the Monkey Tree.'

Eleven

WALES

I arrived at Gatwick Airport and caught the express to Victoria. Stiff and jet-lagged, I could not face taking another no-smoking train, so I gave up my initial plan to go to Bridgend from Paddington and took a cab to the Groucho Club in Dean Street where I got a room for the night. I arranged to meet Bernie Davies for lunch the following day. He would be able to give me a lift to South Wales. I had already promised Gareth I would meet him and Idwal in Blackwood, and I wanted to visit Kenfig Hill. Looking forward to visiting my homeland again, I took some melatonin and passed out. I woke at 8.00 p.m., shook off the rest of the jet lag with a shower and went downstairs. A good friend, Piers Hemu, broadcaster, ex-editor of *Front*, currently working for the *Mail on Sunday* and no stranger to Soho's watering holes, was drinking at the ground-floor bar. He told me Sean Penn was in the first-floor bar. Excusing myself, I rushed upstairs and found Sean.

'Howard! I don't believe it. How's things? Did anything ever happen with the film?'

Talk of a film about my life originally came up when I met Rhys Ifans at Pontypridd Civic Hall during the spring of 1996.

It was the first time I had seen the Super Furry Animals play live and the first gig I had attended since seeing Stevie Wonder in Taiwan ten years earlier. The hall was packed. I took my place anonymously and nervously at the back. The concert was fantastic, an innovative combination of almost every genre I had ever heard from Status Quo to Zappa and tunes that came from God knows where. The crowd bodysurfed, jumped up and down, and waved their arms in pure joy. I went backstage to meet the band. We got on, we giggled, and we enjoyed the booze, the spliffs and the novel experience of being the subject of photographers' attentions. The Super Furry Animals' debut album was about to be released with my photo on the cover as was my autobiography.

A few people asked for my autograph, including a tall blond man with a permanent smile, who held out a packet of king-size cigarette papers and a marker pen. 'Can I have your signature, please, How?' he asked in a quiet Welsh voice.

'Sure. What's your name?'

'No, it's your name I want. On these skins, if that's all right.'

'Of course it's all right. I thought perhaps you might want me to dedicate it to somebody.'

'How do you mean? Dedicate it?'

'Well, like write "To Jack" or something.'

'Jack who?'

'Jack anybody.'

'Fuck Jack. It's for me. I bought these fuckers with my own money.'

'Just my signature?'

'Aye, that's it,' he answered, looking at me as if I was a simpleton.

I wrote a large signature across the packet.

He looked down at the scrawl with disgust. 'I meant every one.'

'What do you mean?' I asked.

'Can you please sign every skin? I'll give Jack some of them.' He started laughing. 'Sorry, How. My name's Rhys.'

I too burst out laughing. 'Good to meet you, Rhys. How do you fit in here?'

'I'm sleeping on Daf Ieuan the drummer's floor until I get a job. I get nervous there, mind. He hits things for a living. Can I ask you something serious?'

'Go on.'

'I'm an actor, a bloody good one even when I'm pissed. If they ever make a film of your life, can I play you?'

'Definitely.' I meant it. 'It's a deal, Rhys. But you have to keep to it.'

'Let's shake on it, How.'

A few years later, Rhys starred in the first Welsh drug film, *Twin Town*, then went on to steal the show from Hugh Grant in *Notting Hill*. In constant demand from Hollywood, he is now a hugely respected actor. But we are keeping our promise to each other.

Shortly afterwards, Robert Jones, executive producer of *The Usual Suspects*, took me out to lunch. He had just bought the film rights to *High Times* – David Leigh's book about my early life – and wanted to make a film about my smuggling antics in Ireland during the 1970s. He asked if I had any ideas about who should play me. I suggested Rhys Ifans, but he was still an unknown quantity. Robert went on to do other projects.

When *Mr Nice* appeared, many other directors and producers expressed interest in making films of my life. I heard from Frank Roddam, who directed the pioneering reality TV programme, *The Family*. He had gone on to direct *Quadrophenia*, often described as the best music movie of the 1970s, and *The Bride*, which is still being regularly screened twenty years after its release. Frank was confident he could interest Hugh Grant in playing me. I again mentioned Rhys Ifans, but to no avail. Hugh Grant turned down the opportunity. Frank blamed Hugh's recent blow-job embarrassment;

it was no time for him to be associated with a dope dealer.

During my 1997 general election campaign the BBC called and asked if I would be interested in selling them the TV rights to *Mr Nice*. I met Michael Wearing, who as head of serials had supervised the new era of BBC costume drama adaptations including *Middlemarch* and *Pride and Prejudice*. Michael and I got on very well and we signed contracts to produce a six-part series based on *Mr Nice*.

On the question of crooks benefiting directly from their crimes, public opinion is clear: banged-up bank robbers should not get to hang on to the cash they steal and hit men must not expect to keep their professional fees if caught. However, opinions vary on whether criminals should be allowed to benefit indirectly. Could a convicted paedophile write and publish something along the lines of Vladimir Nabokov's *Lolita*? Would Osama bin Laden, if caught and eventually released, be permitted to work as a paid consultant on an al-Qaeda film? Should criminals be able to publish and sell their autobiographies? Should gangsters receive fees for advising directors on films about the Mob?

Probably due to my having served a long prison sentence and showing no signs of reverting to dope smuggling, I was generally considered to have paid my debt to society. Accordingly, there was negligible opposition to my writing *Mr Nice*. People could choose freely whether or not to buy it. The BBC, however, derives much of its income from the sale of television licences to the public, who have to cough up without having any say over what is broadcasted into their homes. So, if *Mr Nice* were televised, hard-earned cash would have come my way. This disturbed the BBC's top echelons so much that the project did not progress beyond the script and music soundtrack stage over the next eighteen months, by which time Michael Wearing had left the organisation.

The lack of any visible progress caused many in the film industry to wonder whether some screen rights to *Mr Nice* might still be unsold. Between 1997 and 2000 I received well over a thousand emails from directors, producers, script-writers and actors enquiring about the possibility of making a film. The BBC had the TV rights but the film rights were still available, although they could not be executed until ten years after the first showing on television of whatever the BBC eventually produce. I painstakingly explained this to each person who contacted me, but enthusiasm did not abate. Scripts and offers of free lunches kept tumbling in. The BBC was bombarded with phone calls from interested parties offering money and expertise, but the corporation had other ideas: they wanted to reduce the six-hour series to one half-hour programme. Those who felt it was absurd to condense *Mr Nice* into thirty minutes of film kept on pestering the BBC and buying me lunches and dinners. I did not mind in the least; my social life was great. The BBC then scrapped the thirty-minute idea and put matters on the back-burner.

Performing at the Cheltenham Literary Festival in 1999 I had got to know James Perkins, owner of the highly successful Fantazia record label and the first person to produce and release a DJ compilation album. I enjoyed James's company enormously, and we would often meet for a drink. I ran into him at a party in London at the end of 2000 and explained the state of play with the BBC.

'Howard, I'll buy the film rights off you. It's insane to let a potential blockbuster movie just sit on the BBC's floor.'

'I don't think the film rights are worth anything. And I don't think they'll make a film of *Mr Nice*.'

'Why on earth not?'

'It's too politically incorrect, James. I've led a life of crime without doing that long in prison; I'm making money writing and talking about my criminal past and having a wonderful time. They don't make films about such people.'

'I'd still like to buy the rights. I don't agree they're worthless. Times are moving on, and the film industry is getting more adventurous. How much do you want for them?'

'You can have them for a quid.'

He gave me a pound coin, and I signed them over.

James mentioned the success of *Blow*, a film about American cocaine smuggler George Jung. It was a huge box office hit. James Perkins lost no time in drawing my attention to its success.

'See what I mean, Howard?'

'Yes, but do you see what I mean? George is probably looking at the rest of his life behind bars, and he has formally agreed to testify against his co-defendants. If I became a grass, they would certainly make a film. Just as they would if I died through drug abuse or if an envious gangster shot me.'

James was undeterred, got to work, and went through every relevant email I had received. One was from Nick Graham, a close friend of Sean Penn, stating that Sean was interested in making a film of *Mr Nice*. A few weeks later, Nick, Sean, James and I had a dynamic lunch at one of James's many London clubs. Sean was full of praise for my book and said he had already discussed its film potential with Hunter S. Thompson, Woody Harrelson and Mick Jagger. Sean followed up the meeting with this letter to Fantazia.

As you already know, I am a great fan of Howard Marks' book *Mr Nice* and would like to offer my services to you as your American champion for the film.

As discussed, please accept this letter as commitment of my continued support of the entire project up to and including joining your team of producers. I am willing to take an active role and I can confirm that I will utilise my experience, contacts and knowledge in order to bring this film to the international audience that I feel it deserves.

Yours sincerely

Sean Penn

But the BBC were unimpressed with Sean's overtures when the letter was passed to them and looked for other actors and directors. I hadn't seen or communicated with Sean since then.

'Anything happen with the film?' Sean repeated. 'I didn't get any reply to that letter I wrote.'

'It might happen if I got busted again with a load of dope and got a really hefty sentence. I'm in no rush for that to happen, even if you do play the DEA agent who busts me.'

Sean laughed as I sat down at his table. He introduced me to his wife and a couple of friends. Piers, wondering why I had vanished so abruptly, wandered in and joined us. The booze flowed.

The Groucho shuts at 2.00 a.m and Piers, Sean, and I were up for more drinks, a lot more. Relying on Pier's unrivalled expertise in late-night venues, we left and staggered through a series of dodgy bars. One club refused us entry because we were drunk. Another would not let us in because we did not have enough to pay the entrance fees. Eventually, even Piers ran out of suggestions, so we went to Sean's hotel and silently watched the sunrise through the bottoms of vodka bottles.

I have no recollection of what took place after that until I woke up the following afternoon in my room at the Groucho Club with the most serious hangover of my life wondering who was trying to knock the door down. I managed to open the door and stared blankly at the impressive physical form of Bernie Davies.

'All right, butt? I've been here for bloody hours. Lunchtime, you said, wasn't it? You look fucking rough. I don't think South America has done you much good, to be honest.'

'It's nothing to do with South America, Bernie. I was on the piss all night with Sean Penn.'

'Was you? I wish I'd known. I'd love to meet him. Bit of a boy, I heard, like.'

'He can certainly drink all right. In fact, he is a hell of a good guy. I really like him.'

'Well, we had better get a move on, butt. My Jag is badly parked right outside and I've got to be in Cwmaman by seven o'clock tonight.'

Soon we were tearing down the motorway towards the setting sun. I telephoned Marty to advise him of my imminent arrival in Kenfig Hill.

'How was South America and the Caribbean? Any good?'

'Fucking amazing, Marty. I've got loads to tell you. I discovered where Henry Morgan lived in Jamaica, maybe even the hiding place of his treasure, and I saw a photo of my great-great-grandfather on the wall of a pub in Patagonia.'

'Well I've got something to tell you that you'll find hard to believe.'

'What's that, Marty?'

'John Lennon was Welsh.'

'What? You are having a laugh, aren't you? John Lennon was Liverpool Irish, Marty. Everyone knows that.'

'On his father's side, yes. However, his maternal grandfather George Earnest Stanley, a sailor from Chester, married a Welsh girl called Annie Jane Millward. Her mother, Mary, refused ever to speak a word of English; she hated them so much. Annie had five kids, all daughters, and one of them, Julia, was John Lennon's mother.'

'Are you sure about all this?'

'Hundred per cent. A new biography of the Beatles has just come out. I'm looking at it now in the library. And guess what? The Lennon family attended a Welsh chapel in Penny Lane.'

'So that makes all the rock and roll gods Welsh – Elvis, Marley and Lennon.'

'Don't forget the Rolling Stones, Howard.'

'What! They were Welsh too?'

'Well Keith Richards and Brian Jones sound like Welsh

names to me. I haven't researched it, mind. Maybe you can. That's the sort of thing you do, isn't it?'

The traffic slowed down to a crawl. Bernie spoke up: 'I don't mean to be rude, butt, and I didn't try to overhear you at all, but why does this Welsh pirate, Welsh buccaneer and Welsh cowboy stuff matter a bugger these days? All that finished donkey's years ago. It's too late to be a bloody buccaneer. You were born too late.'

'But you were interested in those Davieses who went to Patagonia from Mountain Ash.'

'As far as Patagonia is concerned, I was just hoping I might find a rich relative in South America. That would be handy. And who gives a fuck whether John Lennon, Brian Jones, Elvis or Bob Marley was Welsh in the first place? They're all dead and gone, most of them. The best music yet is being made now, butt, probably in bloody Wales. In fact, definitely in Wales. The Stereophonics have just had a number-one hit, the Super Furry Animals are making better and better albums and packing out concert halls all over Europe, and Charlotte Church has taken over from Posh Spice. As for Goldie Lookin' Chain, Maggot is on *Celebrity Big Brother*, and the lads are reckoned to be the best hip hop band in the country. Have you heard their latest track, 'Your Missus is a Nutter'? Bloody brilliant. And it doesn't stop with music. Joe Calzaghe is easily Britain's best boxer. Wales won the Six Nations Grand Slam last year. Cardiff City are doing well in football. It won't be long before we're in the Premiership. What did you play in school, butt, football or rugby?'

'Neither seriously, Bernie. I wasn't all that keen on sports.'

'Just out drinking and dancing, I suppose.'

'Not even that. There was nothing happening in the valleys in the sixties. The best thing out of Wales then was probably the M4.'

'You spent all your youth trying to get out of Wales, butt,

and now you're trying to get back in. Are you staying in Kenfig Hill tonight?'

'No. I'm going to Blackwood.'

'In that case, butt, I take back everything I said.'

'What do you mean?'

'I'm going to Blackwood tonight as well.'

'What are you doing there?'

'Same as you, butt. Seeing Goldie Lookin' Chain.'

'I had no idea. I'm going to Blackwood to meet someone called Idwal, an expert on Henry Morgan.'

'Fucking hell! I don't take any of it back. How can you compare experiencing the cutting edge of hip hop with listening to some old fart banging on about a thief who has been dead for yonks? Come with me, butt, I'll get you back into the proper Wales. Today's bloody Wales, not yesterday's. Dirty Sanchez will be there, too. They're a bunch of headers; cut themselves to bits on the stage.'

'I've seen their name on line-ups, but I've never been to one of their gigs. Are they a Latin American outfit?'

'Latin American! They're from the valleys for fuck's sake.'

Latin America and the valleys. Roots and seeds. My memories of growing up now come to me in flickering black and white images. In those days the excitement came from far away – from the radio or treasured Elvis LPs. What I can only call intellectual curiosity took me away from the valleys to Oxford. Then a simple desire for kicks led me to become the world's leading marijuana smuggler.

My recent travels to Latin America in the footsteps of legendary Welsh outlaws and in search of obscure Welsh connections had opened up a world of colour. Now a real live Welsh Valley Commando was driving me back to the land of the Super Furry Animals and Goldie Lookin' Chain and the Stereophonics. This was the place to be. The valleys, here and now.

www.vintage-books.co.uk